ALICIA & ROLF MEDINA

TEAL TRUST
TRANSPARENCY

A guide for self-organizing
and new ways to organize and lead

FUTURE
OF ORGA
NIZING

Published by Future of Organizing AB.

www.futureoforganizing.se

hello@futureoforganizing.se

Cover design: Mia Fallby
Interior design: Wayne Kehoe

Contents

FOREWORD

This is a relevant book for everyone that is part of an organization and can be an inspiration for those who want to make our workplaces healthier with a greater focus on the people who work there.

The authors combine their research with stories and cases from a range of organizations. They share examples and anecdotes from real life, from organizations, and from people that are already using aspects of Teal, but also from companies like Buurtzorg that have come further. They also provide a look back at some examples from the past that help us to understand that this is not something completely new, it is about simplicity and applying practices that make sense.

Their work leads to a practical model called the "DP model," which has 12 different areas that need to be taken into consideration and that are closely related as part of a systemic organism. These areas are people, culture, organizing, leadership, decision-making, transparency & communication, salary model and profit sharing, digital tools & technology, competence & learning, workplace & working hours, social responsibility & sustainability, and finance.

My view and my experience from the journey that I have undertaken at Buurtzorg is that people should be treated as humans, as the individuals that they are. A question that needs to be considered at any time is: "Is this ethical?" This question is not only about how you act; it is also about the way that you perceive people. The values you have and your worldview will determine the way you act. This is what makes a difference and it is a holistic perspective, the wholeness that Frederic Laloux mentions. It is about creating an environment where people can grow as human beings, moving from the view of seeing people as resources to seeing them as human beings.

The authors' description of culture as behaviors, a way of being and acting, is also aligned with what we at Buurtzorg emphasize. For us, culture is about how we behave and how we talk to each other. Can I listen to others or am I only sending messages that could be misunderstood? This connects to different aspects of communication. Communication based on a dialogue is completely different to telling people about your plans, your strategy, your vision, or your mission. Having a transparent dialogue makes these things less important and contributes to another type of conversation.

For example, if the frontline is important, then you should treat the frontline as important. It is about practicing what you preach and about being conscious, aware of what you are like, what you do, and the impact of what you say. This applies to everyone in an organization, regardless of what your working tasks are. Words are very important, and we need to pay attention to what kind of language we use.

A lot of words that are developed within the field of management are very intimidating to many people. Often they do not know the exact meaning of these words and this can have an impact, because people may feel impressed. It also creates a feeling of inferiority and insecurity because they feel they have to do something, but they don't know exactly what. This creates a feeling that people using complicated language know much more than those who don't know the meaning of the words. I know that using the wrong words makes people feel small, but if you use the same language and if you listen to people, you will create a connection to them. For example, if you work in an organization with nurses, you should use the language of the nurses. Otherwise they will feel disconnected: What is he talking about now? It is important to be able to feel the impact of words.

Sensitivity, reflection, and rethinking are an attitude and a behavior and also part of the culture. If people feel free to say what they feel, what they want, that will lead to ideas and innovation for improvements.

Another important thing is knowledge sharing, especially tacit knowledge, what people know but which is not documented. During the last 50 years, our world has moved towards becoming increasingly evidence based. The dark side of this is that the daily practice of frontline work, which is so valuable, is not given as much space. I really believe that we need to find ways in which this knowledge and these experiences can be spread and further developed. This is a horizontal way of sharing where platforms and social networks play an important role.

In social networks, these everyday experiences and learning can be exchanged if people feel free to share. On a platform or social network with a lot of regulations, it will not work. The way to make it work is to keep it open, without restrictions, so people feel that they should respond and come up with ideas. To create this kind of open atmosphere, it is important that the leaders do not give negative responses to things. If I, for example, do not agree, I usually let it go and hope for a discussion. I know that if I say "We cannot say this," people are likely to remain silent.

At the same time, it is necessary to be very clear about what is expected, and what the guidelines are: on the one hand, a lot of space; on the other hand, clarity. We at Buurtzorg have three importance guidelines, namely quality, collaboration, and finance. What is needed for organizations to succeed is a healthy model and a healthy way of doing things based on logic. It should be organic and very clear, because if it is not, it could create a lot of uncertainties and a lot of insecurity. This is illustrated very clearly in this book by several examples that show possible outcomes depending on how safe people perceive themselves to be.

People feel safe when they know what we do as a company, when they know the purpose and the result of the purpose. To get to this point, openness, communication, and transparency need to be in place. Everything is open at Buurtzorg. Everyone can find what they want. It is also about simplification, because when it is possible to understand things, it is also natural to take ownership, responsibility, and accountability.

Alicia and Rolf are bringing an important aspect into the spotlight, an aspect that is very often misunderstood, and that is the view of leadership. The new ways of organizing need to reinvent more or less new forms of leadership. I am convinced that leadership and ownership belong together, and leadership should always create an environment that makes it possible for people to take ownership. When I support organizations, I see that when leadership and ownership are not balanced the organizations have a tendency to fall back into old patterns.

Leadership should focus on the human approach and ownership should not be taken away. When managers say "I give my employees freedom, but they don't take it," they are still caught in the old paradigm. Saying that they *give* ownership is putting themselves in a position above people, because if they have something to give, then they have more than others. Leaders need to be the individuals they want to be seen as; this has an impact on people. People will behave according to their perception, to what they see and feel.

One of the aspects of the DP model is about healthy finances and profitability, which are important for the survival of any organization. Sometimes I am asked: "What happens if a team is not profitable?" But this is not something that "just happens"; it is always a process. Usually the team is doing well, but sometimes it does not work. Then we need to talk about it and try to find the reasons behind it. What can we do in both the short and the long term? Do we think it is a risk or not? It is important to be open and clear and have a normal conversation about it, without pressure. Just raise questions like: What do we do in half a year? Will it continue in the same way? Questions are the forerunners to improvements. Usually the issue will be resolved by itself and the team will find ways to improve the profitability. If it is not possible to solve the situation, it is still important to be clear about it. We need to draw conclusions together, end it, and find solutions for everybody involved. This is part of normal life. Things start, they grow, and sometimes they won't work; and then you end them.

Finding solutions for everyone involved is part of the social responsibility. There should always be connections to other social subjects. Every company can think about what contribution they can make to certain societal issues. For example, if a company makes bread, the approach could be "How can we develop bread that is healthy for people?" Then bread becomes a kind of creative process. It's not only about the slices, but also about making bread that people like, which makes it healthier.

In my opinion, it is possible to give meaning to everything; it is just a matter of choosing an approach. For example, when talking about finance, the conversation could include "We try to sell as many products as possible" or "With our products we try to solve as many problems as possible for those who have financial problems."

I see this book as a contribution to the Teal movement and to the transformation of organizations in general. The hard and meticulous work that Alicia and Rolf have done with their research, as well as the creation of the DP model, is presented in this book in a way that reaches "the many people."

Jos de Blok
The Netherlands
Spring 2021

PREFACE

It is one and a half years since the Swedish version of the book *Teal Tillit Transparens* came out and it has been a joy to see the impact.

We have been conducting speeches, giving talks, running workshops and seminars, giving interviews, and participating in podcasts spreading the message of *Teal, Trust, and Transparency—* both the book and the deeper meaning of the words.

With great humility and pride, we have seen the creation of new organizations based on our book. We have also seen existing ones become inspired and start their journey toward Teal.

The interest in in-depth discussions about the book's topic and content has led to people starting book groups where they meet both physically and online to discuss one chapter at a time. This is far more than we could even have dreamed of.

It is difficult to express how happy we are to see that our book contributes to the creation of better organizations. So many conversations with so many people have taken place in this short period of time, and these have enriched us while bringing new insights to many people.

All this gave us the strength to translate the book into English in order to spread it to a wider audience. This version has small adjustments, and to give the story an even wider perspective, we exchanged two of the invited "voices from the field" with two new ones, one from Denmark and one from Uruguay. These are in the chapters "People" and "Transparency and Communication".

Our hope is that this release of the book will help organizations, teams, and people in general improve the way they organize and work, and to flourish.

Alicia and Rolf
Malmö, March 2023

INTRODUCTION

This chapter begins with a description of the prevailing situation of today's organizations and then takes a look back at the history of organizing work. This is followed by information about why this book has been written, and about our own journey in which, over three years, we explored many organizations and looked for concrete realities. At the end of the chapter, we outline how to read the book and to whom we are targeting.

A CHANGING WORLD

The world is constantly changing, and it feels like both the pace of society and the speed of work are moving faster. Perhaps it is the increasing availability of information that creates this feeling, or maybe it is just that everything is going faster. At the same time, technologies are being developed to replace work that used to be done by people. It is mainly repetitive tasks that are being automated, and machines are actually better than us humans at performing these types of tasks for the very reason that they are machines. Monotonous tasks also tend to affect us physically and mentally in a negative way. Automation of repetitive tasks implies that the work performed by people becomes increasingly knowledge-intensive, which means that we work more and more with our head and heart and less and less with our arms and legs. The interesting thing about a more knowledge-intensive world is that an increasingly large part of the work we do requires interaction with others.

When the assembly line was introduced about 100 years ago, workers were taught to do their tasks and then repeat them over and over again. Of course, sometimes one needed to interact with other coworkers, but only so as not to disturb the ongoing work. Today, much of the human interaction that takes place is to solve problems that have arisen, to develop the business, to make things better, but also because we humans have a need for social interaction. In tandem with this, people change jobs increasingly often. In the past, people went through an education for a specific profession and remained within the same profession and organization for the rest of their lives. Today, it has almost become customary to change jobs frequently and look for new employers. There is also a growing part of the workforce that is not employed by an organization but is instead contracted on a temporary basis, something that comes under the so-called "gig economy." All of this affects how we should organize work today.

During the assembly line's infancy, organizational forms were created where the supervisor (manager) made all the decisions and ensured that the workers followed these decisions and instructions and performed their tasks. But even though these tasks and the way of working have changed radically, many influences from this time remain in the way we organize ourselves today. Most organizations still live in hierarchies of power and authority, i.e. characterized by Command and Control, where decisions are made at the top and communicated down through the hierarchy and where information is filtered at every level as information becomes power.

A question that arises is how this affects people's commitment to work when "those up there" decide and "we down here" are subordinates. We will reason about engagement, commitment, and how engaged and committed people feel at work in the section on people.

Our own experience has led us to the belief that two pillars are needed to be able to create work groups where people feel engaged and motivated, and where everyone gives the best of themselves. These pillars are equality and autonomy.

By equality we mean that everyone is on the same level, that is, that no one is superior to anyone else. Terms such as "subordinates" do not exist, nor do you talk about managers as individuals who stand above the others. Instead, there are people with different areas of responsibility, skills, and specialties, but there are no areas or tasks that are considered better or have more status than others. Things such as promotions as a way to reward people disappear. Reward mechanisms such as being given the opportunity to help others, teach and coach, or just get time to spread your message become important. With equality, status symbols such as having a better office or one's own parking space or belonging to specific management teams, also disappear. Being part of a certain management team is a status symbol in many countries. It happens that people change tasks and roles just to belong to a group or department that has a higher status.

Once upon a time, one of us (writers) was the manager of a support team for a product area within Ericsson. The support team had a lower status than the development team. However, there were several problems in the handover between development and support, which resulted in poor product quality. To improve the handover, the way of working was developed, making people from the support team become part of the development team for a certain part of their time and working on testing the products before handover. The tests became much better and resulted in an improved product quality. But the interesting thing was that suddenly the status of the support team increased, and the development team wanted to include them in the requirements process, working with defining new customer requirements. The support team contributed with knowledge within the product area that was lacking in the development team, which meant that they respected the support people's knowledge. They thus became equals and their knowledge and competence had equal value in each other's eyes. Equally valuing areas of responsibility, knowledge, competence, and specialty is what we mean by equality in this context.

In addition to belonging to a group, it is often a position or title that gives status. In today's organizations, and in society in general, different tasks and roles are constantly valued. Being a manager or supervisor is considered a better position than being a receptionist or a coordinator. Being a director is better and gives more power than being a line manager. Job titles are created with the idea of describing the level in the hierarchy, and the principle is that the higher up in the hierarchy people are, the more power, status, rights, and financial compensation they can enjoy.

THE EMERGENCE OF TODAY'S ORGANIZATIONS

Looking back at the beginning of industrialization in the nineteenth century, industries were staffed with people who did not have the knowledge and skills to carry out the tasks required, and most were illiterate or had very limited reading and writing skills. For that reason, organizations needed to concentrate the power and knowledge in the managers or supervisors. People were given instructions about what to do and how to carry out the work. The manager's role included supervising how people did their jobs, solving all problems, and making all decisions.

This is the background to Frederick Winslow Taylor's "Scientific Management," which emerged when industrialism needed a way to organize the workforce and which enabled the uneducated people who started working in the factories to carry out their tasks. As a response to the evident needs, Command and Control arose, with great specialization and with a focus on workers' productivity. The manager and the supervisor were the ones who had the required knowledge and organized the work, gave orders, and controlled, and the workers adhered to the rules. The workers just followed orders and did what they were told to do. This way of leading has been the dominant leadership style since the nineteenth century. Power was centralized at the top of the hierarchy. Although other forms have emerged over the years, the basic view of the boss and hierarchy with power at the top of each node has been dominant in both organizational and leadership theories.

Since then, and as a response to the development that humanity is going through, a series of theories, models, and movements have been added. Table 1 below presents a brief summary of theories, based on a historical perspective, that have influenced the way work is organized.

Table 1. Overall picture of development and trends since the early twentieth century

Organizational development and trends since 1900	
Decade	Trend/Direction
1900 - 1920	Focus on productivity. Hierarchical organizations with total obedience and with the metaphor "organizations as machines." Scientific Management emerged.
The 1920s	Focus on specializing, efficiency, discipline. Introduction of chord system. The administrative school where responsibility is linked to authority and vice versa. Vertical information paths.
The 1930s	Control by rules. People seen as machines. Bureaucratization of organizations and increased specialization. Introduction of concepts such as limited span of control, line staff, and role descriptions.
The 1940s	Focus on Human Relations where social relationships and nonfinancial rewards have an impact on productivity. Second World War.
The 1950s	Focus on decision-making in organizations. Introduction of concepts such as Bounded Rationality that is built on the notion that the customers' behavior is not entirely rational.
The 1960s	Sociotechnological approach. Contingency theory (situational) where the organizational context is considered.

Organizational development and trends since 1900	
Decade	Trend/Direction
The 1970s	Focus on divisionalization and decentralization. Democratizing of working life and self-managed teams. Systems theory, the learning organization.
The 1980s	Focus on internationalization and culture. Influences from Japan, Toyota Production System, Lean. New concepts such as organizational culture and situational leadership.
The 1990s	Focus on deregulation and globalization. Information technology and the digital revolution. New thoughts and findings: knowledge and service, network organizations, sharing values, longer value chains.
The 2000s	Information technology and the digital revolution. Breakthrough of agile methodologies. Advance in areas such as stakeholder and resource management, processes, and strategies. Focus on coordination of actors, people, and information.
The 2010s	Focus on customer experience, social responsibility, and sustainability. People orientation in a new way and new models such as Teal, Sociocracy, and Holacracy. Gig economy takes off.
2020 - 2021	Covid-19 and working from home. Digital collaboration and radical decrease of physical meetings and gatherings

In addition to Scientific Management, also referred to as Taylorism, one can highlight some of these theories that have had a greater impact on how work would be carried out and organized. Later in this chapter, we will address Eric Rhenman and his work, which was also the basis for what later was called *the Swedish management model*.

A major impact on the manufacturing industry came with Lean Production, which originated in the Toyota Production System (TPS), which emerged at Toyota in Japan during the postwar period. TPS was the foundation of Lean and is based on four basic principles: synchronization, eliminating waste, continuous improvement, and involvement of all employees. With this, each worker would no longer act like a machine and constantly improve the working process. Another important thing was that everyone had the right to stop production if something in the process did not work. The purpose of this philosophy was to enable the employees to become more involved in the work and be part of a systematic improvement work. Lean also became the leading principle in the manufacturing industry. However, the strict hierarchies remained, but people in operational activities began to be considered as thinking people and not only as objects that would perform activities, like pieces in a machine.

During the 1970s, the idea of the learning organization also emerged, where the starting point was that one should learn from things that happened, not least from mistakes. In addition, how an individual person's knowledge could be transferred to organizational learning, i.e learning from each other, became important.

Another philosophy was the agile principles, especially in software development, which were founded in the 1990s and grew strong in the years 2000–2010. From an organizational perspective, these are very similar to the self-managing/autonomous teams from the manufacturing industry during the 1970s and 1980s (see the section on the Swedish management model below). The basic idea is that the team members should organize and divide the work among themselves. There is a supervisor/team leader who does not distribute the work but must support the team and remove obstacles. The team must, as in Lean, work with continuous improvement as a working method and in this way become a learning organization. Agile working methods became a new buzzword that has caught on, and more and more organizations are working with agile transformation where they strive for an organization that can adapt more quickly as the outside world changes increasingly rapidly. Not least in the ongoing digitization, the agile transformation is becoming ever more important.

However, alongside this industrial perspective, work has always been organized around a specific profession. This can apply, for example, to the blacksmith, the doctor, the carpenter, the lawyer, etc. In the past, this type of organization was based on knowledge and skills in a profession that was usually learned at a young age, and where people continued to work throughout life. The licensed practitioner, the master, sat at the top due to his competence in the profession and the others acted more as a support in the organization. These organizations were, and still are, usually quite small and operate in markets and/or areas that change relatively slowly. However, the speed of change in these areas has also increased significantly as a result of the availability of digital information. One can also see that many of these professions over the years have become increasingly integrated into larger organizations, either as employment or as part of a value chain.

What we humans face today is a mixture of opportunities and threats. Today, there is also technology that enables people to communicate and interact in many ways. Digitization has accelerated and information is continuously available. There are many opportunities through technological platforms to understand different cultures and to interact effectively with people from different parts of the world. People can also quickly create contacts with others regardless of location. We have increasingly started to move towards flexibility regarding when, where, and how we work. One of our major challenges, as the world becomes increasingly integrated, is the way we see social responsibility. Another challenge is climate change. These challenges mean that we cannot continue to live in a way where we overuse the earth's resources and produce in a socially unfair way. Today we also see increasing differences in salary in a system that focuses on low costs. In addition, this book was written during the Covid-19 pandemic, which has opened up another dimension that we were not aware of. During the pandemic we could not meet physically in the same way as before. Many people worked from home and only met through digital platforms, which had a big impact on organizing, leadership, and the way of working.

WHAT IS THE IDEA BEHIND THE BOOK?

The idea behind the book is based on the view that the world has changed and that the old paradigms about work and the way of organizing it no longer apply. By maintaining authoritarian hierarchies and a leadership based on Command and Control, organizations are shaped in a way in which only a minority is engaged in work, and sickness, absence, and stress gain more and more ground. In several surveys, we see that engagement in work is falling. According to a global survey by Gallup in 2017 (State of the Global Workplace), only 15% of the workforce world-wide are engaged in their work. The same survey indicates that 18% are actively disengaged in their work, while 67% are not engaged; that is, they do not care. We spend a lot of our time in our workplaces, and spending all this time without feeling a sense of engagement is a waste, both for the individual and for the organization. The fact that every tenth employee is actively disengaged is an even greater waste.

It is natural that people want to spend their time where they feel passion and commitment. The interesting thing is when you see it from the organization's perspective. The clear numbers and conclusions found in Gallup's surveys also show that an engaged employee is six times more productive than one who is disengaged. If you make the assumption that this is fairly accurate, we have a figure for waste from the organization's perspective. It is also quite natural that we become more productive when we feel a passion for, and commitment to, what we do. If we stay with Gallup a little longer, their research from 2019 suggests that we are six times more likely to feel engaged in our work if we are allowed to use our strengths and what we are good at.

If we take the temperature at our workplaces from a health perspective, it does not look good. According to the Swedish Work Environment Authority's survey in 2016, stress-related causes were the biggest single cause of work-related death. A total of 772 people died in 2016 from stress-related causes linked to work. Every third woman experiences stress at work, while for men it is every fifth. The increase in stress-related illnesses in the workplace began in the 1980s and has since continued. If you look at middle managers, they are the group that experiences the greatest level of stress. According to the Swedish Work Environment Authority and Statistics Sweden (SCB), in 2018, seven out of ten middle managers experienced psychological pressure. Many of them worked despite the psychological pressure and were covered by a new concept, namely "sick presence." Sick presence is when you work even though you would feel better staying at home, and this phenomenon is significantly higher among middle managers in particular. And according to hierarchical organizational models, these middle managers are the people who are supposed to make decisions and organize the work of rather disengaged employees who are their subordinates. They are squeezed between the top of the pyramid, which makes demands downwards, and the bottom of the pyramid, which expects the middle managers to make decisions. Today's organizations are experiencing some type of illness. Now we are approaching the reality that the way work is organized today should not be the same as it was 100 years ago. The conditions are simply different.

As a response to this, a series of new methods, theories, and trends aimed at developing the new way of organizing work have emerged. These include, among others: Teal, Sociocracy, Sociocracy 3.0, Holacracy, Deliberately Developmental Organizations, agile, Management 3.0, and a number of other models for self-organizing and decentralization of power. An introduction to these can be found in the section on setting the scene.

WHOM IS THE BOOK AIMED AT?

The main purpose of this book is to present a new model that is the result of the research we conducted from the beginning of 2018 to the end of 2020. Within the scope of this research, we visited over 100 companies, interviewed approximately 300 people in depth, and talked to many more. We call the model the "DP model," which stands for *Distributed Power*. It takes various elements from the new theories as well as from real-life organizational implementations.

We hope that this book and the DP model will guide and inspire leaders, coaches, politicians, consultants, business owners, students, and everyone else who is part of an organization in its journey towards a new way of organizing work. But above all, we hope to be able to contribute to the global "movement" that leads to organizations becoming more human and where we all realize that people must come first, before financial profits and overexploitation of the planet.

THE DP MODEL

The DP model is evidence-based and is considered to be a model based on reality. In addition to the research project mentioned above, we have used our personal experience from 30 years of working life as well as the research and academic work that we have been conducting since 2009. We have also had the privilege of talking with some of the main contemporary frontier-breaking authors and architects behind progressive ways of organizing.

The basic philosophy of the model is based on trust among people, organizing work together, and seeing everything as a whole where everything has an evolutionary purpose, and where we create things together with a sense of respecting and listening to each other without overusing the planet.

The result was a systemic model with 12 areas as shown in Figure 1.

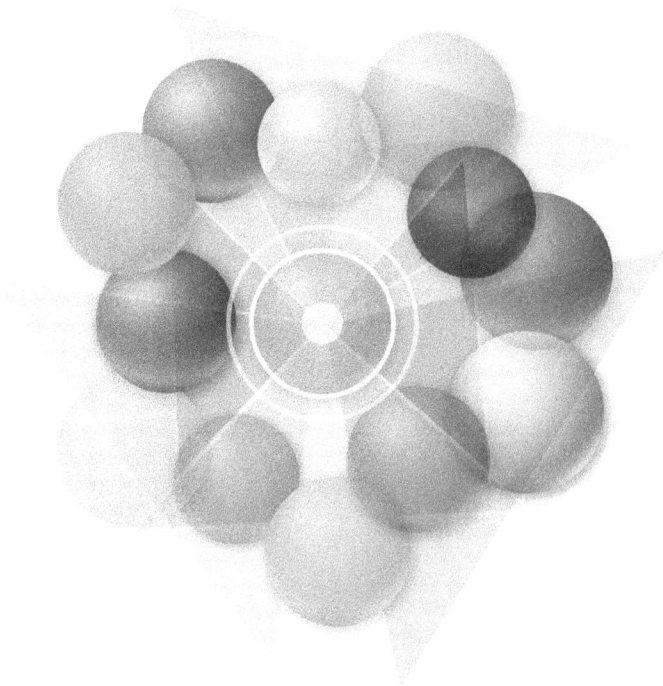

Figure 1. The DP model

The 12 areas are:
- **People**
- **Culture**
- **Organizing**
- **Leadership**
- **Decision-making**
- **Transparency and communication**
- **Salary model and profit sharing**
- **Digital tools and technology**
- **Competence and learning**
- **Workplace and working hours**
- **Social responsibility and sustainability**
- **Finances**

A systemic model means that all parts are connected and influence each other just like parts in a living organism. The new paradigm means that organizations are people-centric. The system may look different, but all areas are included as each organization must find its own creative map for the journey towards a healthier organization where people can flourish and where society and the planet are also considered. Then each organization becomes like a figure created by a kaleidoscope: All areas are included but in a unique way.

OUR OWN JOURNEY

We, the authors, often get asked the question: "When did you start working with the DP model?" This question is not easy to answer. Was it 2018 when we started the specific research project around progressive organizing, or was it earlier? Are there connections to our previous research projects? How much is based on our own experiences from working life?

The answer is that the journey began a long time ago when, as young newly graduated engineers, we entered working life in the early 1990s. Our journey between different organizations and roles, as well as the desire to make the world better, led us, after two decades in corporations, to step into the world of research and start our doctoral studies. In the academic world we learned to look beyond normal business and also to delve deeply into organizational theories, leadership, group dynamics, and philosophical standpoints.

With our doctor hats in our luggage, we continued to work in the business world in parallel with our academic commitments and our writing. Just like many others in academia, we were drawn to international research conferences, scientific journals, and publications. After a few years working in this way, we felt increasingly that there was a barrier between research and business, which is a huge waste. A large proportion of the research results will never reach nonacademics. In the same way, there is an enormous amount of experience and many stories out there in organizations that are never brought into the academic world, partly because of the researchers' distance from the business world. Therefore, we took on the task of trying to make the research useful and attempting to reduce the distance to the business world. Without being able to explain why, we could see how Sweden was losing its early lead regarding democratic organizations where participation had been a given.

Since we have carried out the research project in parallel with working for different organizations, we have also seen with increasingly more open eyes how these organizations work based on the areas that have evolved within the research project.

The result was the DP model, which can be seen as the *Swedish management model 2.0,* and our hope is that the DP model will be a reference for people and organizations around the world.

HOW SHOULD THE BOOK BE READ?

The book consists of four parts, with the first part comprising a presentation of today's situation, an explanation of why the book was written, and a short introduction to the DP model.

This is followed by a chapter with relevant approaches based on self-organizing and progressive organizational models, as well as a brief presentation of the book's protagonists.

In the chapter on the DP model, the 12 different areas of the model are presented as well as a section on the "Voice from the field," where we have invited 12 different people to give their views and thoughts on the areas of the DP model. These people have been chosen based on their knowledge, efforts, and experience in the field they write about. The purpose of the "Voice from the field" is to provide space for stories complementing our own writing.

The 12 sections about the DP model can be read regardless of the order in which they are written. There are clear references between different sections, which allows the reader to use the book as a practical guide.

In each of the covered areas there are examples, anecdotes, and evidence from different cases interspersed with theories and with the authors' analyses and conclusions. On several occasions, the same case is brought up but described in different ways depending on the area of the DP model in which it takes place. To make it easier for the reader to be able to read the different areas independently of each other, there are certain necessary repetitions.

The chapter "The way forward" contains closing remarks, the authors' own journey in the creation of the DP model, and practical tools that support the self-organizing and democratization of organizations.

Throughout the book there are questions and posts that give the reader the opportunity to reflect and make notes that will contribute to the evolutionary understanding of the DP model. These questions and posts are presented in boxes with a small speech balloon and can also be used as a basis for discussions in workshops or training courses.

Important conclusions and thoughts that form the core of the DP model are presented in light-grey boxes. These can be used as guidance in both the communication and development of the organization's principles and as guiding stars in the organization's movement towards self-organizing, decentralization, and democratization. These conclusions and thoughts can also be seen as a summary of the cornerstones of the DP model.

INTRODUCTION: How should the book be read?

SETTING THE SCENE

Before going deeper into the different parts of the DP model, we want to explain the background to the model and what it is based on. In this section we will present some of the case studies we have performed and the experience we brought with us into the research project. In addition to that, we bring up various current progressive models. Often what is considered new is not completely new. We present some examples of this as a conclusion to the chapter.

THE BOOK'S PROTAGONISTS

The book is based on real cases from a long-term research journey out in the field. During this journey we have been able to see, and not least feel, how it looks in different organizations. We have also been in contact with several protagonists and leading figures within different theories and approaches with the purpose of capturing their thoughts. With their input in combination with all our case studies and experiences, we have created the DP model.

In our search for various existing forms of organization that are not based on Command and Control, we have studied several well-known and, in this context, less-known international organizations in depth. We have done this by using available data as well as direct contacts via communication channels such as LinkedIn, e-mail, and online meetings.

One of our goals has been to ensure the relevance and authenticity of the stories, and for that reason we have always gone to the source to look for evidence. On this journey we have learned that many famous stories are based on secondary sources and that these are unfortunately spread and retold by many people without having verified that they are true.

We have also looked back in time and found organizations or working groups that had elements of self-managing organizations. Since there is something to be learned from these cases, and from history, we have chosen to include some of these examples throughout the book.

In small businesses and start-ups, power and decision-making are distributed in the organization in a way where self-organizing seems natural. The difficulties arise when the company grows. Therefore, we decided to study in depth some organizations with more than 100 employees by following them over a longer period of time.

Our selected case studies are presented in the next section so that you, as a reader, can get an idea of what types of organizations they are and in which area they operate. We will refer to these many times in the coming chapters, so there will be some recurrences.

We have also had the privilege of having a dialogue with many of the leading researchers and figures in progressive forms of organizing.

Swedish case studies

Over a period of three years, we visited and studied many companies and thereby gained many insights. Not all of them can be described here because it would take half the book. In this section, we have therefore only chosen to highlight the companies that we have followed for a longer period of time, as well as some companies that, in some sense, stand out in a positive way and that have contributed to the design of the DP model. Below is a brief description of these companies.

SVENSKA RETURSYSTEM

Svenska Retursystem (SRS) is owned equally by Svensk Dagligvaruhandel (SvDH) and Dagligvaruleverantörers förbund (DLF), both trade associations with the purpose of promoting an efficient, innovative, and sustainable fast-moving consumer goods (FMCG) industry. In 2019, SRS had 152 employees, which had grown to 171 by 2021. The headquarters are located in Stockholm and the company has production and logistics facilities in Helsingborg, Mölnlycke, Örebro, and Västerås.

Since 2001, SRS has operated a deposit-based return system for standardized load carriers such as plastic boxes and pallets. SRS provides standardized services for its customers. From the store, the boxes and pallets are returned for washing and then sent out again into the system. When the boxes and pallets wear out, they are recycled. The system contributes to reducing the entire industry's environmental impact by replacing millions of items of disposable packaging every week.

SRS's role in the sustainability flow is illustrated in Figure 2 below.

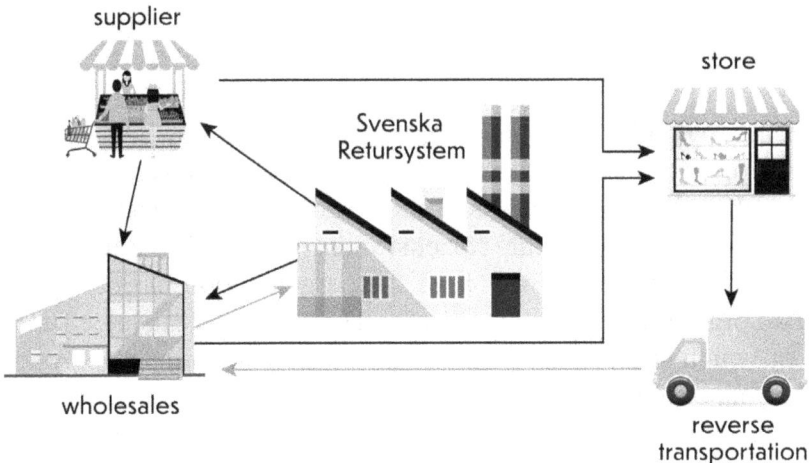

Figure 2. SRS's role in the sustainability flow

SRS has followed, and is following, a cultural journey with a focus on systematic and continuous improvement of work. This journey has moved the company from a traditional hierarchical organization with power concentrated in the management team to one that is largely self-organized with multiple cross-functional groups. The transformation has also led to the distribution of power to cross-functional groups and the dissolution of the management team.

CENTIGO AB

Centigo is a Swedish management consulting firm with its headquarters in Stockholm and offices in other parts of the world. The company was founded in 2002 and had 290 employees in 2019. All three founders had a background in IT and management consulting companies such as Accenture. Their philosophy is, and has been from the beginning, to create a different company where the entrepreneurial spirit would be a cornerstone in the organizational culture and with an involving instead of directing leadership.

The company is part of the Business Wellness Group (BWG) together with several other companies that have a similar philosophy and culture. Centigo offers services in organizational and business development, change management, and strategic IT.

One of the principles from the beginning has been that the company will not have a CEO; this is because they believe that this role does not fulfill any function. The CEO role exists solely to fulfill the requirements of the Swedish authorities; instead, someone is responsible for customer relationship and someone else for the business area. The organization basically has two organizational types of units. These are the business unit, for which someone is responsible and to which the employees belong based on knowledge areas, and the customer team. The customer team includes employees from different business units who work on projects for a particular customer. Centigo wants to symbolize the interface between these types of organizational units with an internal market where the consultant can work in one or more customer teams but always belongs to a business unit (see Figure 3).

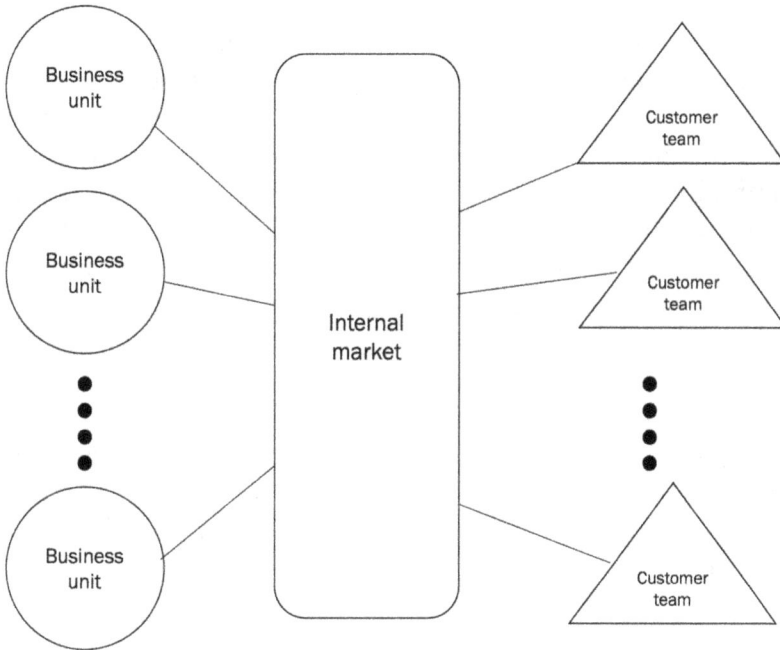

Figure 3. Centigo's organizational structure

Because Centigo strives for all board members to have a solid commitment, there are no external members on the board. They also have the principle of being financially independent and have therefore never looked for venture capital. The employees could apply for co-ownership and the board decides who becomes a co-owner. Thirty-six employees are co-owners at the time of writing.

Strategic decisions relating to company structure are made by the board, while major financial decisions are made by the operational management team, which consists solely of shareholders. The decisions concerning daily operations are made by the employees themselves.

The company has no managers, having been founded with the goal of being self-organized.

JAYWAY

Jayway is a software development company that was founded in Malmö, Sweden and combines design and technology to develop ideas into products and solutions. The company was founded, among others, by Thomas Dagsberg in 2000 and in 2019 had approximately 250 employees organized into ten so-called "studios." In 2018, it was bought by the French company Devoteam. In 2019, Jayway had five offices located in Malmö, Halmstad, Stockholm, Copenhagen, and Silicon Valley.

The organization is based on agile teams that design and develop different types of software. They try to create an ecosystem by involving customers and partners, as well as constantly developing their employees. Furthermore, they have a strong belief in open-source software (which everyone has the right to read, modify, use, and distribute) and are a major player in their field of business.

STUDSVIK

Today, Studsvik is a listed company group that supplies services to the nuclear power industry.

The company was founded in 1947 under the name AB Atomenergi 'and at that time, 57% of it was owned by the Swedish state' The remaining 43% was owned by a mix of municipal and private companies.

When the company was formed, its purpose was to construct experimental reactors and develop methods for extracting uranium from Swedish deposits. After gradually altering direction, the company changed its name in 1978 to Studsvik Energiteknik AB, and then in 1987 to Studsvik AB, which is the group's current name. In 2019, Studsvik had around 1,000 employees in seven countries.

Tõive Kivikas, who was an associate professor in physics, was recruited in 1990 to the position of CEO of Studsvik AB. His assignment was to liquidate the company, which had been unprofitable for several years. Tõive rejected the task and, with his leadership style and human approach, developed the declining company into a successful business that expanded abroad and is today a successful and innovative listed company. In the autumn of 1996, Studsvik AB became a subsidiary of Atle, with the venture capital company Euroventure Nordica II as a minority owner. A year later, Tõive was dismissed.

BEETROOT

Beetroot is a Swedish-Ukrainian IT offshore company founded in 2012 by Andreas Flodström and Gustav Henman. The company built its operations in Ukraine from the start due to the large availability of competent system developers. Andreas and Gustav were young and had recently graduated from Chalmers University of Technology, Gothenburg, Sweden, and they were convinced that a company should be run based on trust. Over the years, they have incorporated several elements from self-organizational methods and are on a journey incorporating even more of these aspects.

Today, Beetroot has offices in Stockholm and in several locations in Ukraine, where all offices are characterized by having a home-like atmosphere without a strict dress code. The company has approximately ten employees in Sweden and 500 contracted programmers and IT specialists in Ukraine. Through its business model and organizational culture, they have changed the often rather impersonal offshore operations into a kind of extended in-house team. In 2016, the ownership structure changed, and Andreas and Gustav today own 61% of the company. The remaining 39% is distributed as follows: 25% is owned by a large investor, 11% is distributed in different proportions among three other investors, and the remaining 3% is owned by the employees (both from Ukraine and from Sweden).

Beetroot also runs the Beetroot Academy, which has trained more than 3,000 IT talents in Ukraine.

BJÖRN LUNDÉN

Björn Lundén Information AB was founded in 1987 and has approximately 130 employees. The business is conducted in Näsviken, Ljusdal, and Stockholm in Sweden, with its headquarters being in Näsviken.

The company offers modern software solutions and practical tools for handling corporate tax and declarations, accounting, salaries, and personnel issues. The organization is known for its self-organized principles, and they were one of the pioneers in Sweden in introducing a flat organization where everyone has influence and where decisions are made in a democratic way. Since the beginning, the focus has been on the connection between work, family life, leisure, and personal development. Working hours and the amount of work are flexible and the employees plan their days and the scope of work themselves.

The company has grown a lot in recent years and some organizational changes have been introduced. An example of this is a new role called "group manager," which is not a formal manager but a person who focuses on coordination. There are currently eight group managers. As Björn Lundén himself today is retired and no longer active in the company, the current CEO, Ulf Svensson, owns 66% and the remaining 34% is distributed among three other owners.

Ulf was one of the first employees of Björn Lundén Information AB and follows the vision of the founder.

HOLMA FOLKHÖGSKOLA / HOLMA FOLK HIGH SCHOOL

Holma Folk High School (in Swedish, Holma Folkhögskola), in this book referred to as Holma, is a school for adult education with most of its operations in Höör in the southern part of Sweden and provides courses in permaculture for around 200 students per year. The people's high school sees itself as a tool for change and aims to benefit biological as well as human diversity. One of their mottos is to make people grow in community with each other. The school is today organized according to Sociocracy with a systemic and holistic approach. Each unit is self-organized and there are goals and objectives for each part of the organization. The school's principal, Andreas Jonsson, is one of Sweden's leading experts in Sociocracy, both in theory and in practice, and he has a big heart and the willingness to make our society much better.

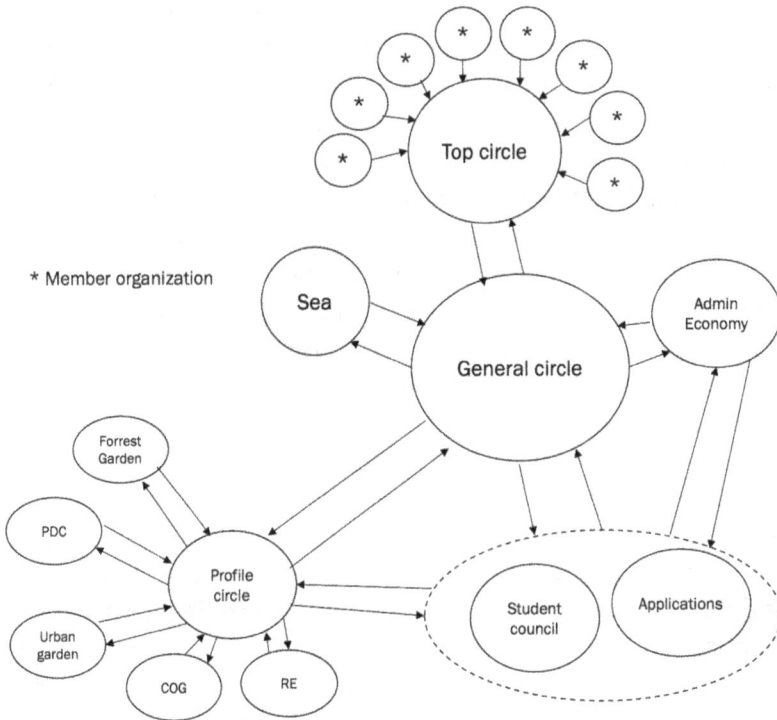

Figure 4. Holma folk high school's organization
Source: Holma folk high school

International case studies

We have also studied both well-known and, in this context, lesser-known international organizations. Since we have been looking for evidence and concrete results, we chose to immerse ourselves and delve deeply into the organizations mentioned below.

K2K AND GRUPO NER

K2K Emocionando was founded by Koldo Saratxaga in 2005. Since its inception, the company has dedicated itself to transforming organizations that want to evolve from the traditional hierarchical style to what they call the "New Style of Relationships" ("NER" from *Nuevo estilo de relaciones* in Spanish).

The company is 100% owned by Koldo and in 2020 consisted of eight facilitators with proven and successful experience in managing organizational change based on a radical management model where people increase their knowledge and autonomy, thereby improving the organization as a whole. They have converted about 70 organizations of different sizes and different industries, mainly in the Basque Country, to become self-organized. Many of these organizations were bankrupt when K2K took on the task of leading the change journey.

Grupo NER began as a network created by K2K and gained legal status in 2010. In 2020, the group had a total workforce of around 2,700 people in around 30 companies. The group consists of different types of organizations, in terms of legal form (stock companies, cooperatives, and also nonprofit associations) and size (from small and medium-sized companies to large companies with hundreds of people in different countries) as well as industry (manufacturing, public administration, education, services, etc.).

BUURTZORG

Buurtzorg is both a Dutch company and a foundation founded by Jos de Blok in 2006 that offers care services to patients in their homes. The entire organization is based on autonomous teams of up to 15 nurses who together manage all tasks. The central part of the organization is very small. In 2020, there were 14,000 employees in the Netherlands, with good profitability. Buurtzorg became known through Frederic Laloux's book *Reinventing Organizations* from 2014. Today, Buurtzorg is present in 24 countries, and Buurtzorg's success story continues throughout the world.

FREITAG

Freitag is a Swiss company that makes robust and waterproof bags, backpacks, and sacks from old tarpaulins, bicycle tubes, and seat belts. More recently, they have also created a completely new and biodegradable textile that is produced in Europe.

The company was founded in 1993 by the brothers Markus and Daniel Freitag, who still own the company. Since 2016, Freitag has made the journey from traditional hierarchy to self-organizing based on Holacracy. Today, several hundred products are available in 28 Freitag stores as well as over 300 retailers around the world. In 2020, they produced yearly approximately 700,000 bags and accessories and had 250 employees. As part of the company's circular strategy, there is a swap service, and when we followed up on this in early autumn, 2020, 5,999 users had at that time "swapped" 4,450 bags.

PATAGONIA

The company is headquartered in Ventura, California and manufactures clothing and gear equipment for outdoor adventures. The company was founded in 1973 by Yvon Chouinard and today has more than 1,000 employees. Yvon started climbing mountains at a very young age and made a living by making tools for mountain climbing. In 1970, together with Tom Frost, he created America's largest company in this field. He became increasingly interested in outdoor clothing and gear, which has been Patagonia's focus ever since. The company is known for its way of looking at sustainability and works, for example, with reusable materials and also takes responsibility for its products throughout the value chain. In addition, they are also known for their inclusive approach to all employees and suppliers. The company has taken a clear stance on both political and environmental issues. For example, they have boycotted the Outdoor Sports Retail Expo & Conference in Utah, sued former President Trump, called on municipal councilor Ann-Sofie Andersson in Östersund municipality, Sweden, to stop the construction of the Långforsen power plant, and boycotted Instagram. These are just some examples of having a systemic view of business and society as a whole.

CHOBANI

Chobani is an American food company that specializes in yogurt. The company was founded in 2005 by Hamdi Ulukaya, who bought a facility in the town of South Edmeston, New York, that had been closed by Kraft Foods. Ulukaya hired several of the former Kraft employees as well as a "yogurt master" and launched their brand in 2007. They are today one of the largest players in the American market and have expanded to several countries with approximately 2,300 employees.

Chobani is like a fairy tale, and reading what has been written and listening to the founder and also the CEO on his TED Talks, it is so interesting that they could become one of the best examples of a systemic organization. Unfortunately, despite several months of trying, we have never managed to have a conversation with a single person from the company. On several occasions it felt like we were close; we had correspondence via LinkedIn and e-mail but then the people became very busy and could neither have a shorter Zoom meeting nor a phone call. In the end, we were told that they did not want to participate in our study or stand up for any interview. Since we seek evidence through information from the source and in this case cannot get it, we leave it to the reader to explore further. If what is published is true, Chobani is a very good example of organizing.

Case studies from our own experience

We authors have approximately 30 years of experience of having worked in various types of organizations and roles, mainly in different types of leadership positions. This experience, combined with having taught and researched in organizing, leadership, team development, competence, and more, has led to an overall picture of the view of modern organizing.

Below are some of the larger Swedish organizations in which we have worked for a long time and to which we refer in the book. In some of these organizations, we have also carried out previous research projects in the shape of in-depth case studies.

ERICSSON

Telefonaktiebolaget LM Ericsson is one of the world's largest manufacturers of equipment for building networks for mobile communications. In 2012, the company was the largest in this market with a market share of 38%. Ericsson is a Swedish telecommunications company with an international focus and was founded in 1876 by Lars Magnus Ericsson.

We have both worked at Ericsson as employees and as consultants, and our first leadership experiences came from Ericsson.

SONY MOBILE COMMUNICATIONS INC./SONY ERICSSON

Sony Mobile Communications Inc. is a multinational telecommunications company founded on October 1, 2001 as a joint venture between Sony and Ericsson. It was originally formed as Sony Ericsson Mobile Communications and was headquartered in London, until Sony acquired Ericsson's stake in 2012.

We have both worked at Sony and Sony Ericsson in different roles, one of us as an employee and the other as a consultant for different periods of time. We have actively pursued larger projects and held leading strategic roles. Sony was also a case study in a previous research project that aimed to investigate how to manage competence in knowledge-intensive organizations.

IKEA

Ikea is a multinational conglomerate that designs and sells furniture, kitchenware, home accessories, and other goods, sometimes combined with home services. Ikea was founded in Sweden in 1943 by the, at that time, 17-year-old Ingvar Kamprad and has been the world's largest furniture retailer since 2008. At the end of 2019, there were 433 Ikea stores in 52 countries. Since then, Ikea has mainly grown through online sales and smaller stores more centrally located.

We have worked within Ikea as employees and consultants and have also in recent years worked with "Lead, Work and Organize," a global transformation program that affected all employees within the Ingka group (the retail part of Ikea). In addition, we have acted in various roles within the digital transformation that is carried out in the company.

ASTRAZENECA

AstraZeneca plc is a British-Swedish multinational pharmaceutical company whose products are sold in more than 100 countries. The company was formed on 6 April 1999 through a merger of two pharmaceutical groups, Swedish Astra AB and British Zeneca Group plc. The head office is in Cambridge, UK. In 2019, the company had 70,600 employees worldwide.

One of the authors has held senior positions within AstraZeneca and has also been part of a larger organizational transformation that touched several countries.

AXIS COMMUNICATIONS

Axis Communications AB is a Swedish manufacturer of network cameras for the physical security and video surveillance industry. The company was founded in 1984, has headquarters in Lund, and in 2020 had approximately 3,700 employees. During the 2010s, it was seen as one of the fastest-growing Swedish technology companies.

Axis Communications was the subject of our largest case study in a previous research project that aimed to investigate how to manage competence in knowledge-intensive organizations.

PROGRESSIVE ORGANIZATIONAL MODELS

In this section, we will present some of the organizational models that can be considered progressive. According to the Cambridge Dictionary, progressive ideas or systems are those that encourage change in society or in the way things are done.

Not all progressive organizational models or all progressive activities are always systemic. Something that is systemic refers to the whole, that is to say that the whole organization is taken into account and not just some parts of it. Some progressive models focus on being innovative and doing things differently but neither look at the people nor at the whole.

Today, there are various organizational models that put the people in the center and that are based on self-organizing principles. Several of them have existed for a long time and have grown strong in various types of business. Here we present those that we believe are progressive, have the human perspective, and to some extent are systemic. These also form the basis of the DP model and have contributed as part of a framework for analyzing different companies and case studies.

Agile

Agile frameworks became famous in the early 2000s when 17 men (no women) who were working with different software development methods met in Oregon in February 2001. When they met, they created the Manifesto for Agile Software Development. The reason for the meeting was that traditional project models (called "waterfalls" because the projects were carried out as a sequence of phases) were not suitable for software development. In the traditional project models, the planning phase is usually long, and a lot of things become out of date when the time for implementation arrives. In addition to this, the methods were in general quite rigid where the goal of these traditional methods was to follow the plan and processes. At this stage, a bureaucratic tendency with a lot of documentation and formalization had also emerged.

The Agile Manifesto is based on the following principles:

• Individuals and interactions over processes and tools
• Working software over comprehensive documentation
• Customer collaboration over contract negotiation
• Responding to change over following a plan

These were supplemented with 12 principles for software development and with some standpoints that are the basis for the creation of an agile culture. These positions are focus, courage, sense of obligation, respect, openness, and transparency.

Agile frameworks have since spread to areas other than software development and many organizations are trying to introduce different types of agility to deal with the rapidly changing world around them. Several different methods have emerged such as Scrum, Kanban, XP, and more. Many of the methods have Lean as a starting point and Lean terminology is also used there (for example, Kanban and Kaizen).

But agile mindsets were not born in 2001. In software development, they have their origins in iterative and incremental development that existed as far back as the 1950s. The first major projects with this approach were carried out in the 1970s. During the 1980s, different types of methods were developed, for example EVO (Evolutionary Delivery vs. The Waterfall Methods), which was published by Tom Gilb in the journal *ACM SIGSOFT Software Engineering Notes* in 1985.

EVO had three basic principles:

- Deliver something to the actual end user
- Measure the added value for the user in all important dimensions
- Adjust design and goals based on observed reality

The early agile methods were a reaction to the bureaucratic engineering methods that took a long time and did not take into account the fact that the outside world was changing. Looking at the principles of an agile approach compared to EVO, they are:

- Adaptive
- Iterative and incremental
- People-centered

This means that you must adapt to the changing world around you, develop products and services in stages, and have a focus on the people in the organization.

Although there are a lot of discussions about methods and frameworks, agile is more of a culture. An agile team, for example in Scrum, is self-organized by nature. When it comes to organization within Scrum, there are only three roles, namely Product Owner (Customer), Scrum Master (Team Facilitator), and Team Member. The team also works with continuous improvement of its work processes, usually in so-called "retrospective meetings" after each iteration. Scrum is today the leading method in product development, above all in system development.

Many organizations that try to adopt agile ways of working fail, partly because they are otherwise organized according to a hierarchy of authority (see the section on organization). An agile transformation involves implementing the agile principles mentioned above, namely being adaptive, iterative, and incremental as well as people-centered.

Another difficulty is the traditional budget models found in many organizations where budgets for various initiatives are decided based on a strategy process. The budget process can take up to a year before a budget decision is made. When eventually the budget is approved, the initiatives can start, which can also take some time, and throughout this process much will probably change. An agile approach is to deliver added value at the right time, which becomes difficult with a fixed budget that may have a different focus.

The weakness of agile methods and frameworks from an organizational perspective is that they lack a governance model, which, however, is found in both Sociocracy and Holacracy. In the chapter on the way forward, we reason about how to combine Scrum and Sociocracy in order to have a holistic view and governance of different Scrum teams.

Sociocracy

The French philosopher and sociologist Auguste Comte is considered to be the founder of Sociocracy and its philosophical position when in 1851 he created the word that aimed to define a new way of governance. The word comes from the Latin "*socius*," which means a friend or ally, i.e. people who know each other and belong to the same group or society, while the suffix "cracy" comes from the Greek "*kratía*" and means leadership or rule.

But it was not until 1926 that the first known sociocratic organization was formed. The Dutch educator and pacifist Cornelius Boeke and his wife, the social activist Beatrice Cadbury, formed a very different school for the first time. The Boeke-Cadbury couple were Quakers and the idea started with the fact that they needed a school for their eight children, and therefore they started, in their home, what they called the "children's common workplace"

(Werkplaats Kindergemeenschap). The school was based on their philosophy of peace and the Quaker approach, whose values are integrity, equality, simplicity, community, stewardship of the Earth, and peace. The school worked very well and 20 years later it had become a school with 400 children. At that time, the school was divided into autonomous groups that made decisions through the consensus model, which we present in detail in the section on decision-making.

Many years later, in the 1970s, Gerard Endenburg in the Netherlands developed a governance model for organizations called the "Sociocratic Circle Organization Method" (SCM). Gerald had been a student in Boeke's school and had therefore gained insights into how groups could self-organize but realized that a new way of making decisions and resolving conflicts was needed to be able to be used in other kinds of organizations and, above all, in the business world.

Sociocracy is organized using circles. A circle can be a department, a project, or a work group. When a circle becomes too large or too complex, subcircles are created. If a circle is no longer needed, it is dissolved. In this way, Sociocracy can be compared to a fractal where different circles are created when needed; for example, if you need to make a major change, you can create a circle with several participants who support the change with their skills. Through the book, we will explain how Sociocracy works in various aspects of organizing.

In decision-making, it was realized early on that it was not possible to exclusively apply consensus in larger organizations and therefore the "consent method" was developed, which we present in detail in the section on decision-making. This decision-making method is based on a reverse approach compared to consensus. In the consent method, people do not make a decision by saying yes to a proposal; instead it is about striving for no objections to the proposal. It is important to be able to explain, in a fact-based manner, why one has an objection in order to improve the current proposal. In short, the consent method is about being able to accept the proposal even if it is not what you have as your own preference.

By the mid-1980s, the basic principles of Sociocracy were established:

- decision-making according to the consent method
- appointment of representatives using the consent method
- semi-autonomous circles as organizational units
- feedback as a principle using double-linking.

These principles will be further explained with concrete examples in the parts of the DP model where they are relevant.

Many Dutch organizations started to use SCM, but it took a few years before the method spread around the world. The spread started in 2007 when Sharon Villines and John Buck published the book *We the People*, and in that way the method reached the wide population of English-speaking people around the world.

In the USA, SCM is called Dynamic Governance (DG).

Sociocracy For All (SoFA) is a global nonprofit organization founded in 2016 and had in 2019 approximately 160 members and a handful of employees. Its purpose is to ensure that everyone has access to resources, education, and the opportunity to meet others on the same journey. The organization is financed through training and coaching, membership fees, and donations. Ted Rau is one of the founders of SoFA. He co-wrote with Jerry Koch-Gonzalez the book *Many Voices One Song*, which was published in 2018. The book is a detailed manual for implementing Sociocracy based on SCM principles.

You can read more about SoFA at:
https://www.sociocracyforall.org/

Sociocracy 3.0, also called S3, was launched in 2015 after being developed through the collaboration of James Priest and Bernhard Bockelbrink, who are originally from England and

Germany, respectively. They realized that SCM did not provide sufficient support for the management and organization of the operational work and therefore they began to develop a new framework, which led to S3. S3 integrates concepts and methods found in agile methods, Lean Management, Kanban, Design Thinking, Teal, and several sociocratic governance methods (SCM/Dynamic Governance, Holacracy®, SoFA). It is free and compatible with all agile frameworks, including Scrum.

James's background was in educating children and young people from socially disadvantaged groups in England. Bernhard had a background in system development with extensive experience in agile methods. The framework reflects both of these backgrounds.

One of the biggest differences between S3 and SoFA as well as SCM is that the structure of the latter two can be seen as hierarchies of domains, while S3, which focuses more on collaboration among different stakeholders, can be seen as a guide around how collaboration and interactions are managed, which is that which constitutes the organizational structure.

Sociocracy 3.0 consists of seven basic principles and a collection of ten independent and principle-based patterns.

A pattern is a process, procedure, or guideline that serves as a template or guide for succeeding at a challenge or opportunity. The patterns can be adapted to different contexts and used in no particular order (see Table 2).

Table 2. S3, principles, and patterns

7 principles	11 patterns
Empiricism	Sense-Making and Decision-Making
Consent	Evolving Organizations
Equivalence	Peer Development
Accountability	Enablers of Co-Creation
Transparency	Building Organizations
Effectiveness	Bringing in S3
Continuous improvement	Defining Agreements
	Meeting Formats
	Meeting Practices
	Organizing Work
	Organizational Structure

You can read more about Sociocracy 3.0 at:
https://sociocracy30.org/

The Sociocracy Consulting Group, Sociocracy For All, and Sociocracy 3.0 are nonprofit organizations and publish all their material under a Creative Commons license.

Holacracy

Holacracy was developed in the United States by Brian Robertson over many years by experimenting with new ways of organizing and leading. The influences came from Sociocracy but he also took inspiration from other methods and concepts such as agile methods and procedures.

Brian Robertson discovered Sociocracy, and the work that had been done in the Netherlands, by accident and was impressed by how well it matched what he and his partners had created.

He also found in Sociocracy several organizing principles, such as double-linking, which he added to his model. But he realized that there was a radical difference in approach: Sociocracy was centered around people and therefore the organization and the principles also happened around people, while Brian and his partner, who had a background in system development and went very far in both experimentation and the introduction of agile methods, focused on the organizing of work. In 2006, they coined the new name "Holacracy" not only to be able to highlight the difference but also to emphasize that it is about managing the whole, of which the people are a part.

There are many similarities between Sociocracy and Holacracy, but what can give the impression of being big differences is above all the language. Often, these two methods do not have the same name for the same thing.

But what really differentiates Holacracy from Sociocracy is a stricter governance, for example by validating objections and letting a facilitator end the discussion if he or she thinks the objections are not valid. In Sociocracy, everyone is invited to raise their voice and to do so in turn.

Many consider Holacracy to be more rigid, strict, and controlling, which is seen as positive for some and negative for others. This depends on which glasses you are wearing. In Sociocracy, it is the circle/team that chooses its leader, and this must be accepted via consent of the parent circle, while in Holacracy, the leader is called the "circle leader" and is chosen by the leader of the parent circle. The latter is similar to traditional organizations where a department manager selects/appoints a group manager or supervisor. The same thing happens when something new comes up, for example a problem; then it is the circle leader who is responsible for making sure it is solved. Holacracy may also appear to be more efficient in the way they handle meetings because they make a stricter division between tactical and operational issues.

For more about Holacracy see:
https://www.holacracy.org/

Since culture and context play a role in the choice of approach, it is not strange that Holacracy, which has emerged in the United States, is more driven and result oriented than Sociocracy, which has its roots in Holland and was originally designed according to Quaker principles.

The different sociocratic methods are connected; most of the elements they have in common, but there are also things that are unique to each of the methods.

Teal

Teal, or the blue-green paradigm, was coined by the Belgian Frederic Laloux. During his ten years as a management consultant at McKinsey, he gained experience and insights in different types of organizations. This sparked his interest in diving into the subject. He carried out some autonomous studies at several companies in different industries, and in some of these he conducted in-depth studies. The results of Laloux's studies and reflections are described in his book *Reinventing Organizations* (2014), and this is where Teal is presented and introduced to the wider audience. The book has spread globally, has been translated into 20 languages, and by 2020 had sold more than 700,000 copies.

The book's name comes from a new paradigm around organizing that has been emerging around the world, which led many to rethink how organizations should be formed and managed. Laloux believes that a global liberation movement is taking over, where the leaders driving the change do not know each other, are based in different countries, and have not been aware that there are other leaders carrying out the same transformation. In spite of dissimilarities, Laloux thought that there are remarkable similarities in what they want to achieve and their perception of organization.

Laloux's book describes an evolutionary model that is characterized by Integral Theory, which was created in the 1970s by Ken Wilber and which is based on the fact that everything is connected and has an evolutionary development. Wilber's model describes how our awareness develops, and he uses different colors to symbolize level and perspective. Teal is the level of consciousness where we view everything from a planet-centered and integrated holistic perspective.

Teal Holism	Wholeness	Self-organized or systemic companies and organizations	
Green Pluralism	Idealism	Non-profit organizations, social networks, culture-driven companies	
Orange Performance	Materialism	Traditional companies, Political organizations	
Amber Conformism	Control	Catholic church, military, public organizations, schools	
Red Impulsivity	Power	Street gangs, mafia	

Figure 5. Organizational evolution

The red paradigm is characterized by powerful and charismatic leaders who control the organization through their power. These leaders control chaos and instill both fear and respect. Organizations in this stage are characterized by division of labor into cells and specialization of work and have clear operational goals. Examples of these organizations include the mafia, street gangs, and mercenaries.

The amber paradigm. Here we can see the first forms of hierarchical structures with specific roles that are usually defined in detail, as well as control mechanisms. Another characteristic is the existence of long-term goals and implementation of processes. Examples of these organizations include governments and public schools, but also traditional churches.

The orange paradigm. This paradigm is also based on hierarchies but with a focus on profit, and the organizations are characterized by competition. They are characterized by the fact that innovation is important, which gives rise to the introduction of research and development departments as well as the introduction of metrics and follow-up. Everyone has the opportunity to advance because what governs is the performance in relation to the follow-up of the organization's goals. There is also a very strong focus on the shareholders. In these organizations, commitment is often found to be low. Examples of these organizations include large and international corporations.

The green paradigm. These organizational forms have emerged as a reaction to the sense of futility that employees may feel in the orange paradigm. Here, employees can find meaning in their work and they are generally more engaged. Hierarchy is still present but there can also exist another kind of hierarchy based on relationships and not on formal roles. The focus is on customer experience, there is a striving for balance between the stakeholders and not just the shareholders, and the company's culture and values are central. Individuals have more responsibility for their competence, but there is still a hierarchy that limits their autonomy and influence.

The blue-green paradigm, also called "Teal." As with the previous paradigms, this has arisen as a reaction to previous organizing principles and strives to create freedom and eliminate the rigidity and dehumanization that existed before. This is done by abolishing hierarchies and creating room for participation. The focus is on wholeness, self-organizing, and evolutionary purpose, and, from an organizing perspective.

DDO

DDOs, or Deliberately Developmental Organizations, were introduced in 2016 by Robert Kegan and Lisa Laskow Lahey from Harvard Business School through their book *An Everyone Culture*. The book is based on an article from 2014 that they wrote together with some other researchers. The authors describe the model as radical and as having the aim of "unleashing the company's potential." They take the position that all people have potential and that everyone wants to develop. With this position, they believe that it is wrong to want only a few people to participate in different types of programs; it is about getting everyone to develop through their daily work.

A DDO is organized around the belief that organizations thrive when there is a culture that supports that people's strongest motivation is to grow. Its motto is: "Working is learning and learning is the job itself." The point is that adults can develop and grow.

Kegan and Laskow's position is that in most organizations, almost everyone is doing a second job that no one is paying them to do—namely, hiding their weaknesses, trying to look their best, and managing other people's impressions of them. There is perhaps no more waste of company resources than this. The ultimate cost is that neither the organization nor its employees can realize their full potential.

A DDO consists of a balance between the following three parts:

Edge: Here we get our challenge, are spurred to grow and learn, a drive for self-improvement.

Home: Here we are supported so that we can flourish in times of failure, weakness, and vulnerability.

Groove: Here we build methods and create feedback loops.

There are some characteristics here that are similar to Teal and agile philosophy, such as the importance of creating a learning company culture, room for personal development, self-organization, and transparency. But the big difference is that a DDO aims to get people to move faster than anyone thinks possible. There is also a strong focus on profit margin by making people grow; profits are expected to grow as well. The examples of the introduction of DDOs that exist today are organizations that are hierarchical and where decisions are made by managers and where there are traditional roles. The difference from the traditionally hierarchical organization is that there is a high level of transparency and that everyone has an opportunity (or an obligation) to grow and to learn new things, and that continuous feedback is built into the culture.

WHAT IS NEW?

In the current discussion about organizing, there is a discussion about "the new way" regarding organizing in the future and it is described as a revolutionary approach. We know that it is not really that new and we have found examples both in and outside Sweden that show that this is the case.

Former protagonists

Falu copper mine in the region Dalarna in Sweden is one of these examples where ore has been mined for several hundred years. As early as in 1347, an organization was created that was very advanced for its time.

The new way of organizing the mine was established after the king, Magnus Eriksson, visited Kopparberget. The king was enraged that the old documents relating to the operation and distribution of the mine from his ancestors had been neglected. Then he wrote a new letter of privilege, which was very detailed and formed the basis of how the work at the mine would be organized. According to the mining privileges, among other things, miners were not allowed to join any foreman who would plead their case and rule over them. However, there were supervisors whose role was to coordinate the work.

Until the eighteenth century, the mine was organized in such a way that a shareholder in a smeltery, a miner, employed his own hands to pick up his ore. In that way it was a very loose organization. The organizational structure was very similar to a modern limited company and the work groups were self-organized. The fact that the work groups worked in some kind of autonomous team had many advantages because the work was associated with great risks. By having a group mindset, you protected each other and each other's tools and also gave room to organize the work so that it could maximize the team's deliverables.

During the seventeenth century, Falu copper mine was the world's largest copper producer and the country's largest workplace with more than 1,000 employed workers and with an organizational structure not so different from Buurtzorg in the Netherlands, which is one of our case studies (see the protagonists section). From the eighteenth century onwards, the organization moved towards becoming more and more centralized.

Another example is Scandinavian airline SAS from the 1980s, which underwent a major change when Janne Carlzon was appointed president and CEO in 1981. His innovative way of looking at the employees, believing in their competence and focusing on the customers' needs, helped him to turn the loss-laden company into a company with a large profit. Janne turned SAS from an authoritarian hierarchical organization to a flatter organization with only a few levels in the hierarchy. One of the authors met an employee in the 1990s who described the impact on the way of working as follows:

"We had no managers at the airport, we planned all our activities together in the team. There was always one of us at the desk meeting our customers. There are always changes in airline traffic; flights can be delayed, which affects other flights and so on. In these situations, we have to rebook our customers onto other flights. But sometimes some customers were not happy with the changes, especially business travelers, and wanted to talk to the manager. What we did then was that the one at the desk went back to our office to find someone else from the team.

That person put on a jacket with many stripes and went out to talk to the customer. The customer was almost always satisfied after speaking with 'the manager'."

Janne Carlzon's experience and thoughts are described in the book *Tear Down the Pyramids!* from 1985. His position was that a customer-driven organization cannot be led by autocratic leaders who sit at the top of the hierarchy without knowing what is happening further down. The leaders must instead be visionary, be able to inform and teach in an educational way, and be able to inspire the employees.

Decisions must be delegated to those who do the work and not concentrated on those at the top of the nodes of the hierarchical organizational chart.

Another example is the success story of the Swedish state-owned company Studsvik during the 1990s. Tõive Kivikas got the assignment to take over the CEO role and shut down the company as it had been running at a loss for a long time. In addition to the financial losses, the working environment in the company was not good—partly because of the negative image that the media presented, partly because of the management of the company.

The staff did not feel well, they did not have much faith in the future, and sick leave was high. The average age of the employees was 53 and the opportunities to get new jobs were not that great due to the fact that they were highly educated with specific and highly specialized skills that were not much required in other industries. Figure 6 clearly shows the financial turnaround the company underwent.

Studsvik Group - Profit

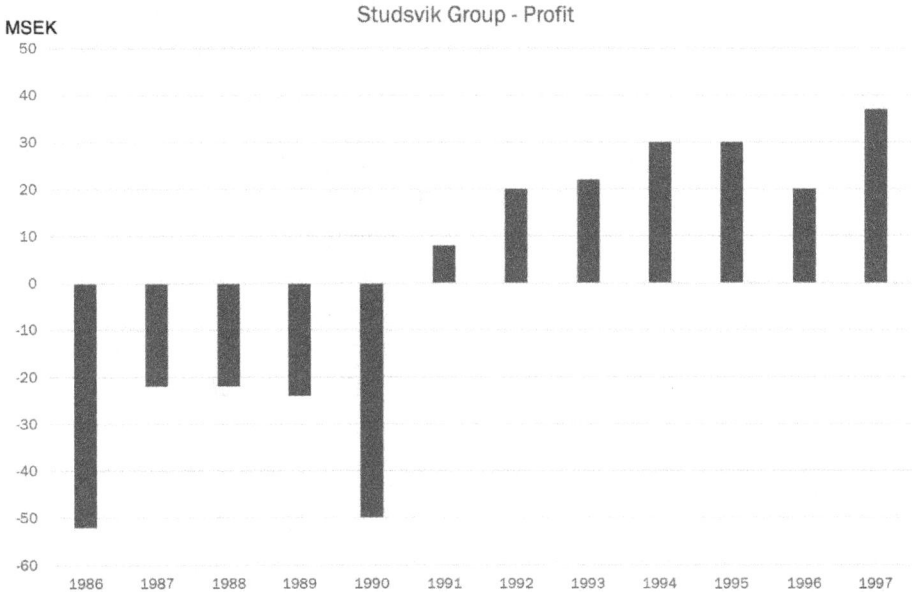

Figure 6. Studsvik Group's results 1986–1997

How was it possible to break such a trend and go from a loss of 50 million to a profit of six million in one year? The answer is simple: through a different leadership that put the people in the middle and through a distribution of power where decisions were made by those who had knowledge, and not by Tõive as CEO or by other high-ranking managers.

Tõive explains that his success is based on the following six insights and positions:

1. The staff are the company's most valuable asset.
2. The staff have the knowledge.
3. The staff have the ability.
4. The staff want to do a good job.
5. The staff do not always get the opportunity to show what they are really capable of.
6. Tõive's task: Create insight and consensus and give the staff the opportunity to show what they really know and are capable of.

He also adds that a creative culture can only be created when you (as a leader) dare to take risks and leave control to others.

Studsvik was transformed into a thriving company where innovation took off and created positive headlines around the world. Several companies spun off from Studsvik and a revolutionary new way of handling radioactive waste was created. No one had to be fired and Tõive's leadership style generated added value in all respects. This took place 30 years ago and we know that it was not an isolated phenomenon, as there were other Swedish companies that, under humane and democratic leaders, created organizational cultures where people thrived and could develop.

The Swedish management model

Have you heard of Eric Rhenman? If not, you can take comfort in the fact that you are not alone, as most of the Swedes we ask have not. In reality, very few have!

In his book *The Company as a Controlled System* from 1964, the metaphor of a company as a system whose components are connected and interdependent is presented. He had a strong focus on the relationships between stakeholders and believed that the principles of Scientific Management created bureaucracy. Eric Rhenman believed in a democratization of working life and self-government.

Dividing his time between being an academic and a management consultant, he took on the role of bridging the gap between research and reality. For that purpose, in 1966 he formed SIAR (Scandinavian Institutes for Administrative Research).

He was a docent at the Stockholm School of Economics, a professor of business administration at Lund University and at Harvard Business School, and is considered one of the founders of what is known as the Swedish management model.

Today, there is not much talk about the Swedish management model, but other trends such as agile methods, Teal, and Sociocracy are in the spotlight when it comes to organizing and the way of working. In a report regarding the Swedish management model from Guller's group published by Vinnova (2007, p. 14), the following can be read: "The vacuum (within the Swedish management model) that, for example, the professor and consultant Eric Rhenman and his company SIAR left behind itself has not been filled by any Swedish actor. There is thus no strong advocate for spreading the model among today's management consultant firms. Instead, it is international consulting firms such as McKinsey, Boston Consulting Group, Bain, and Deloitte that dominate."

It has been a few years since the report was published but these claims are still relevant. One can ask why the Swedish model has gained less power since the 1990s. How is it that Swedish companies and organizations, which have traditionally been less bureaucratic, less formal, and flatter with a tendency towards decentralized leadership, have become more hierarchical? Furthermore, how is it possible that the tradition of creating work environments where there are good employee relations and an atmosphere characterized by competent employees who take responsibility for their work and have high loyalty and initiative has been transformed into workplaces where only 14% feel engaged?

The answers are, above all, among the effects that have accompanied globalization. With this, new ownership structures have emerged and created demands for quick returns and strong governance. This purpose is in contradiction to the traditional Swedish management model, which is based on a long-term perspective and faith in the employees. Another explanation is that, again as a result of globalization, more company leaders from cultures that are more hierarchical, and where there is a widespread tradition of Command and Control, have entered the management of Swedish companies.

In their book *The Nordic Secret*, Lene Rachel Andersen and Tomas Björkman attribute the origin, spread, and establishment of the Swedish way to, among other things, the massive movement that was set in motion through the folk high schools in the

Nordic countries and thus laid the foundation for the Swedish management model.

In 1900, there were 100 established folk high schools in Denmark, 75 in Norway, and 150 in Sweden. In these formative centers, young people who were about to enter working life could learn and experience independence and develop democratic values for six months. Several of the people we interviewed refer specifically to the massive public education in the form of study circles, folk high schools, and a well-functioning apprenticeship system as the cornerstones of the Swedish (and Nordic) approach, not only regarding business but also in society at large. These people also mention that today's situation in Sweden, where workplaces are less democratic, is partly due to the fact that many of the current business leaders were formed in business schools where they learned completely different values than those advocated at folk high schools.

Within the framework of the Swedish management model, it is mentioned that both Scandinavian Airlines, under Jan Carlzon's management, and Volvo, under PG Gyllenhammar's management, with their inclusive way of making decisions, were examples. PG was a pioneer when it came to including union representatives in the management room, and this was long before it became a legal requirement. ABB, under Percy Barnevik's leadership, is regarded as an early example where decentralization was on the agenda and where local traditions were encouraged to set the framework for local operations. Another example is Ingvar Kamprad, who created Ikea. With his way of creating an organizational culture with soft values coined on participation and trust, and where everyone can reach everyone else within the company, he was also part of the Swedish management model.

Can you think about which organizational leader or company could be a living example for the Swedish management model?

The answer is not obvious and not easy. Many give examples of public activities or municipalities. This is not so strange because the Swedish management model is based on a series of factors that collide with the short-term profits that many companies demand today. Instead, the model fits more with the human service that public services aim to provide.

It is time to go back to the good values and develop these further in a progressive way where people are at the center, and which also generates financial prosperity for the owners, employees, stakeholders, and society. However, it is important to also take into account that the outside world has changed, work is different, technology has developed, and we have more and more relations with other countries.

THE DP MODEL

In this chapter, we will describe the 12 different areas that constitute the DP (Distributed Power) model. In each part, we present several concrete examples from our case studies as well as from other organizations. These are alternated with brief background theories. Since our purpose is to highlight successful examples and implementations, we anonymize the organizations that have less successful stories.

The distribution of power is what we consider to be the common denominator of all the models and theories regarding progressive and systemic forms of organization that we have delved deeply into, all the case studies that we have analyzed, and the experiences from our long working life.

As the world faces many challenges, a fruitful and sustainable way to deal with these organizations is to view them as living organisms that are part of a larger ecosystem. It means having a systemic approach and a philosophy where everything is connected and constitutes a system where the whole is greater than the sum of its parts. The DP model fills this empty space.

The DP model can be seen as a systemic approach that can help organizations to implement the improvements or transformations needed to face the future.

PEOPLE

The first area of the DP model is people. It is about people constituting the core of an organization, which is not something new. During the 1990s, many companies were created with names referring to people, for example Human Capital and Human Entrance.

The idea behind HR (Human Resources) as a function, as a special competence, and specific role was initiated from the need to focus on the people in organizations. What differs over time is which part of the person the organization believes it needs (this does not always match the real needs). During industrialism it was the <u>hands</u>, during the post-industrial era, which is also called the "information technology era," it was the <u>brain</u>, meaning knowledge, and in the current era, often called the "digital era," it is the <u>brain and the heart</u>, which also includes feelings, meaning the whole person.

The evolution has led, throughout the ages, to a change in the view of people and organizations. In the same way as when feudalism transitioned to the industrial era and people were free to take up an employment, we can today see a kind of global movement where employees are no longer just bringing in arms, legs, and brains to their organizations but also their own thoughts and feelings. This is what Teal is all about—a holistic approach where people are allowed to bring their whole selves into the organization. Organizations that remain in their old ways of thinking create suffering in terms of stress and burnout. This is the root cause of why only 15% of employees are engaged in their work. A consequence of low well-being is also the reason why many employees are considering changing jobs.

A survey conducted by the Manpower Group in 2019 shows that almost seven out of ten employees in Sweden are thinking about changing, or have already decided to change, jobs (see Table 3 below).

There are no major differences in relation to age, gender, or being a manager or not.

Table 3. Are you thinking about changing job?

	All	Male	Female	Below 29 years	30–45 years	Older than 45 years	Managers	Nonmanagers
Yes	29%	24%	32%	27%	28%	31%	34%	28%
Considering	39%	43%	35%	36%	41%	38%	40%	39%
No	32%	33%	33%	37%	32%	31%	26%	34%

Source: Manpower Group, 2019

The development in terms of sick leave due to mental illness has risen significantly in Sweden, from 30% in 2010 (quarter 1) to 48% in 2019 (quarter 1). Thus, every other sick leave in 2019 was caused by mental illness. Not all of these sick leaves are due to work, but the majority of the stress-related cases have been caused by work, or at least work has contributed to them.

We can see that these figures are similar in many other comparable countries.

In organizations that consider themselves people-centric, well-being must be one of the most important metrics. It should be just as obvious to be able to see numbers that report well-being in the same way as profit and turnover. The DP model advocates that the key to people's well-being and engagement in organizations is to ensure an environment and a culture where psychological safety prevails.

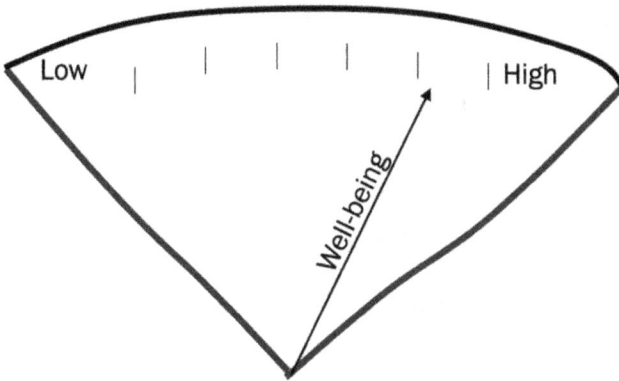

Figure 7. Well-being KPI

PSYCHOLOGICAL SAFETY IN THE WORKPLACE

The term "psychological safety" is widely used today and has become trendy, but the concept was coined by Warren Bennis and Edgar Schein as early as 1965. They saw this as an essential aspect in being able to develop organizations towards a less bureaucratic culture. Their belief was that psychological safety needs to be present for people to feel safe when implementing changes in an organization.

Since Bennis and Schein's work, many researchers have devoted themselves to analyzing and understanding various links between psychological safety and performance, well-being, commitment, learning, and innovation.

One of these researchers is Amy C. Edmondson from Harvard Business School, who has been researching this topic since the 1990s. Her findings and thoughts reached a wider spread after she was hired by Google to run one of their internal research projects, "Aristotles," which started in 2012. The purpose of the project was to find out what factors distinguish successful and innovative teams. One hundred eighty different teams were included in the study. The results showed that the common denominators for successful teams were that the team climate was characterized by high trust, that people dared to communicate ideas at an early stage to get feedback, and that they dared to review and criticize others' ideas. What characterized these teams was that the members felt that:

1. They could share thoughts and ideas without the risk of alienating themselves.
2. They could admit mistakes without the fear of being blamed.
3. People had respect for each other's feelings.
4. The team members were good at reading and understanding their colleagues' reactions.
5. Everyone in the group had the same amount of space and, for example, had the space to speak equally as much during meetings.

The term "psychological safety" has been further developed by, among others, Timothy R. Clark, who has created a model consisting of four stages. He believes that we humans thrive in environments where we are respected and where we can (1) feel included, (2) feel safe in learning, (3) feel safe in being able to contribute, and (4) feel confident in challenging the status quo. It's about being able to do all of this without fear of being ridiculed, marginalized, or penalized in any way. The four steps are summarized in Table 4.

Table 4. Four stages of psychological safety, updated from Clark (2020)

Stage 1: Inclusion safety	Feeling accepted and involved in a social context. Being able to interact with others without fear of exclusion, embarrassment, or punishment, which increases confidence, resilience, and independence.
Stage 2: Learner safety	Feeling safe in being able to learn and develop. Being able to ask questions, give and receive feedback, experiment, and even make mistakes. This without feeling afraid or stupid.
Stage 3: Contributor safety	Feeling that you can contribute and make a difference. Feeling confident that, as a full member of the team, you can contribute with your skills and abilities and thus create added value. This with commitment and enthusiasm.
Stage 4: Challenger safety	Feeling safe in being able to make things better. Feeling safe in being able to challenge the status quo without negative consequences or the risk of harming your personal position or reputation. With sincerity come innovation and creativity.

The content seems like obvious stages, but in reality, employees are very often confronted with situations where there is a lack of at least one of these four stages.

Think about situations where you have felt excluded. What were the consequences?
Also, think about what other feelings they brought up and write them down if possible.
How good is the psychological safety in your work group(s)?
Make an analysis of the four steps.

There are many situations where the environment at first glance appears to be good because people feel nice and relaxed. We are going to share a story of a meeting at a company where we were hired to help them with their digital journey.

There were three digital experts participating in the meeting, two IT architects, four developers, and a business representative. The atmosphere was good before the meeting. Everyone laughed and one of the participants showed some pictures from his last vacation. Others shared personal stories, including the fact that one of them had broken up with his partner. Our client was proud of the atmosphere in the group and was totally convinced that there was 100% psychological safety in the group.

In fact, everything fell apart during the meeting. The experts just asked questions to each other and used many terms and abbreviations that the others did not know or understand. As a result, the rest of the participants felt excluded. Some wanted to ask questions that could lead to learning something new but did not dare because of the fear of being considered less knowledgeable and therefore less worthy. The youngest of the participants wrote down some thoughts, ideas, and questions but said nothing during the meeting. When we looked afterwards at what he had written, there were very good ideas that would have contributed to the meeting itself, but also to solving the problems the group was facing.

The business representative discovered that the experts had misinterpreted an important business requirement and asked questions about it, but the conversation contained a lot of terms that he really did not understand. The explanations he received were also exclusionary because of the terminology, which also lost the message that there were misinterpretations around the contractual requirement.

The meeting ended with loud laughs, hugs, and plans for an afterwork.

Now, when you have read the example above, we would like to ask you to look at what you recently wrote down and think again about how good psychological safety is, or has been, in the organizations where you have worked.

Everyone contributes to whether an environment is safe or not. Therefore, it is important to analyze and examine oneself regarding one's own contribution to psychological safety. It is through reflection and with increased self-awareness that healthy organizations are created.

Many organizations have some way to go when it comes to how we treat each other and how psychologically safe our work environment is. Kristoffer Holm at Lund University conducted a study on this subject in 2019. It showed that 73% had been exposed to uncivilized behavior from a colleague and 53% from their manager, and that 66% had themselves treated someone else badly. Everyone is involved in creating psychological safety!

> Within the DP model, we consider psychological safety to be the most important prerequisite for innovations and adaptation to a rapidly changing world. Only those organizations that succeed in this will survive the next two decades.

THE GOOD ORGANIZATION

In order for employees to feel good, be engaged, thrive, and produce in a satisfactory way, good organizations are needed. This is so obvious that it is difficult to understand why it is that not all organizations are good in the sense that they put people first. The explanation lies in the fact that organizations are created and are led by people with both good and less good qualities and that many people have inherited the view that an organization should work according to Command and Control. Furthermore, most of today's organizations have been created with other purposes and for other reasons than ensuring the well-being of employees. Real change does take time.

Historically, it is possible to identify many people who realized that the view of people in relation to work situations had to change. Will Schutz is undoubtedly one of those who has made a significant contribution to the development of people, groups, and organizations through the model he developed in the 1980s, *The Human Element*. At an early stage, Schutz created collaboration with human resource developers and organizational consultants from Sweden and Japan. Sweden is also one of the countries where many leaders, managers, organizational consultants, and coaches have undergone training within The Human Element, something that was started in the early 1990s, and which has also contributed to a positive impact in Swedish organizations.

The model has several perspectives and several dimensions that together constitute a whole. The basic dimensions of the model are:

1. Inclusion: belonging or being outside
2. Control: the degree of power, influence, and self-determination
3. Openness: the degree of truthfulness and transparency of oneself and others
4. Meaning: gaining attention or being ignored
5. Competence: perception of oneself and others as competent or incompetent
6. Appreciation: liking oneself and others, and being appreciated

These six dimensions are applied to four perspectives, which can be summarized as:

- My relationship with others
- Others in relation to myself
- Myself
- Others

We are happy to see that much of what is included in the new theories and models are actually variants of the cornerstones found in The Human Element. Due to trends in terminology and concepts, things are expressed today in a different way, but they are very similar.

K2K and the NER group, whose motto is based on creating and managing relationships, can really be considered as living examples of organizations where The Human Element is applied.

This is not something that they themselves communicate, or perhaps are even aware of, but they are the conclusions that we draw from their way of being.

When Tõive Kivikas let the employees at Studsvik come up with proposals about which products and services could be considered for further development, he actually used all six dimensions in the model above. He began by including all people in the discussion by developing principles. He was extremely open when he told the people that he did not know the way forward, that the situation was serious, and that they only had a few months to turn around the critical situation in which they had been for a long time.

The people in the organization were given control, i.e. influence and power, and Tõive believed in their competence. In addition, everyone in the organization felt they had a meaning because everyone's opinion was considered. Furthermore, he created a new culture of showing appreciation to others and to themselves for accomplishing almost the impossible, which was turning large losses into profits in a short period of time.

In other words, Tõive followed all the steps of The Human Element without knowing it. He acted according to his basic view of how people are viewed and how engagement is created.

THE HUMAN BEING IN THE CENTER

Most people do not want a job where they work eight hours a day just to make money, they want to be a part of something and also contribute to a higher purpose. Therefore, it is important that there is a purpose for the tasks as well as for the organization that they work in. An organization can be seen as a way of structuring work, but it is above all relationships between people. For K2K this is the essential thing and the reason why they formed the NER group, where everything is about relationships between people. Because of this approach, an important principle for them is to not dismiss anyone because of a financially critical situation. Instead, in bad times everyone helps each other. This became very clear during Covid-19 when some of the companies in the group had to reduce salaries, but everyone could keep their jobs.

The DP model states that good and systemic organizations can be created when, and only when, people's needs and wishes are considered. A people-centric organization means organizing around people's competences and interests instead of around structures and processes. It is about adopting an approach where adults are treated as adults and where people are more important than organizational structures. To transform organizations into healthy work environments, control systems should be replaced by a culture where trust, responsibility, and freedom prevail.

Organizations that are people-centric must have principles that guide daily decision-making and provide advice on how to act. The principles must reflect the belief that people come first and should state how values are to be fulfilled.

A good example is from the company Gore, which, ever since the company was founded in 1958, has had four values with associated principles as shown in Table 5.

Table 5. Gore's four principles

freedom	We believe in each other, and we will allow, help, and empower our fellow Associates to grow in knowledge, skill and scope of responsibility.
fairness	Together, we are responsible for sustaining an engaging Enterprise built on inclusiveness, striving to be fair with each other and everyone with whom we do business.
Commitment	We make and keep our own commitments to demonstrate personal responsibility to each other, our teams and our customers.
Waterline	We are all shareholders, and we will consult with the appropriate Associates before taking an action "below the waterline" that could cause serious damage to the long-term success or reputation of our Enterprise.

Another example from our case studies where the values and principles that guide the organization are centered around people is Jayway, whose principles can be seen in Table 6.

Table 6. Jayway's principles

People first	We value community. We make time to have fun together, celebrate together, and share struggles together. It's important that everyone gets to enjoy being at work so we welcome people for who they are, keep our offices family-friendly and make our studios feel like home.
Humble Brilliance	We love what we do, and we're good at it. Pursuing excellence goes far beyond our work; it's our passion. We take pride in being technological groundbreakers, obsessively creative in finding ways to improve the human experience.
Respectful Autonomy	With great freedom comes great responsibility. Our teams have freedom in how to solve tasks — we trust each other to know best how to do our work. Our clients trust us with their success so we take the time to challenge ourselves and make decisions we stand behind.
Evolve through Curiosity	Giving and asking for help is second nature to us. Everyone is expected to contribute to our competence development. It's the campfire we gather around to teach, learn, and master our skills. We are experts at becoming experts in things that don't exist yet
Be the change	Our company is built by us for us. Not everything is perfect, but everyone is free to take action to make things better. We prioritize economic, social, and environmental sustainability and make choices we can be proud of long term. We are the change we want to see in the world.

These values are of extreme importance because the new generations want to see people-centered principles and not just principles that deal with the approach to financial transactions and the way of doing business. In the very near future, we will see that organizations that do not shift their focus from the financial to the human and include caring for the planet will have difficulty attracting and retaining staff.

WHEN PEOPLE BECOME THE ORGANIZATION'S ONLY AND/OR MOST IMPORTANT ASSET

If you go back to industrialization and the construction of production lines, most of a company's capital was tied up in fixed assets in the form of machinery, equipment, buildings, etc. This is how most organizations worked until the turn of the millennium. At the end of the twentieth century, knowledge-intensive work, i.e. working with the brain instead of with arms and legs, increased rapidly. One of the most important reasons was what was then called "computerization": Computers and networks made it possible for us to communicate and work in a completely different way than before. Since then, this development has accelerated and the attempt is being made to automate work that is repetitive. This is actually a positive thing since most repetitive work wears out our bodies.

The proportion of knowledge-intensive work increased dramatically around the turn of the millennium. By knowledge-intensive, we mean that knowledge is being transferred more and more quickly and people have to learn new things faster. Knowledge also became increasingly accessible through the development of the Internet. We are also starting to interact with each other more and more remotely. We send e-mails, chat, have digital meetings, etc. This is increasing more and more, and especially today, and during the Covid-19 pandemic, it has exploded.

As we mentioned earlier, today we use the brain and the heart more and more instead of arms and legs. But organizing has not kept up with the change at the right pace and has most often been a step behind. At the end of the twentieth century, many new companies were created whose only asset was people. Many of these companies belonged to what was then called the "first IT era," the "IT bubble," or the "IT boom." Our financial institutions were not prepared to be able to financially value these types of companies, which meant that most of them were overvalued.

One of the most fascinating companies in Sweden in the latter part of the 1990s was Framfab, or Framtidsfabriken as it was first called. The founder, Jonas Birgersson, was one of the IT pioneers and a very charismatic person who was also known for his orange fleece sweater. Framtidsfabriken was created by some young students in the city of Lund, in the south of Sweden, with Jonas at the head. They created a different kind of business where everyone was equal and wanted to have fun together, while making money. Jonas was not a traditional executive but more "one of the bunch." He always emphasized that the employees were the company's only asset. Framfab used to invite all the employees for a beer on Friday afternoons and Jonas used to say that after the Friday beer the company had no assets because then everyone had gone home to have a well-deserved weekend. Jonas Birgersson and Framfab contributed to changing the view about the importance of people instead of processes. Framfab was also part of the IT bubble, which was characterized by overoptimism and ended up in an economic disaster, but that is another story.

Some of our case studies, for example Centigo and Jayway, are children of this evolution. Centigo started its journey in the early 2000s with the idea that everyone should be a small-business owner, but in a larger organization. They believed that individuals would do what he or she was best at and develop his or her ideas, but still belong to something bigger. They invested in young entrepreneurs who wanted to develop themselves, but also to develop new things, new innovations. Thomas Dagsberg created Jayway around the same time and with the premise that they would be the best in software development, Java, and agile development methods. In both companies, people were considered the only asset.

THE EQUAL VALUE OF PEOPLE

As this book is being written, the Black Lives Matter movement has been sweeping the world for a few months, and many abuses that have their basis in discrimination, both in society and in organizations, have once again been highlighted.

Although all people have equal value, this does not mean that everyone should have an opinion on all things and be involved in all decisions. As we discuss in connection with the chapter on decision-making, decisions must be made by those who have knowledge in the area and, if possible, by those who will be affected by the decision. Sociocracy For All has the motto "Many voices, one song." This motto means that all people in the organization have equal value, and also that diversity enriches. Any form of exclusion due to gender, origin, sexual orientation, or disability also means that the organization is missing competent people who could add value.

An ongoing trend in many organizations is to put *diversity and inclusion* on the agenda. This is done by training staff and hiring people from groups that have previously been discriminated against. This is a big step, but we within the DP model believe that it is not enough because organizations still have some work to do regarding the equal value of all people. One of the companies that we have worked with for 15 years is, according to its own statement, consciously inclusive. This is an international organization and people have different levels of education. In recent times, many openly gay people and transsexuals have been employed, which is very positive. However, the company has failed to put the systemic mindset in relation to diversity and inclusion as this only applies in certain areas. For example, there are almost no people with physical disabilities of any kind among the more than 2,000 employees who work at the head office in Malmö. There is only one elevator in the four-story building, which is mainly used for transporting goods. The reason is that the culture in the organization rewards physical activity and sportsmanship. It is positive that the staff should keep in good physical shape, but they forget about those who have physical disabilities. Nor is there any employee who wears a veil, despite the fact that a significant proportion of the population in Malmö are practicing Muslims.

In a systemic organization, the workforce should be a representation of the surrounding society.

PEOPLE'S RELATIONSHIP TO WORK

When it comes to why we humans work, there are two explanations that dominate. One is that we only work because we need money to survive. The second is that everyone must have something to do, and it is through work that we create meaning in our lives. We believe that there are actually several things to consider.

For example, you might think that a nice environment is required for people to thrive, but there are many examples of work that is heavy and is carried out in dirty environments where people thrive, are engaged, and proud of what they do. One of the authors of this book worked at Swedish Steel (SSAB) in Oxelösund during the 1990s. SSAB produces steel and during this period coal was part of the production and coke was produced in a part of the company's area called the "coking plant." This was a very poor physical working environment, objectively speaking: The air was black with coke dust, sulphureous smoke rose from the furnace where the workers worked, and the noise level was high. The coking plant was situated next to a beautiful archipelago, so the environment was somewhat surreal. In any case, the coking plant had very low sickness absence and, on average, a high number of years of employment, as well as positive results in employee surveys. This was because the people enjoyed being together and the dirty environment nevertheless contributed to a great sense of community among the employees. People were also proud to work at the coking plant. Nowadays, this type of unhealthy work environment is not allowed in Sweden, but the example shows that community is important to us humans and that we generally enjoy being part of a context. People can feel good and engaged, even when the tasks are not fun.

Another aspect that must be considered is people's lives as a whole. Some work may not be uplifting in itself because it is repetitive, but there are other ways to create value in it. We visited a pick-and-pack warehouse in Denmark where we met an employee who had worked there for over 20 years and was satisfied, happy, and engaged in work. He helped many of the new employees and contributed to reducing stress and increasing well-being within the group. When we asked why he enjoyed and liked his work, he replied that it was because the work was easy, so he had energy left to do many fun things in his spare time. He grew plants, painted paintings, and built miniature houses. For him, work was an enabler and therefore he enjoyed himself and could not imagine working with anything else or anywhere else. This is also part of systemic thinking where the work is part of a whole.

So when we look at the statistics of Manpower's survey that we presented earlier in this section, we suggest that the high number of people who are thinking about changing, or have decided to change, jobs do so because the working climate is not good, because they do not get the opportunity to use their skills or develop their interests, or because they want to make the balance in life work.

Managers with meaningful tasks account for a large part of the stress-related sick leave. One of the reasons is that their situation is not good overall—for example, because work takes all their energy and there is not much energy left for other activities or family life. Another reason is that they cannot participate with "their whole true self" at work but must play an expected role based on which their performance is measured.

People in the Western world spend a third of their time at work and the time has come to demand that work enrich our lives in one way or another. This can be through self-realization, learning, fellowship, value creation, financial participation, or meaningfulness.

The DP model places people at the center. The remaining 11 areas that make up the model relate to people being the most important asset in all organizations, regardless of industry or purpose

Voice from the field: Cristina Sánchez – People Operations Manager at BrokenRubik, Montevideo, Uruguay

Cristina is trained in fields related to the humanities and project management. She has worked in public organizations with policies related to digital transformation and people's access to information. Currently, she works as People Operations Manager at the IT-company Broken Rubik. She believes deeply in people and organizations as vectors of change for a more equitable and sustainable world.

Knowledge has been the guiding light for humanity in the most remarkable aspects of its development. Creating and sharing knowledge is one of the principles of the movement that connects us and makes us better, day by day, in our lives. In the 21st century, we are witnessing the revolution of specialization. Specialized knowledge has become the most demanded form of knowledge in work environments, but one aspect must remain central when promoting knowledge and its specializations: the comprehensive view. Related and relational knowledge. And that has to do with understanding people as a whole.

In work environments, we often say that one's "personal and professional life should be kept separate." Is that possible? Can we leave our personal experiences, beliefs, and experiences aside when applying "professional knowledge"? I don't think so.

This book repeatedly speaks of well-being as one of the determining factors in generating healthy environments. Well, at BrokenRubik, we believe that there are healthy ways to mix one's personal and professional life, and we believe that promoting that union in our teams at work generates a sense of belonging, commitment, and better work results.

Let me give you an example. If a colleague has to take their kid to get vaccinated and the medical appointment schedules coincide with work hours, it is BrokenRubik's responsibility, not only to allow but also to promote a culture in which that the colleague sees leaving work for a couple of hours to take their child to get vaccinated as a possible and desirable option. Fostering parental co-responsibility helps develop more conscious masculinities and undoubtedly proposes better ways of inhabiting the world and relating to each other. This results in personal development that will undoubtedly have a positive effect on professional development. Not only do you have to be great in JavaScript, but you also have to be able to accompany your son or daughter when they have to get a vaccine, because to build a better society, we must work as companies on intersectionalities (in, for example, feminism, the inclusion of diversity, attention to disability, and zero tolerance for racist, sexist, or discriminatory attitudes).

Our vision for managing people consists of thinking about work environments not only as healthy and comfortable spaces but also as places where personal life plays a role, based on a respect for and understanding of human relationships as a fundamental part of development. Our proposal is to replace competitiveness between people with collaborative work, indifference with empathy, and overblown growth with responsible scalability. We want to generate spaces where conflicts are analyzed, and where words are the tool to understand frustrations and achievements. This is, according to our conviction, the best way to grow our company.

In my daily work at BrokenRubik, promoting a comprehensive view means knowing the concerns and aspirations of my team. We must not confuse respect for privacy with indifference. One way to balance that aspect is to generate spaces where my fundamental task is listening. I do not ask inconvenient questions about my colleagues' personal lives, but I am willing to listen to what they want to tell me. What I know about the people I work with will help me understand their context and better support their needs.

Something is fundamental for this proposal to be successful and achievable: This vision should not belong only to the human resources department. It is not the sole property of the human resources manager. These practices must be permeable at all hierarchies and in all work teams. For that, the message that the highest positions convey is fundamental: If they believe in this form of relationship and carry it out in their daily lives, this culture will permeate the character of the company and will build trust between employees and employers, as well as an agreement based on the belief that the company they work for cares about what happens to them.

CULTURE

Culture is a concept that has many dimensions. The first thing that comes to mind is probably the national culture with the cultural characteristics that exist within different countries or regions. This dimension of culture also affects us at work. Another dimension of culture is the one related to professions or occupations—for example, the culture of doctors, lawyers, salespeople, and so on.

A third perspective can be the specific culture that exists within different industries, such as the steel industry, the public sector, or logistics. In this book and in the DP model, however, we provide a broader perspective on culture that also includes organizational culture and identity. The DP model assumes, among other things, that the establishment of a strong and well-functioning organizational culture is the basis for the areas that make up the model.

What do we include in the concept of culture? There is a lot of research on culture and what most people agree on is that organizational culture is when a group shares values, beliefs, goals, and expectations that persist over time, even if the members of the group change. This definition should mean that the people in an organization share its values and live accordingly, and that new people do not affect the culture. Many of us have probably seen that the culture is affected by people who come in with different values and, above all, behaviors. It is also not always the case that all people in an organization share the organization's values. This can mean that there are differences between the culture that the organization claims to have and how people behave in practice. In these cases, the culture in the organization can be said to be weak, which can contribute to a dysfunctional organization.

On the other hand, a culture is strong and well-functioning when the gap between what is said and what is done is small, and also if the culture persists even when people with a different view of life connect to the organization. It has to be said that it is not likely that all people in an organization share all of the organization's values; there is always some kind of gap.

A concept associated with culture is identity. An organization's identity can be described as what other people and organizations expect it to be and what it stands for. People experience identification when they feel at home in a particular culture or environment. A certain profession, for example doctors, lawyers, or a specific industry, creates a feeling of belonging and identification. They share language, approaches, ways of thinking, being, and dressing, and so on. Identity is very much about feeling a "we," for example "we teachers" or "we doctors."

> *Now we would like to ask you to stop reading and think about different organizational cultures that you have experienced. Where have you felt at home? Where is the same language spoken as you speak? Perhaps you are part of an organization or association where you feel identification with the group?*

During our many years of working life, we have come across many organizations that use values or phrases on posters or coffee mugs, usually values that are considered to be positively loaded. It can be "openness," "participation," "simplicity," "We always share," or similar. But culture is not what is written on the walls; the culture of an organization is about how people behave. For example, you can consider which behaviors are rewarded and which are punished. A culture should be strong and well-functioning in order for it to be a positive asset for the organization. A danger, however, is that it is so strong that it hinders new ideas and influences and creates "not-invented-here" behavior.

The DP model highlights the need for a strong and well-functioning organizational culture, which means that it supports the organization's goals and that the individuals in the organization can clearly describe and understand it, i.e. that people's behavior and actions must be consistent with the values. A culture should be able to be experienced with the senses, it should be felt, it should be seen, it should sound. In addition, individuals should be able to identify themselves with the organization's culture.

In the coming sections, we will discuss some cultural areas that, according to the DP model, are important for creating the foundation of a good organization.

CULTURE BUILDING AND CULTURAL DEVELOPMENT

In order to create a strong and well-functioning culture, an organization needs to have clear aims and principles as well as the right expectations of people. Do people know and understand their roles and the plans and goals of the organization to such an extent that they can work together to achieve those goals? According to the DP model, too much effort should not be put into breaking down the company's strategic goals at group level and down to the individual level. This type of activity tends to become ineffective as the goals become too old before they have been broken down to the individual level, while at the same time they can become quite diffuse and contribute to low flexibility. The focus must instead be on understanding the organization's purpose in order to be able to answer the question: Why do we exist?

As mentioned earlier, each circle within Sociocracy has a clear purpose for its existence as well as principles. Every decision must be in line with the purpose of the circle, which makes it easier to focus on the group's goals and build community. Sociocracy also provides a method in case purpose and principles need to be adjusted, providing both flexibility and clarity. We have seen over the years, and through our work in different organizations, that when clarity of purpose and goals is lacking, the group tends to discuss things that are not relevant, which can create a culture (i.e. a way of being and how people behave) where discussions take over and where facts are not fully considered. But it is not enough that there are clear documents or descriptions about the goals and purposes on the intranet; people in the organization must understand these in order to achieve the desired result. In the case of the SRS focus groups, the overall aim and objectives were quite clearly described. The focus groups were supposed to work on development issues (the tactical level), but in many cases, and for a long time, the focus groups tended to discuss operational issues that did not really concern all members of the group, leading to inefficiency, and even frustration. SRS was aware of the problem and actively tried to continuously review the purpose and working methods for the focus groups.

In order to maintain and further develop a strong and well-functioning culture, organizations need to constantly work with their culture. We call it managing and nurturing the culture. By answering the following questions, you can map whether the organization is working to nurture the culture.

» Are the people in the organization active and free to get involved in creating, for example, events, cere-monies, or rituals with the aim of strengthening and communicating the organization's values, philosophy, and purpose?
» Do employees share and understand the core values and vision that unite the organization's culture?
» Are those who are good carriers of culture noticed?
» Are those who deviate from the culture noticed in a constructive way?

The values that are most often expressed in phrases or slogans must also be reflected in behavior. In a previous study, we analyzed Axis Communications based on an organizational learning perspective. Axis used its values in its daily work. One of the slogans was "always open," which meant that you should always be innovative, find new ways, and give responsibility to the team. In daily work, this phrase was often referred to when you needed to solve difficult problems or organize yourself. One leader referred to this value when he said: "We give the team a high degree of freedom to organize themselves and use the way of working and methods that suit them best."

In many organizations, a common phenomenon is that subcultures evolve in different parts of the organization. These subcultures can lead to different types of behaviors that can make cross-functional work difficult or can cause individuals to join different groupings and create a "them and us" situation. If all "us" can still cooperate, the problem is not as big as when the behavior suggests that "us" are right and "them" are wrong. There is then a risk that the culture loses strength, that it diverges, and that the other areas that make up the culture, and which we discuss in this section, deteriorate.

Since a strong and well-functioning culture requires people to feel identity with the organization, it is important to create opportunities for people to socialize both inside and outside work. Are people emotionally engaged in their work and in the organization, and do they feel motivated to be part of achieving the organization's strategic goals? In the introduction, we discussed the level of engagement at work and the consequences of low engagement. At Jayway, people felt a high degree of engagement because there was space to test and try new things. It was an allowing organization where people were given the freedom to work in areas where they have their strengths, and this leads to higher engagement. This in turn results in a stronger identity with the organization. When Jayway started in the early 2000s, the founder, Thomas Dagsberg, introduced so-called "innovation weekends." Many employees gathered in the office over the weekend and tried new things while having fun and socializing with each other. They did this outside working hours and without pay. The company was responsible for food and drink. Traditions and rituals were also created—for example, a family day at Bakken in Copenhagen (a famous amusement park that also claimed to be the oldest in the world) in August every year. Recruiting family members and friends was also something that was encouraged. Loyalty with the company was very strong at this time, and in a hostile attempt in 2006, when the passive owners wanted to oust Thomas as CEO and sell Jayway, the employees stood by Thomas. A large majority resigned even though they had no new employment at a time when the job market in Sweden was not so good. It ended with the owners being bought out and Thomas continued as CEO and co-owner along with several of the employees. This is one of the most fantastic examples we ourselves had the honor of experiencing, and it shows that a successful culture creates a strong identity with the company and thus loyalty.

DISTRIBUTION OF POWER AND PARTICIPATION

The degree of authority across the hierarchy shows whether the organization is centralized or decentralized. In the section about organizing, we discuss different types of hierarchies, including where hierarchy is symbolized by power and authority. In organizations characterized by a high degree of authority at the nodes of the hierarchy, people gain more power the higher up they are. A power distance is created where decisions are expected to be made by the managers. Often, this kind of organization leads to a culture where information is filtered to a downward line of decision and power, and with control. This also has a negative impact on people's engagement and willingness to contribute to the organization and the ability to innovate. This reflects the Scientific Management and Command and Control organizations that we discussed in the introductory chapter. If the degree of authority is reduced, it usually means that decisions and responsibilities, in whole or in part, are decentralized and distributed to those who carry out the work. This is what is called *empowerment*, meaning that the manager gives part of his power to the employees. The positive effects of distributing power were clear at Centigo where the founders did not want hierarchies of power from the beginning. The creation of a democratic culture at Centigo has led to the consultants having greater freedom, wanting to contribute to developing the organization and customer relations, and being more engaged in the company's business.

SRS was a hierarchy of authority before the company began its cultural journey. This was visible in the way that the functional managers were expected to make all the decisions and in the fact that there was a lot of rivalry and there were many conflicts in the management team. It went so far that there was an open conflict between two senior managers. In the cultural change, mandates were moved to cross-functional teams where tactical decisions were made, while operational decisions were mostly made directly in the functional teams. Ultimately, the management team realized they were not needed and dissolved themselves as a management team. Instead, a priority cross-functional group was introduced in which all the functions were represented. In this way, power (decisions and responsibilities) was distributed within the organization. This is a good example of how to reduce the hierarchy of authority and at the same time create a higher degree of openness and involve more people in decision-making.

Reducing the concentration of power has a positive impact on how people participate and how they are encouraged to participate in various activities in which they listen to others, as well as feeling that they can express their opinion without negative consequences. This is in line with Amy Edmondson and her theories about psychological safety, which means that people dare to participate and share their thoughts.

People have different personalities and some people seek more connection to others than other people, while some may prefer to work for themselves. This is good as we can solve problems and tasks in different ways and complement each other. The difference with the cultural identification is that, in a culture characterized by participation, I feel that I want to participate and people listen to me, and that I can express my opinion, which also counts. When participation and your engagement are low, you go to work, do your job, and go home.

This is regardless of how much you want to participate in other activities. Sociocracy has participation as part of its model and the expression "Many voices, one song" is used, which is based on the fact that everyone should be able to express their opinion and that decisions should be made where everyone gives their consent. Team meetings are based on rounds where everyone gets the chance to express their opinion, or say they have nothing to add. The advantages of using rounds where everyone gets to speak in turn are actually twofold: Everyone has the opportunity to express their opinion, and since all participants know that they will have the opportunity to speak, they can also listen to the others in peace and quiet.

To be able to manage these kinds of meetings, we developed, 20 years ago, a method called "REPI" (Reflection, Elaboration, Participation/Practice, and Investigation), which is based on rounds. We present REPI in more depth in the chapter "The way forward." For two decades, we have used this method in many different contexts, such as brainstorming, training, requirements, coaching, change journeys, decision-making, and more, with great results.

Participation must also apply to decision-making; both Sociocracy and Holacracy are based on consent for decision-making (see the section on decision-making) and each member of the circle has the right to object to a proposal if they can justify their objection.

Several of the new organizational philosophies and models are based on the fact that individuals should seek to belong to teams where they feel that they can contribute. This is a way to encourage participation.

Have you ever joined a team or had to attend a meeting where you did not feel like you contributed much? How did it feel?
In which situations do you consider yourself involved? Are there differences between feeling involved in the "doing" and in the decision-making?

An organizational culture that promotes specialists and working alone often has a low degree of participation. This also applies if there are many different roles in the organization and each person has their own tasks without sharing or collaborating with others. A higher degree of participation is created if the team has a shared responsibility for solving tasks and works together. An organization that distributes and decentralizes power creates a higher degree of participation.

THE DEGREE OF TRUST AND OPENNESS

An open culture must be characterized by trust, as without trust it is not possible to create good organizations where people can flourish. According to research, about 3% of employees do not keep to agreed rules and use the organization or its funds for their own purposes. A question that the organization's management and business owners must ask themselves is whether it is really reasonable to create governance and control that restricts, and in many cases frustrates, the remaining 97% just to minimize the risk of the 3% acting in the wrong way.

An organization that distances itself from Command and Control must be built on a high level of trust. The attitude of its members is then based on everyone doing their best to fulfill the organization's goals and purpose. By default, this becomes a culture with principles and accepted behaviors.

During the Covid-19 pandemic, it became very clear that organizations that had a high level of trust in their employees, and that already had mechanisms in place for staff to be able to do their jobs outside the normal workplace, were able to meet the situation in a better way. For these organizations it was much easier to transit to work 100% remotely, while organizations where trust did not exist had a harder time. Some of the latter organizations required employees to wear cameras, or to send screenshots of their activities to managers, respond within five minutes to chat, and more. This was proof that there was no trust in the people working in the organization. Why hire people you don't trust?

In a research study from 2002, Dirks and Ferrin demonstrated that there is a strong correlation between trust and job satisfaction, organizational engagement, and the desire to stay in an organization.

Another dimension of trust is about believing in people's ability to perform their work and be able to develop, as well as believing in people's potential and letting them try and test different things. Ikea has been a leading company in this area: Employees in general have great opportunities to develop regardless of background; this is because of a culture where everyone is seen as a talent. It remains to be seen whether the reorganization changes these aspects of the culture.

Trust is also about believing that people can manage information without having to write specific agreements. Having to sign confidentiality agreements before entering a meeting does not create a culture of openness; rather it will lead to the opposite. Yet there are organizations that do exactly this despite the fact that it has no other effect than to signal a lack of openness and trust and to create fear.

We mentioned earlier that SRS created a higher degree of openness when distributing power from the management team to the organization. SRS worked a lot to create openness and transparency, both to distribute all information as quickly as possible and to introduce new digital platforms for sharing information. When we conducted a quantitative survey as part of our study at SRS, transparency was the area that was mentioned as being the most successful area of improvement.

> We are convinced that an open culture where information is shared without being filtered through hierarchies, where you can, and dare to, openly raise all thoughts and problems, and where you speak to each other in a respectful manner, creates a basis for productive collaboration and innovation.

Tuff Leadership Training, which is a Swedish company specializing in communication and conflict management, uses a method they call "moose head on the table." The founder, Karin Tenelius, coined the term "moose head," which meant that there was something big in the room that was disrupting the collaboration but no one dared to mention, much like "the elephant in the room." Tuff Leadership Training trained and supported SRS in communication and conflict management, and SRS began using the moose head by starting each prior meeting or focus group meeting by asking if there were any moose heads on the table to discuss. By doing this, they wanted to remove any tensions or potential conflicts before they arose. Raising issues in an open way can sometimes be difficult but it creates a greater naturalness in the communication with each other because people do not have to swerve around difficult things. This will lead to a culture where feedback is a natural part of the daily work.

Consider for a moment whether there are "moose heads" in your organization or working group. What consequences do they have for the work or for people's well-being? Why do they exist?

We advocate that team meetings or other types of recurring meetings should start by asking around the table if there is anything that causes irritation or interferes with being able to do a good job. What is important is that there is a culture that stimulates speaking openly, constructively, respectfully, and with a focus on the subject matter. If the organization does not have an open culture, these rounds could have a negative impact on people's feelings and behaviors.

The focus should be forwards and not backwards. By this we mean that if someone has done something that is perceived as wrong or contrary to what has been said before, the focus should be on talking about what we can do to avoid this happening again in the future. For example, if a colleague is repeatedly late for work meetings, the discussion should be about what needs to be done to avoid it from happening again and about the consequences of being late. When the focus is forward, the risk of conflicts and bad relationships is reduced. Constructiveness is about looking forward, not backward. In the chapter "The way forward" we present the R&F (Retrospective & Feedforward) method, which is based exactly on this approach.

In hierarchies of authority (see the section on organizing), information is often pushed down from the top of the hierarchy to the bottom. At each level, the information can be filtered and sometimes manipulated. In our previous working life, we ourselves participated in such filtering, which occurs, for example, when the management team informs their subordinated managers, who in the next wave inform their subordinates, and so on. Many people in the organization know that something is going on, the managers disappear into meetings and rumors are spread. This type of behavior counteracts openness and, in many cases, creates distrust in the organization.

In one of Sweden's largest companies, a major change program was carried out from 2018 to 2020, where the company, with the support of one of the major international management consulting firms, would make a major transformation of the company. Information leaked out and rumors arose. This had a direct impact on people's motivation and productivity. "Am I one of those who will have to go?" and "Does my role still exist?" were two of the questions that many asked themselves. The consultancy firm drove the change with the attitude that no communication would take place until everything was ready to be announced. The consequence was that many became suspicious and had difficulty accepting the change, which in reality was necessary. A culture that had been open since the organization was founded was quickly transformed into a culture of silence where people did not dare to express themselves, and a lot of energy was spent on speculation.

If the transformation program had been based on openness, the employees could have been involved in the change and acceptance would have been higher, as too would the impact on motivation and productivity. The latter is what AstraZeneca did when the organization in Lund, Sweden was to be shut down. All employees were informed at an early stage and as soon as the decision was made, despite the fact that the change would take place a couple of years in the future. The management team took time to inform and explain what would happen and what was realistic to expect from the transformation. The openness was high, and the aim was to provide concrete, relevant, and very direct information.

INNOVATION, CHANGE, AND LEARNING

Innovation is often seen as radical product inventions such as the mobile phone, streamed music, the electric car, the refrigerator, and other similar things. But this is only a small part of all innovations, and we start with changes from several perspectives. One way is to constantly improve the way of working by keeping what works well and changing what works less well. Another perspective is to find new ways to communicate with customers or other types of stakeholders. Product innovation also means how to improve existing products or use them for other purposes.

The pharmaceutical industry can be used as an example where already approved drugs are used as treatment for other diseases. For example, AstraZeneca has created new pharmaceuticals for new uses based on previously produced ones. Their product Entocort, which is used for stomach and intestinal diseases, was developed by using previous research on Pulmicort, which is used for asthma and chronic obstructive pulmonary diseases.

Many companies want to be innovative but have not taken on the task of "building" an innovative culture.

Innovation was very important to Jayway and a natural part of the culture, which gave rise to the introduction of innovation weekends right from the start. Axis Communications had introduced a system whereby each employee could use at least two weeks of their working time to test completely new things that were not part of the daily work. Specific days were organized where people from different departments could work together to find new product ideas. On these days, there were also patent engineers on site to help see if people could proceed with patent work. The interesting thing was that the culture of innovation also led to increased openness regarding, for example, working methods. Different departments could, for instance, choose working methods and project models themselves without being guided by a centrally decided model. They chose the way of working that suited them best. The company is one of the fastest growing in Sweden, largely thanks to their innovative culture. The reason for that is that the innovation comes "from below" and is not guided by any strategic plan. Within the DP model, we advocate that it is better to try or test a new idea than to implement a well-known but bad idea.

Innovation can be compared with quality. A few decades ago, when customers and evolution in the world began to demand not only new products and services but also quality, roles such as quality managers or quality coordinators were created. Quality departments or teams were also started. At the beginning of this development, it seemed that quality was something that was added to the product or service once it was finished. Over time, it became obvious that quality is something that must be built into every step and right from the start. It has become a common approach. Innovation is now moving in the same direction. There are new roles in innovation such as innovation managers, innovation consultants, and innovation departments. In addition, there are numerous training courses in the area. But innovation, like quality, is something that must be present at every step, and the way to get there is to create a culture that promotes innovative thoughts and approaches.

Learning can be considered from different perspectives: organization, team, and individual. From a cultural perspective, we want to focus more on how an organization learns and how to make use of what individuals can do and what they learn. It is important to consider how people's knowledge and abilities are used and how people are encouraged to develop and to be curious about new things since there is a connection to how to encourage experimentation and innovation. Engagement is based to a large extent on being able to use one's strengths and also having the opportunity to learn new things and explore new areas. Jayway created a culture where people could explore and test new areas, which led to several of the employees becoming experts in their fields. They were invited to speak at conferences, be part of various networks, and more. This shows that when the culture encourages learning, the people and thus also the organization develop. One of the interesting things about Jayway was that knowledge sharing was encouraged, which stimulated organizational learning.

Organizational learning is also based on sharing knowledge across functional boundaries. This can be done in different ways. One way is to stimulate people to move in the organization and by appreciating and respecting knowledge and proficiencies other than those that are important for one's own field. In this way, you can get different angles on challenges and problems. Another way to share knowledge across functional boundaries is to stimulate cross-functional collaboration, as SRS did with its focus groups. They involved people from different functions to drive the business forward in a specific area, allowing people to learn from each other. It is very clear that an organizational culture that stimulates learning has a greater ability to be innovative and adaptive to changed conditions.

An innovative culture is based on constantly finding new ways and solutions, and in that way, people are stimulated to learn new things by collaborating across functional boundaries, and innovation becomes a part of daily work.

EMPHASIS ON RESULTS OR ACTION ORIENTATION

Organizations can be classified as being either results or action oriented. In a results-oriented culture, the organization is characterized by a focus on results; initiatives are started where the most important parts are the goals and the outcome. In addition, there are measurable key figures that are reported frequently. The opposite is an action-oriented culture where many initiatives are started but may not be completed; there is a lot of discussion, there is a lot going on, but it may not always result in many outcomes. As a rule, a results-oriented culture is a bit tougher than an action-oriented one.

SRS was clearly action oriented. The list of various improvement initiatives was long, but it was difficult to get anywhere. The meetings were quite long with a lot of discussions and involvement, but not so many results. When we studied SRS, they were in the middle of their cultural journey and they tried to find ways of working together, which contributed to the strong action orientation, which is characterized by many meetings and many conversations about how things should be done.

If you look at Ikea, this culture is also strongly action oriented—many meetings and many ideas that lead to various initiatives and decisions being made that could eventually be revised, turned down, or discussed again. This usually leads to a slower work pace, but not necessarily a lower business efficiency. Many people thrive in this type of environment, which is also noticeable at Ikea, where people are positive, want to discuss, try different paths, etc.

The opposite to Ikea was Sony Mobile, which was strongly results oriented. In the 2000s, when Sony Mobile was called Sony Ericsson, the pressure was strong to deliver new mobile phones continuously. This created a culture of focusing on results and getting products out quickly, rather than developing new, high-quality, competitive models. Working as a project manager at Sony Mobile meant steering towards the goal, and time was usually the most important parameter. Towards the end of the 2000s, Sony Mobile lost market share, not least when Apple launched its iPhones. As a result, many people had to leave the company in Lund.

On the other side of the motorway in Lund there was, and still is, the fast-growing company Axis Communications, which supplied surveillance equipment based on intelligent camera technology. Many who left Sony Mobile became employees at Axis, which had a great need to employ. Since both companies operated in the same technology area, it was a natural step to cross the motorway, which also became a saying in Lund: "to cross the motorway."

The biggest difference between the companies was the culture. Axis has a culture similar to Ikea's with a strong action orientation and strong innovation focus. In this culture, people have time to experiment and test different ways of solving problems.

We interviewed a newly employed project manager at Axis who came from Sony Mobile. The project manager's biggest frustration was time and pace. Everything took a long time at Axis and deadlines were not respected; instead the engineers constantly wanted to test a little bit more. The project manager was used to working in a culture that was characterized by a strongly results-oriented environment and ended up in a strongly action-oriented world with frustration as a result. This example shows that culture plays a big role in how work is carried out. If a person is used to working and acting in a specific culture, it takes time to adapt to a new one, especially if the person eventually ends up in a culture that works differently.

It is necessary to understand that there are big differences in approach depending on whether the culture is action or results oriented.
Adapting to new cultures is about learning new behaviors and relearning, which takes time.

TO DARE

Trust was previously mentioned as an important area for a person to dare to take on things and dare to make mistakes, and also to try new things that make work more interesting and fun—all this in order for people to develop and take new steps. Spotify has a principle in its culture whereby people should try to make mistakes as quickly as possible and, moreover, that you should celebrate them. The latter is celebrated in a "fail-fika," which aims to learn and find new ways to learn. And this is where trust comes in: To be able to celebrate one's mistakes, the culture must be characterized by mutual trust. "If I am sure that my mistakes will not be used against me, I dare to admit them."

Ikea is another company with a strong culture and where mistakes are part of the daily work. This is largely based on Ingvar Kamprad's historical quote: "Only while sleeping does one make no mistakes. Making mistakes is the privilege of the active—of those who can correct their mistakes and put them right." This created Ikea's unique innovative development where people dared to try new things, and if they failed, they just said: "It's just a matter of taking new steps."

Here we see two examples of innovative companies that almost invite employees to make mistakes, and where trust is linked to daring, and if we dare, we will fail sometimes, or even quite often.

What exactly is failure? After all, this is a negative word that at Spotify and Ikea is positive. Thinking further about trying and testing, it presupposes different results that are not always what was expected. In order to get a great result, maybe there is a need to try ten or 100 different ways, right? Then the previous nine or 99 attempts are not failures, but steps on the way to success.

Trying and testing are different ways of being able to succeed and develop new products, ways of working, approaches, and so on. And with that come some attempts, which may not be great, but are steps on the way forward. They can provide new insights, create new ideas, or find the way forward. There are companies that start ten new initiatives where they only let one continue. The other nine are not failures, they are the basis for one to be able to continue.

Another area of organizational culture is the level of risk-taking in the organization. Do the people in the organization prefer to take only safe routes or do they take risks? In a culture with low risk-taking, employees tend to hide mistakes and try to maintain the status quo. Risk-taking can in many cases be linked to the industry you operate in, but even within industries there are different levels of risk-taking.

Industries that are governed by strong legal requirements are often less prone to risk than those that do not have a strict regulatory framework around them. The public sector should have a culture where people are less prone to take risks, but without hiding mistakes, which is more related to openness and trust. However, these activities would be promoted by a high-innovation culture where you follow the regulations but are still innovative in relation to the general public. Risk-taking and innovation are related and are two sides of the same coin, as a culture of high risk-taking can lead to radical innovations. Actually, the level of risk-taking should be related to its context.

If we go back to AstraZeneca, there is a natural innovative culture within the pharmaceutical industry. The interesting thing was that between 1950 and 1980, a team of researchers with a very innovative but also risk-taking culture was created in Hässle AB in Gothenburg (later part of Astra and even later part of AstraZeneca). The risk-taking was not in the form of taking risks with the research procedure, but of believing in what you were doing and not giving up. The risk-taking was therefore in making long-term investments. One of the drugs they believed in was Losec, which later became by far the biggest blockbuster and most successful product for Astra and AstraZeneca. However, the Losec project was very close to being shut down on several occasions, but the research team believed so strongly in the product that they continued. During the early 1990s, the product became the basis of Astra's success story and their cash cow for several decades. Losec was the greatest success of the research team at Hässle, but they also developed several other products through a balanced innovative and risk-taking culture within the framework of their legal prerequisites.

The Studsvik case, which we presented in the introduction, is clear proof that it pays to take risks, especially when it comes to venturing into new areas based on the skills the staff have. This came about due to changed leadership that gave the employees space to think differently and try new paths.

It's about daring to invest in untested areas and seeing it as an opportunity instead of focusing on the risks. In order to succeed, one must dare to fail, and failure must be seen as a learning experience.

DIFFERENT CULTURE IN DIFFERENT PARTS OF THE ORGANIZATION

The question can be raised as to whether organizations have the same culture throughout. In most organizations of a certain size that we have worked in, studied, or been in contact with, we have found subcultures. In many cases, this phenomenon was linked to profession or country. For example, in manufacturing companies there is a big difference in the culture between the research & development, production, and logistics departments.

One of the authors studied a Swedish company involved in high-tech products a few years ago. The company's culture was based on openness, collaboration, and support for each other. The culture was strong and functional within the research & development department. In conversations with the employees within the company, they often came back to the basic values and worked accordingly. Among other things, they had created incentive models where individuals could only be promoted to experts if they helped others, especially new employees. The company was rapidly growing in high technology in a fast-growing market where the logistics department was not part of the core business but rather was considered a lower-status organizational part. As the logistics department, in turn, was solely focused on operational work with a strong emphasis on deliveries, they developed their own subculture according to Command and Control. This part of the company was strictly hierarchical, encouraging directive leadership and following up on details, which made it difficult for people to grow. It was clear that the strong and functional culture within the research & development department did not exist within logistics.

As there is always a dynamic when organizations grow rapidly and recruit people with different experiences, it can, in some cases, be a challenge to maintain the culture and the behaviors that people in the organization have. This can create subcultures. On the other hand, culture must also develop as the outside world changes. Ingvar Kamprad created a strong and well-functioning culture at Ikea, but since the context in which Ikea operates has changed, the culture may also have to be adjusted. On the other hand, the basic culture, such as experimenting, trying new ways, openness, and more, is the basis for Ikea to continue to grow and create new innovative business opportunities.

Another area that most often affects organizational culture and can lead to subcultures is the organization's international spread. When we worked at Sony Mobile, we saw how the difference between different national cultures affected the way work was done. Sony Mobile had its origins in a joint venture between Sony and Ericsson with a Japanese and a Swedish culture. These two national cultures are quite far apart, which in many cases led to misunderstandings and uncertainty over how to act. On the Swedish side, they did not understand the process of how, in the Japanese way, to start different strategic initiatives, while on the Japanese side, they did not understand that it was possible to distribute responsibilities to different individuals, and instead they continued to act through their hierarchy. Despite several initiatives in intercultural awareness, many different cultural clashes arose.

Have you seen companies or organizations act based on profession or national culture? If so, has it affected you? How has it impact the organization in general? How were the decisions made?

In many organizations there are subcultures depending on work areas, geographical spread, and more. The subcultures often lead to different behaviors that are not always in line with the organization's values and can stand in the way of collaboration across borders.

Voice from the field: Gustavo Razzetti – CEO, Fearless Culture, Chicago, USA

Gustavo Razzetti believes that most organizations do not lack ideas or talent, but what is missing is a nurturing culture. He created the *Culture Design Canvas* tool to help organizations become more human, agile, and innovative. He is also the author of three books (*Stretch for Change*, *Stretch Your Team*, *Stretch Your Mind*) and writes articles for, among others, *Psychology Today*, *Medium*, and *Forbes*.

How to create an organizational culture

Can workplace culture be designed? That's the question I always get when I tell people what I do for a living. People still think that culture is something that just happens organically. A recent study by Glassdoor shows that companies with a strong culture outperform the S&P 500 index, delivering almost twice the gain. It's not surprising that the 2020s is meant to be the decade of culture-first organizations. Every company has a culture, either by default or by design. However, successful cultures don't happen by accident; they are purposefully designed and built. Here's how.

1. Apply user-centered approach to culture design

Design Thinking revolutionized the way organizations solve problems and develop new products and solutions. The reason for its success? It provides superior solutions, lowers risk, and facilitates employee buy-in. Company culture benefits from a user-centered approach, too. Intentionally designing what your organization stands for requires starting with the user in mind: your employees. Most leaders miss an opportunity when they try to define their culture on their own. They fail to get early buy-in by not getting employees involved in the process.

Airbnb decided to reduce the number of core values when it realized that people could not remember them. Rather than simply choosing their preferred ones, the company invited every employee to help them select which values inflated or deflated Airbnb's culture.

Instead of having a small committee defining your company culture, involve people in the journey.

2. Company culture is more than just values

Culture is about creating the right environment so people can do the best work of their lives. It goes well beyond perks such as ping pong tables or crafting fancy corporate values.

Your organization's culture is "the way people feel, think, and do things here" – it encapsulates the collective emotions, mindsets, and behaviors. The Core is the foundation of culture, defining what the company stands for. It includes Purpose and Core values but also crucial priorities and the behaviors that are rewarded and punished. A strong culture is action driven, not just filled with good intentions.

The emotional culture captures how people feel about the organization. It starts by promoting psychological safety – the belief that people can speak up, be themselves, and share their ideas without fear of criticism or punishment. It also involves how feedback is used to learn and grow from each other. Last but not least, team rituals play a key role in shaping collaboration and bonding.

3. Focus on the journey, not the destination

Most executives believe that their culture is like a journey that they can control. They think about moving the culture from "Point A" to "Point B" – just like entering the final destination on a GPS and following the most direct route to get there. However, cultural change is more like sailing than driving. Regardless of what the GPS tells you, you'll have to deal with a lot of unexpected forces, such as tides, storms, wind, and currents. All those elements will affect your navigation, forcing you to adapt and course-correct.

Culture change is a never-ending job. Rather than being obsessed about reaching the destination, leaders must understand that the journey is what really matters. It encourages people to enjoy the trip while also being more aware (and appreciative) of the progress made together.

4. Design doesn't mean control

Letting your company just happen can be as harmful as trying to control it. Culture change cannot be achieved through a top-down mandate. It's a co-creation process with your team that requires integrating both planned and organic elements. Designing a culture does not mean imposing how people should behave but creating collective norms of what's expected from each other and what is rewarded, too.

Japanese landscapers plan ahead, but adjust their design based on people's feedback. Once they have designed a park, they let people walk freely without having a clearly defined walkway. After some time, by looking at where the grass had worn away, they pave people's favorite paths. Culture design is not about imposing a rigid path but setting the environment. Let people choose the way.

The Culture Design Canvas

After many years of experience in the marketing, innovation, and leadership world, I realized that organizations do not lack ideas but a conducive culture. But how can you design that culture?

For decades, organizations have benefited from Alex Osterwalder's Business Model Canvas. Inspired by his work, and after several iterations, I came up with The Culture Design Canvas – a simple-to-use tool that allows us to design company culture in just one page.

The Culture Design Canvas helps organizations map, design,

and evolve their culture in a visual, human-centered way. Since making the tool public over a year ago, it has quickly gained tracking with 20,000+ professionals and organizations using it across the world.

The CDC, for short, includes ten building blocks that capture the three elements of company culture: the core, emotional culture, and functional culture.

An intentional, human-centered design can help you shift your company culture from good to great. Focus on the user – your employees – and involve people along the journey.

Culture design is a never-ending job. Effective design requires providing room to breathe and evolve. Let the best behaviors organically emerge.

THE DP MODEL: **Culture**

ORGANIZING

The first thing that comes to mind for most people when talking about organizing is an organizational chart, and mostly with a hierarchical structure.

For us, organizing is much more than just a structure with an organizational chart and a description of the different roles that exist in an organization. The DP model also includes classification, distribution, and coordination of tasks as well as cooperation and steering. Put simply, it can be seen as what organizing should be like in order to solve tasks in the best possible way'.

The traditional way of organizing has been as a series of nodes, where each node in the hierarchy can be seen as a way of classifying work around a function, geographic market, product, competence, or some other classification, meaning that hierarchies are based on purpose or commonality.

In our research and through many conversations, we have been able to ascertain that there are misconceptions about what a hierarchy is and why it exists.

Before you continue reading, we would like to ask you to think about what kind of image you see when you think of a hierarchy. What words come to your mind?

The first image that appears to many when talking about hierarchies is a hierarchy of authority because we are influenced by the Command and Control approach that comes from Scientific Management, which we presented in the introduction chapter. By default, we get an image of a bureaucratic structure where power is held by a few and where decision-making is slow and directed downwards in the hierarchy. For a few years we have been gathering results from the little exercise you just did, and we can say that words that come to mind when people think of hierarchies include "control," "governance," "bureaucracy," "administration," "power," "titles," and "vertical management." In some way, hierarchy is linked to less desirable ways of organizing, to something negative. Therefore, many of the business leaders we interviewed mentioned that "we are nonhierarchical" or "we are a flat organization." What do they really mean by "nonhierarchical" and "flat organization"? Our analysis is that people actually feel and see hierarchy as something negative, but as something that is needed to manage an organization and that there is no alternative to a hierarchical structure.

Before we talk further about hierarchies, we would like to describe some different types:

1. **Hierarchy of authority** is where managers have the authority to hire, fire, promote, assign tasks and priorities, and make all decisions. The employees are guided by their manager in all matters. The managers or decision-makers are appointed by higher levels in the hierarchy and power always comes from a superior. There is a culture of control, centralized power, filtered information, and high levels of specialization.

2. **Hierarchy of responsibility** is where the managers are ultimately responsible for the results and the work is performed by those below them. Here, some of the operational decisions can be made by the working group and in many cases by those who have knowledge of the subject, thus there is slightly less centralized power. Employees can guide and direct others in their working group, i.e. others who are at the same hierarchical level. The managers are appointed by higher levels of the hierarchy; therefore, power also comes from above.

3. **Democratic hierarchy** is when the managers/leaders make decisions but they have been elected. Therefore, their authority is considered to come from below. They can also

be "deposed." This could, for example, apply to associations or political parties.

4. **Network hierarchy** is where the nodes are only a structure and can be seen as autonomous units with a certain independence. These units cooperate and have relationships with other nodes and in this way form a whole. Here the power is not centralized, and the hierarchy can be seen as a logical order or classification of the work and/or people and there is an interdependence between the nodes. Network hierarchies may differ. On the one hand, they can be loose, where there is one or more main nodes while the remaining nodes are more or less completely autonomous, including in terms of economic and financial management. They can also be intertwined where the nodes are grouped and where there are strong connections and dependencies.

But back to the question of why many business leaders say "we are nonhierarchical" or "we are a flat organization." Could it be that they do not want a hierarchy of authority but instead want employees who take responsibility in the organization, perhaps a hierarchy of responsibility? That they are trying to get away from the negatively loaded word "hierarchy"?

In the DP model, we see hierarchies as a way of categorizing, grouping, and distributing work.
There are different types of hierarchies, and the differences need to be highlighted. What matters is the distribution of power and not just the structure.

In all the organizations we studied and analyzed that indicated that they did not have a hierarchy, we found a shadow or proxy hierarchy. This is because it is in the nature of both people and organizations to be able to classify and structure. However, because during the last decade hierarchies have become almost synonymous with misuse of power, bureaucracy, and inefficiency, many people do not want to classify their organization as hierarchical. We see that it is more about a trend in the use of language but hierarchies remain as structures. What is changing is how power is distributed in the hierarchy.

Even Laloux and the Teal paradigm, which we presented in the section on progressive organizational models, mentioned organizations free from hierarchies. But there are hierarchical structures in the examples presented in his book. What is different is that governance and power are distributed.

The best way to organize is to structure work through principles that make sense, such as by products, services, regions, industries, customers, processes, markets, technologies, competencies, and so on. Since it is a classification, there are almost always subcategories. An example is a product structure in the form of a hierarchy as in Figure 8 below where the product is built up from its parts. In the same way, an organization can build up through its parts. Larger organizations may have to be structured in different parts or dimensions. We will reason more about this below.

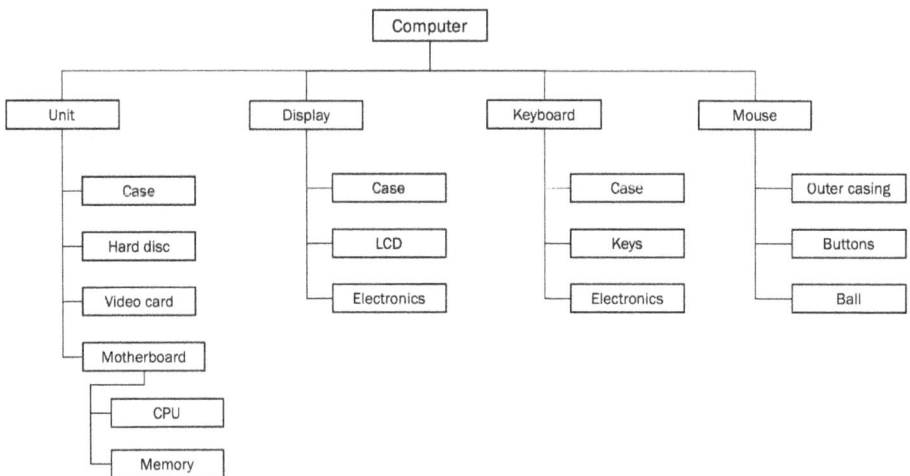

Figure 8. Example of product hierarchy

ORGANIZATIONAL UNITS AND FORUMS

Organizations where power is distributed and that are organized according to the network hierarchy consist of different teams or working groups. These teams can have a variety of names depending on the organization that created them, and also on the method or theory that is used.

At Spotify, a team is called a "squad," and several squads form a tribe, which could correspond to a department in a traditional organization. There are also chapters that correspond to functions (functional areas), and guilds that are an internal group of employees with the same interests, either private, professional, or work-related. The principle is that there must be a balance between a high degree of independence, cooperation, and coordination (see Figure 9).

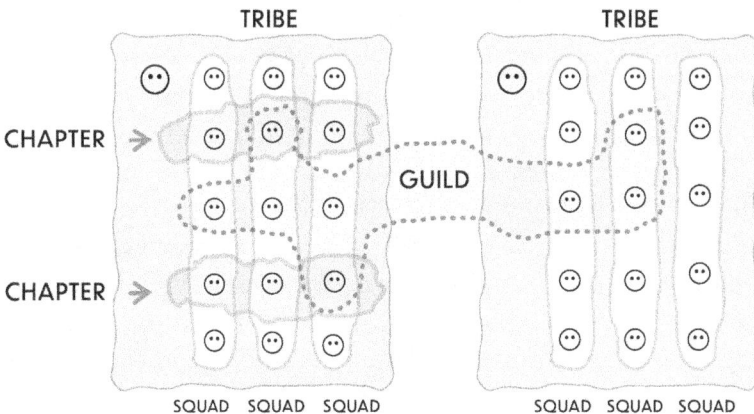

Figure 9. Spotify's organizational units

At Chronoflex, teams are called "speed boats," while at Favi, they are called "mini factories."

Spotify's organization can be compared to other types of matrix organizations where the functional organization is drawn in a horizontal direction while, for example, the product organization is drawn in a vertical direction, as exemplified below in Figure 10.

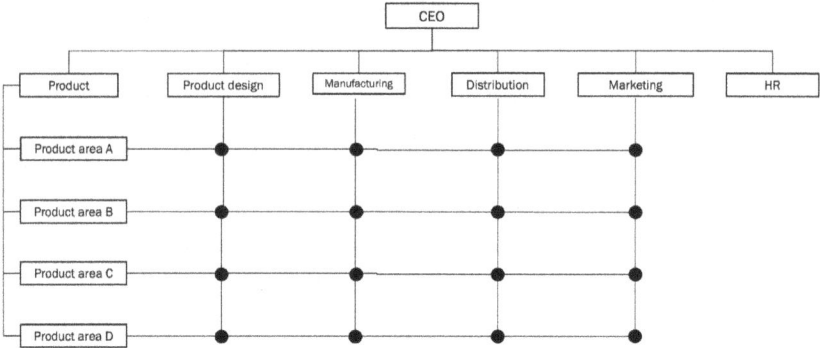

Figure 10. Example of matrix organization

Spotify's organization is considered to be an innovative organizational form, but a comparison between Figure 9 and Figure 10 shows that their organizational structure is a type of matrix organization. This shows that it is not the organizational structure that causes innovation at Spotify.

One of our case studies, SRS, was previously structured in a hierarchy of authority where managers made all decisions and ensured that these were implemented in the functions. The cross-functional work did not work because the organization suffered from internal politics. The management realized that they could not continue to work in this way and started what they called a "cultural journey." After a period of time, the hierarchical structure still existed with functions organized in traditional areas such as operations, market, finance, etc., but the management team was dissolved. Instead, the "power" was distributed to cross-functional teams called "focus groups" (the name can be misleading because they are not focus groups according to Lean or marketing theories, rather they are groups that have a focus on an area) and a steering group with representatives from the different focus groups, called the "prio group." The latter became the forum where all company-wide initiatives and decisions would be managed, including the prioritization of various initiatives, budgeting, and resources. The strategic plan was developed by a group with selected members, and the final decision about the strategy was made by the company's board of directors.

The second thing SRS did was to let each function decide whether it wanted a formal manager or not. This meant that the functions that did not want to have a manager created self-managing teams, while the functions that chose to keep the manager role continued with the previous organizational structure. The functions managed the operational activities, while the focus groups took care of the business development in a total of eight areas, which could include sustainability, business development, logistics and production, administration (internal processes), and so on. All office workers within SRS were encouraged to be part of at least one focus group in order for everyone to experience participation. The challenge for SRS was that the focus groups tended to address far too many operational issues, and the mandates of the self-managing functions and the functions that had a formal manager became different. It can be said that SRS in its transformation has gone from a hierarchy of authority to a mixture of responsibility and network hierarchies. Looking at how SRS wants to define its culture, it is very close to an intertwined network hierarchy where the nodes are grouped and where there are strong connections and dependencies.

Centigo clearly indicated that there were no hierarchies and that, right from the start, they wanted to build a boss-less organization, where every employee would have the feeling and drive of being a self-employed person in a larger organization. "You can't have a boss if you are working for yourself," as one of the founders expressed it. Entrepreneurship, independence, and being able to choose and make use of people's ideas were emphasized as important parameters. Centigo built its operations on three principles: objective (independence), ambition-driven, and collective leadership (being able to make one's own decisions within the frames of what a person can control).

If you look more closely at the organization, it is a classic matrix organization where all employees belong to a business unit where the people have similar areas of knowledge, which constitutes the first level in the matrix. The business unit has a partner as the business unit manager who is responsible for traditional managerial tasks such as salaries, skills development, and more. An interviewed consultant referred to the business unit as the "department." The second link in the matrix is the customer dimension in that Centigo has customer teams for different customer segments. The customer teams are led by a customer coordinator (a customer coordinator compared himself to a KAM – Key Account Manager) and each employee can belong to one or more customer teams. The consultants can always decline an assignment, which means that the customer coordinator wants to present attractive assignments. However, there are financial incentives and internal pressure on people to have assignments that in practice make it difficult for more junior consultants to say no. Priorities are managed through dialogue between the business unit responsible and the customer coordinator. This shows that Centigo has a network hierarchy with strong elements of hierarchy of responsibility as the organization consists of different nodes that are intertwined with each other. However, the business unit coordinator and customer coordinator are appointed by the management team and are ultimately responsible for results and the work that the consultants perform. Since each new consultant gets a more experienced coach and mentor, this becomes a great way to be onboarded to the company.

Looking at Sociocracy, Holacracy, and S3, circles are used as an organizational unit and depend on the purpose. A circle normally has no more than ten members, and if the circle gets bigger, it is divided into several circles. The interesting and powerful thing about the circles is that they have very clear purposes and areas of responsibility. The members of the circles are free to organize themselves in the most efficient way within these areas of responsibility. The organization can be seen as a fractal rather than a hierarchy and can in principle be any size. Some circles can be temporary and considered as support circles if required.

All three models have a top or initial circle that defines the purpose of the organization and its policies.

Another thing that distinguishes these models from traditional ones is double-linking. Each circle has a leader who is appointed by the "mother circle." This leader creates prerequisites for the circle and is then responsible for communication from the parent circle to the circle, the top-down link. This can be seen as the traditional leader. But since the circle is responsible for organizing itself, the circle's members appoint a person, a delegate, who is responsible for communication from the circle to the parent circle and thus the rest of the organization, the bottom-up link. Both of these represent the circle as equal members in the parent circle. The advantage of this is that it is not one person who participates in a kind of management group and becomes a filter for the team. Instead, there are two people with different responsibilities and that can capture different perspectives. This increases transparency and strengthens communication between the various organizational units. To translate double-linking into a traditional organization, the department or team would always be represented by two people in, for example, a management team, one responsible for information downwards and one for information upward.

The unasked question becomes: Isn't there more administration this way? The answer is no. Many misunderstandings are removed, it is easier to make decisions, etc. By having a representative from the team with the same rights as other members of the management team, it would be ensured that the team's perspective is considered and without filtering in the flow of information. This creates better transparency and reduces the time usually needed to get the team's acceptance for, for example, decisions.

The strength of models such as Sociocracy, Holacracy, and S3 is that decision-making, conflict management, the team's (circle's) area of responsibility, and more are given. The members of the circle organize its work within the frames of its area of responsibility. A support circle can be created in the case that a circle needs to perform special tasks. Should this be transferred to a project organization, the project would be organized in different circles where the top circle corresponds to a steering group, in which the project organization is represented by the project manager and one more person, the delegate. This would strengthen the project's representation in the steering group with a person who, for example, has a strong focus on the content of the project.

Most organizations have some type of structure similar to the dimensions in matrix organizations, which are divided based on a specific area but also operate in another dimension, for example product or customer. This also applies within self-organizing.

ABOUT MANAGERS AND ORGANIZING OF WORK

One of the basic theses of the DP model is that it is people in an organization who organize themselves, it is not managers who organize work and instruct people on what to do. This is what has given the name "self-organizing" to organizations where working groups have a certain level of autonomy and independence. The team decides how to carry out their work in the best way within the frames of their area of responsibility. Organizing and coordinating tasks are actually two different things. A team almost always needs someone who has a coordinating role so that nothing falls through the cracks or dependencies are missed.

In many of the companies we analyzed and in general discussions and debates around self-organizing, there are misconceptions. Many call such an organization "without managers" and believe that the tasks that were the manager's responsibility simply disappear, because they were "administrative" and are not needed in a more agile or flatter organization. Regardless of the choice about how to organize there are still certain tasks that need to be done, such as coordinating work.

A traditional management role includes several tasks, for example:

1. Administration of personnel (managing time off, rehabilitation, well-being, recruitment, introduction to work, salary setting)
2. Leadership (competence development, coordination, follow-up, performance management, conflict management, communication)
3. Organization of work (priorities, who does what, planning, budget)
4. Decision-making
5. communication, collaboration, and participation in management teams and steering groups

These tasks remain regardless of how work is organized. We have seen examples where several of these tasks were forgotten when the organizational form was changed or a more modern organization that did not follow the traditional model was established.

An example from one of our case studies is the responsibility for rehabilitation in the case of long-term sick leave. An employee became ill because he had worked too much and had not taken a vacation. Since the person belonged to a team that met mostly virtually, no one in the work group had noticed the high workload and signals. When it was time to start rehabilitation, the company needed to think about how this could be solved – not only because it was needed, but also because it is a legal requirement that there is a person who is responsible for rehabilitation and has contact with the Social Insurance Agency. The solution was that a colleague took on the rehabilitation responsibility. This example shows that traditional managerial tasks are still needed even if there are no formal managers and that those tasks must be distributed within the organization. It can involve tasks that many people are not very keen on doing. One of the most difficult tasks is the salary process, which we discuss in more depth in the section on the salary model and profit sharing.

In all organizations there are activities and decisions of different natures. We categorize these decisions as strategic, tactical, and operational. In the company Patagonia, the strategic decisions are made in what they call "Picking Mountains," which are considered to be the conversations/meetings where the management team or the board chooses the mountain (the symbolism comes from the founder's great interest in mountaineering). The teams in the organization must then climb the "mountain" in the ways they consider most appropriate, i.e. make operational decisions. The manager's role during climbing is to be a coach and mentor. The team organizes the operational work independently. Depending on the size of the team, there are operational leaders who work with the tactical level together with a group of people. A common misconception in self-organizing is to think that everyone should be involved and make all kinds of decisions, which can in fact be devastating for the organization.

Self-organizing and a systemic approach is not necessarily about taking away all managers, it is about distributing power and decisions being made by those who have knowledge and/or are directly affected by the decision. It is very important to categorize activities and decisions into strategic, tactical, and operational matters and clarify responsibility for these.

ABOUT ROLES, COOPERATION, AND GOVERNANCE

Organizing based on distributed power and distributed decision-making does not necessarily mean that there are no roles. A role is actually a number of tasks that usually belong together in some way and for which there is some form of responsibility. A board of an association needs, for example, a chairman and a secretary. A number of tasks with associated responsibilities are linked to these roles. A team at school may have a supervisor who coordinates the activities, and so on.

Looking at Patagonia, which has a flat organization but uses an organizational structure similar to a functional departmental structure, we find, for example, a CEO, a Marketing Director, and a Digital Creative Director. In addition, there are also specific roles that have been created because they are needed to manage various initiatives, for example Head of Environmental Strategy. Each of these department heads has employees who report to them, and the heads are responsible for the achievement of departmental goals. What is significant for Patagonia is that all people regardless of their role can be "reached" by all employees, that there is no hierarchical reachability. Being "reachable" by everyone means an organizational culture that allows a person to go to the top manager without involving his or her immediate manager (which is typical of an organization based on Command and Control and which is usually called "respecting the hierarchy"). One thing you gain with this is that the organization becomes more open, and information is spread faster without being filtered in the hierarchical structure. Patagonia has in this way combined a traditional organizational structure with an open culture where everyone is considered equal. The latter is a basis for distributed power.

Centigo also has a flat organization: business unit manager and consultant. There are no managers between these two parts. The business unit manager is always a partner and part of the company's management team. In the second dimension, there is a customer manager who is responsible for the relationship with various customers. For the consultants, there are a few different roles based on experience and seniority. For example, if you come directly from university, you become a *Consultant*, and after a few years you are offered the opportunity to become a *Business Consultant*. When accepting the role as Business Consultant the salary model changes from an almost completely fixed monthly salary to a model based on how much income the consultant generates. For that reason, there are quite a few roles and the organization is flat. What Centigo also does to facilitate the training of new consultants is that they get a coach who is one of the experienced consultants but not the business unit manager for the business unit to which the consultant belongs. The coach's task is to ensure that the consultant builds a strong network, finds the right fit in the organization, and receives consulting assignments that are in line with the consultant's objectives. A coach can be seen as a role at Centigo. Looking at the traditional managerial tasks, the business unit manager performs most of these. For example, the consultant has development talks with the business manager. He or she also handles the payroll process, any rehabilitation needs, etc.

HOMOGENEOUS TEAMS AND THE SAME TYPE OF TASKS

A famous case of autonomous teams is Buurtzorg, which is a Dutch organization in the home care sector. Almost everyone in the organization is a nurse who cares for patients who need rehabilitation or other types of healthcare in their homes. The company is organized into small (max. 15 people) autonomous teams. Each team plans its time, recruits new employees, and makes decisions related to how the team designs the work. These teams are supported by a slim central unit consisting of about 50 people who comprise coaches, purchasers, economists, customer administrators, and strategic business developers. When the number of patients increases in an area and there is a need to grow, the group is divided, and new people are hired. In this way, the rule that a team does not have more than 15 members is followed. Each team is also autonomous in terms of financial results. If a team is not self-sustained, i.e. not financially viable, it is dissolved.

What is specific to Buurtzorg is that it is homogeneous in terms of professional group because all are nurses. In addition, the work is of the same nature in all autonomous teams, namely providing care at home. There are different types of care but it is always about care, meaning that all teams do roughly the same things and have a geographic area of responsibility. Looking at Buurtzorg from a hierarchy perspective, they would be categorized as a loose network hierarchy as there is a main node (the central unit) while the remaining nodes are completely autonomous, including regarding economic and financial management (see Figure 11). The autonomous teams exchange experiences and support each other, but otherwise they act completely independently.

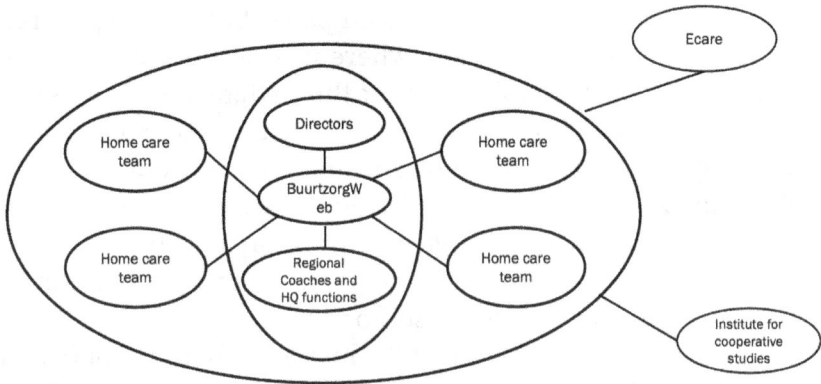

Figure 11. Organizational structure for Buurtzorg in the Netherlands

When consultants, speakers, and researchers today talk about self-organized teams, they often use Buurtzorg as an example of how self-organizing should work. The dilemma is that many businesses have a more complex reality, which means that many business leaders do not think this works for them – not because Buurtzorg's business is simple, but because it is relatively homogeneous, meaning all teams do roughly the same thing. There are other organizations such as schools and treatment centers that also have homogeneous professional groups and the same type of tasks, but the vast majority of organizations consist of a number of different professions and various tasks that require different types of competence and skills.

The reality for many companies is that it is not possible to organize themselves into small autonomous teams without considering the big picture. In a company where there is research and development, production, logistics, sales, marketing, purchasing, IT, and so on, it is not as simple, and it is obvious that these teams cannot become autonomous in the same way as the teams at Buurtzorg. This is because there is a clear dependency among the teams and also a need for different types of skills and tasks.

Another thing that characterizes Buurtzorg is that there is no strong interdependence in the tasks within a team and even less between different teams. Each patient can be considered as a separate entity. In cases where it is necessary to discuss what action or type of treatment the patient should receive, someone else with experience in the team is consulted or, if needed, support from someone in another team could be asked for. Buurtzorg also has a well-developed digital system support for communication exchange within the organization.

Now you might be wondering why Buurtzorg is one of the most frequently cited examples in self-organizing.

The answer is quite simple: We humans like to simplify and talk about things that sound fantastic because then there will be many people who want to listen. Buurtzorg has been on a fantastic journey and has developed into being by far the market leader and a company where many nurses want to work. Buurtzorg is a very good example and indeed proof that it is possible to create an organization that is based on principles other than Command and Control and that creates motivated employees, satisfied customers, and better financial results. However, there are few organizations that can use the same type of organizing.

The degree of homogeneity and the types of tasks must be taken into account when organizing work in general but above all within self-organizing. This also includes the degree of dependence between the people and the teams.

SIZE AND COMPLEXITY OF THE ORGANIZATION

In smaller companies with owners with a healthy view, decisions are generally made by those who have knowledge and/or, if possible, those who are affected by the decisions. In this type of organization there are, in most cases, transparency, dynamics, and flexibility, which are a must for survival. If a journey must be undertaken in these smaller companies to work according to the philosophy of the DP model with equal value for all, equality by removing status symbols, better distribution of profit, etc., the journey is not as complicated as for a larger organization. It's like comparing mini-golf to golf: There is a higher degree of complexity and, according to our experience, not only are different types of activities needed, but also different types of support depending on the size of the organization.

SRS is a company with many different functions. In 2018, they had a total of approximately 150 employees, of which approximately 50 were counted as white-collar workers. They started their cultural journey based on a strong Command and Control structure where functional managers were expected to make all decisions and communicate downwards in the organization, as well as a situation with silo thinking, conflicts, and a lot of internal politics. The company's CEO and parts of the management team realized that this was unsustainable, even though the financial results were quite good, largely thanks to the market being good and the product being wanted on the market.

Employee surveys showed that people were not happy. Instead, they wanted to make a cultural journey towards an organization that was more sustainable, where they worked across functional boundaries, where they took responsibility, and felt trust in each other. External support was brought in to work with communication and solve conflicts, but the real trigger was when the company's CIO was leaving the company. The IT department was asked if they wanted to test working without a manager and they chose this way forward. They created their own organization and chose a CIO who was not the head of a department but rather a representative in the management team and responsible for strategy and budget. The managerless department was successful and several functions are managerless today. The challenge for SRS has been that some functions still have their manager while others have no manager, which creates an imbalance. Representatives in different forums can sometimes have different mandates, which has affected decisions and cooperation. What also happened during the SRS culture journey was that the management team had less and less to do and finally decided to dissolve themselves. All previous management team tasks were distributed to various cross-functional forums.

SRS undertook a journey from a hierarchy of authority to a combination of responsibility and network hierarchy. At Centigo, the founders had the idea from the start that there would be no traditional managers (even though business unit managers do a lot of traditional "managerial work"). The company was founded in the early 2000s with the philosophy that employees should take on personal responsibility and that there should be transparency and trust among employees. Their challenge has been to maintain this during a growth where in 2019 there were approximately 290 employees. From this case we can see that it is increasingly difficult to have full transparency in information and communication, especially as many employees are working at different customers' offices. In this situation there is a need to develop communication platforms and constantly work on sharing information.

Jayway also started in the early 2000s with the philosophy of being innovative, transparent, and having equality and strong trust. This was the founder Thomas Dagsberg's basic philosophy, which permeated the company's culture. For example, Thomas disliked bonuses because they made people focus on the wrong things. All managers would also have exactly the same salary and definitely no bonuses.

But despite the founder's strong values, several challenges also emerged here in maintaining the company's culture as it grew. The company was divided into several different areas based on technology and methods, and created hierarchies and new titles such as Vice President, which could actually be compared to a consultant manager. After some time, the founders realized that they had to do something and decided that there would be only one Jayway. Unfortunately, several of the first employees had left the company in the meantime, which also affected the culture. However, they tried to develop the company and created a more modern organization based on agile principles.

If you compare SRS, Centigo, and Jayway, you can see that they have had different cultural journeys, which have been based on their own prerequisites. What is comparable is that all of them have had founders or company leaders who are strongly rooted in wanting to create a good organization with a positive and strong culture that is based on transparency, equality, and decentralized decision-making and where the employees should be able, and willing, to take their own responsibility. The other commonality is that size matters. It is easier to create a culture with common values when you are a small organization. When the organization is large or growing, particularly if that is happening rapidly, the values are challenged by other behaviors that pull in different directions. If this is put in a context where it can be compared to a global and large organization such as Ikea, despite a strong culture with a cultural DNA that sits in the walls, the organization tends to become "deep," meaning that there are many hierarchical levels. Ikea also have their own special managerial tradition. With managership, hierarchies of power are created, which is why within the DP model we choose not to use the word "manager," but rather only use the word "leader."

One of the strong recommendations we have within the DP model is that each organization must create its own creative map, that is, draw and shape its own cultural journey. Copying someone else's journey can be a dangerous way to go, especially if the organization differs in size and/or complexity, which has implications for how to organize.

Voice from the field: Ted Rau – Program Director and Operational Leader Sociocracy For All, Massachusetts, USA

Ted Rau is co-founder of Sociocracy For All and co-author of *Many Voices One Song*. Ted cares about system changes for more equality and sustainability and that also create more human organizations and relationships. Ted is transgender, has five children, a PhD in Linguistics, and is a German/British citizen living in the US.

Among other roles, I am the operational leader of the General Circle of a nonprofit organization that makes sociocracy accessible to as many people as possible through resources, training, networking, and consulting. We touch about 100,000 people per year.

In preparation for this piece of writing, I went to look up how many circles of paid roles and volunteers our organization has right now. It seems to be 33 circles today. It is very likely that this number will change soon, or maybe it is already outdated! I lead an organization that I don't fully oversee.

What is it like to be in the "center" of a decentralized organization? It's a little bit of everything. There is pride in all the projects completed and awe of all the things happening that I didn't even know had started. There is trust because I know and trust the people in linking positions.

There is also some anxiety – I attribute this to old-paradigm thinking still very much present inside me. "I am the Executive Director, and I should know everything that is going on! I am responsible! What if something goes wrong?!" Right after thinking that thought, I remember, again: Things have gone off track before here and there, and almost every time, the people around were able to take care of the issue. And if they can't, then the next "level" does. And if it can't, then the tension will find its way to my peers, the General Circle, and me. I don't need to be the person who knows everything.

The system of interlinked, decentralized circles holds us all.

In good moments, being at the center of a decentralized organization is like sitting in a meadow – everything around me is humming with activity. I lift up a rock and am surprised to find creatures crawling underneath. I look further away in the distance and I see there is even more to discover, even beyond my reach.

The metaphor of sitting in a meadow also works in another way: One has to tread carefully. You can't bulldoze your way through the system. When talking to others in roles or circles, it is clear to me that they are in charge of their domain. I need to listen well, pointing my antennas out towards their situation, while never impinging on their authority. I have no power over them, and I need to keep asking myself: "Is this my place?" If it is not, then I wonder, "whose domain is this in?" or "who needs to know this?" Maybe I can fill information gaps, otherwise I can only try to listen closely. The members of other circles most likely understand their own issue much better than I do. What I am learning here might be relevant elsewhere. If I see weak spots in the ecosystem, I give feedback to relect it back and let the system learn more about itself. If it's the right time, a conversation will create the clarity for action.

For example, I noticed in our organization that circles in one branch of our system often relied on information and decisions in another part of our system. This, mixed with some lack of clarity, created tension and bottlenecks. I was not the only one to notice, it had been brought up by others. My job was to amplify those voices because I saw what they saw as well, and to make sure a conversation can happen between those who could make the necessary changes. The wisdom was already in the system and the people.

The complexity that we are surrounded with renders heroes unnecessary – there is no scenario in which I could possibly step into a circle that is not mine and "fix" an issue. It might be fixed short-term but that wouldn't be sustainable. Back to the image of the meadow, a top-down reorganization of domains would be like ripping a branch off a tree and telling it to grow on a different tree. It just doesn't apply.

In a system like this, all circles need to become their own communication center. They need clarity on what information from their circle needs to be communicated to other circles, roles, or parts of the entire organization. There never seems to be an end to how much clarity and coordination are required and how many reviews "should" be done, and communication needs to be effective and prioritized. Systems need attention and maintenance. For a whole year, we decided to devote our energy to reconsolidation of existing operations instead of growth. The constant change is exhausting for some. To me, I see that the next stage in our evolution happens with ease if we ourselves are ready for it.

Sometimes imperfections and quirky solutions remain in place longer than I am comfortable with. In those moments, I hold my breath a little. For example, we are a multilingual organization. In our current system, there is a Training Circle for the overall organization, holding in its domain all training offers. Yet, several circle connections removed from that, in a completely different department, there is a circle offering similar training offerings in Spanish. Should this be? Yet, despite being a little messy, it works, mainly because each of those circles gives each other space in making their own choices. And we talk to make sure our choices move us in the same direction – alignment coming from our voluntary commitments, not the structure alone.

What brings me joy is the willingness of everyone to contribute and do their roles well, with joy, affection for each other, and passion for the organization. I strongly believe that people are at their best when they are choosing what they are doing, how they do it, and what bigger context they are contributing to. More than once, when things were slow-moving or faulty, I've gotten impatient and tried to throw money at a problem to fix it instead of strengthening the ecosystem so it can heal itself. So far, that hasn't worked a single time. A system tended to, and people who understand the system around them, by far outrun extrinsic motivators.

LEADERSHIP

It is almost impossible to have a clear and uniform definition of leadership; there are so many definitions and it is not our ambition to value these. Within the framework of our research, we have come across almost 70 different definitions. In most cases, leadership is described in relation to management.

Sometimes leadership and management are used as synonyms and sometimes as a way to differentiate these by saying that management is about personnel administration, planning, co-ordination, budgeting, and is linked to a role, while leadership is about qualities that are linked to human relations such as managing others, communicating, guiding, inspiring, etc.

One of the definitions that is widely spread comes from Peter Northouse (2007), who believes that leadership is a *process* through which a person *influences* a *group* of individuals to achieve a common *goal*. There is a limitation in saying "common goal" because it can be about a goal that a single person has or that only part of the group has. Therefore, we think that Bruzelius and Skärvad's definition is more useful because they define leadership as follows: *As an influencing process with the aim of getting other people to act voluntarily and committedly to achieve certain goals* (2004, p. 365). This definition is timely because it addresses two important aspects, namely voluntariness and commitment. This is in contrast to many definitions aimed at authoritarian leadership, which is linked to the view of the leader and the manager directing subordinates. Like many other aspects of organizational theory, leadership has undergone an evolution, and this should be reflected in how it is defined.

There are usually three types of leadership that have their basis in behavioral theory: authoritarian leadership, democratic leadership, and let-go leadership. An authoritarian leader makes all decisions himself, does not take into account what others think, and gives orders and controls, while a democratic leader, on the other hand, involves the employees. The third category, a so-called "let-go leader," lets things happen without taking action. For us, such a classification is outdated because leadership is not only linked to management.

We see leadership from a wider perspective, namely as a characteristic and capability that does not have much to do with the role people have in the organization. For example, when a person clarifies a task for another by exemplifying, using metaphors, or simplifying, and then ask questions that help the other person to prioritize or find new solutions, the first person is utilizing leadership regardless of the organizational role the person holds. This way of seeing leadership also includes the internal processes that take place within people themselves and that influence their decisions towards certain goals, i.e. self-leadership.

In the DP model, leadership is considered an influencing process with the aim of getting oneself or others to act voluntarily and committedly to achieve certain goals. Therefore, we believe in everyone practicing leadership.

PRACTICING LEADERSHIP AS A MANAGER

In most traditional organizations, the managers are expected to be the ones who practice leadership, meaning that in addition to the tasks that are included in the managership (planning, distributing the work, administration, etc.), leading the group towards the goals is also included. It is within such a paradigm that concepts such as formal and informal leadership have emerged. The basic idea is that only the person who is the manager has the formal right to practice leadership. If another person in the group leads others, this person is considered an informal leader and thus not legitimate based on the organization's rules. In many cases it is also considered a threat.

Take a moment and think about people you have worked with who have practiced leadership without having a leadership role. Why and how did they do it?

How managers practice leadership depends on a number of different parameters, with one of them being the organizational culture. In an authoritarian culture, all managers tend to use authoritarian or at least nondemocratic leadership to a higher or lower degree. In organizational cultures that are inclusive and open, managers tend to be democratic, even those who are essentially authoritarian in nature.

There is some debate in academia over whether some personal characteristics are more suitable than others for leadership. We believe that McGregor's (1960) thoughts about Theory X and Theory Y are the basic principle that governs how we look at people and thus the choice of leadership style. In Theory X, the basic idea is that work is not natural or attractive to humans and that humans are lazy by nature and do not want to think for themselves or take responsibility. Because of this, they must be controlled and directed, even forced. Controlling managers, who in some cases behave like tyrants, are often very dedicated people who work hard and long hours. Most managers of this type want the best for the organization and can therefore become despots. They believe that it is only themselves who are doing their best; the rest must be beaten into compliance.

Theory Y is the opposite, the belief that people consider work meaningful, like to take responsibility, and develop positive attitudes to work depending on experience. Based on this, people need to be guided and encouraged to achieve their own goals while meeting those of the company. The DP model is based on this approach and places people at the center.

Most organizations are designed according to the principles of hierarchy of authority, which we present in the section on organizing, and reward managers who lead according to Theory X. In contrast, Teal, sociocratic, agile, and other forms of self-organization see the world as Theory Y.

As we mentioned in the introduction, seven out of ten middle managers, according to the Work Environment Agency and Statistics Sweden (SCB) in 2018, experienced psychological pressure, and on top of it all, many of these work despite no matter how they feel. One explanation is that many of these middle managers act in an organizational culture that is not in line with what they themselves believe – for example, if a manager with values according to Theory Y works in an organization where the culture is based on Theory X. The norm says that in this culture the manager must control the subordinates (employees are called "subordinates" in this type of culture), while the manager's own values say that employees must be encouraged and that they will take personal responsibility.

Another explanation is that middle managers operating in hierarchies of authority live with strong expectations from both their managers and their subordinates. There is an expectation from the bosses that the manager should be proactive and organize the work, and from the subordinates that they should be able to make decisions and be a central point for all kinds of uncomfortable issues. The middle manager gets stuck in a hierarchy of authority characterized by positions of power.

There is no doubt that this type of organizing has strong roots and it is manifested in the way that many consultants, psychologists, rehab organizations, and others express themselves In a presentation from an organization that provides services for managers with stress-related problems, we found this recipe: *Create a flatter and more equal hierarchy with less distance so that it becomes easier for middle managers to switch between giving and taking orders.*

"Giving and taking orders" and "a flat organization" are contradictory. In a flat organization you do not give and take orders. It is actually easier to give and take orders in a strictly hierarchical organization based on power and authority. In a flat organization, the middle manager will be squeezed even more if he or she has to give and take orders.

In the case of Studsvik, it is very clear that the CEO, Tõive Kivikas, through his leadership, changed an entire organization even though it was a hierarchy of authority. What is also interesting in this case is that Tõive did not know much about different leadership or management theories. Instead, he acted based on his own beliefs and feelings, and on how he wanted his managers to treat him so that he could feel motivated and engaged and thus could contribute to the organization in the best possible way. He followed his intuition, trusted the employees, believed in their competence and ability, and used a leadership based on these beliefs. Tõive used his position of power as manager and CEO to change the organization in such a way that the hierarchy became flatter, decisions were distributed, and the organization took its first steps towards self-organizing.

Politics is often characterized by authoritarian leadership. Göran Persson (Swedish prime minister 1996–2006) can be used as an example of almost tyrannical leadership. During his time as a municipal councilor in Katrineholm, Göran Persson received the epithet HSB (in Swedish "Han Som Bestämmer," in English "He Who Decides") and has said: *A prime minister and leader of a party is always alone, always alone. There are certain topics and questions where only you can decide, no one shares that responsibility with you, it is yours. Always alone but at the same time never alone because I always have people around me* (Madestam, 2009).

What distinguished Göran Persson from other leaders of the Social Democratic party was that he became extremely dominant in his leadership style and was accused several times of bullying, both internally in his party and by several leaders of other parties. During Göran Persson's time as leader of the party, the Social Democrats became a strong hierarchy of authority where power was concentrated in the leader of the party alone. This led to a leadership crisis within the Social Democrats, and it has been very difficult for them to find the kind of leadership they are aiming for, a leadership that fundamentally has other values.

Looking around, it is possible to find quite peculiar views of management and leadership. One example is a Swedish company that trains managers and leaders, which writes the following on its website: *It is clear that it is possible to be friends with your employees, but your leadership becomes more difficult. There is a risk that this will lead to conflicts and misunderstandings. If you were friends with an employee before you became a manager, it is a good*

idea to be clear about the different roles. "As your friend I think ..."
"As your boss, I would advise you to ..."

What did Göran Persson say? *Always alone but never alone be-*
cause I always have people around me. A bit of a shame that those
who train in management and leadership have this attitude.
Maybe they think managers should only be friends with other
managers, and all nonmanagers can be friends with each other?

In certain contexts, people want to avoid sensitive situations.
An example is that around the time of the merger of Astra
and Zeneca, a principle was spread among managers that one
should not hire friends or people they knew, as this could lead
to inappropriate dependencies and not being able to make
"tough decisions." During this time, the two companies would
be integrated with each other, which would lead to dismissals
of personnel.

> **Reflect for a moment: How do you view management**
> **and leadership? What distinguishes a good leader?**

BEING A LEADER

What does it mean to be a leader and is it possible be a leader
without being a manager and thus be considered an informal
manager? The answer to these questions may vary depending
on the philosophy applied. According to Taylorism and Scientific
Management, the manager is the only true leader, end of discussion. It is all about managers and subordinates. Should a
subordinate act as a leader, he or she automatically becomes
an informal leader and that is not a desirable situation. This is
obviously an outdated way of looking at leadership. Because leadership is about influencing both oneself and others to achieve
certain goals, and also something that all people in a group practice to some extent, whether they are aware of it or not.

As with Theory X and Theory Y, mentioned earlier in this
section, most individuals have different orientations of emphasis.

Some are more focused on people and human relationships; others focus more on tasks and results. Research has shown that leadership is obviously affected by these orientations. Like many other aspects concerning people's development, these two orientations are neither static nor that one is used exclusively.

A common misconception within self-organizing is that there are no managers and by extension no leaders in the organization. All organizations need leaders, but leadership does not have to be held by just one person. It can rotate, be exercised by several, or vary over time.

SITUATIONAL LEADERSHIP BASED ON COMPETENCE AND DEVELOPMENT LEVELS

Most of the early theories of leadership focus on the leader and are about characteristics and personality. During the 1970s and 1980s, the focus shifted from the leader to the group and to the people. Hersey and Blanchard developed back in the 1960s (further developed in the 1970s and 1980s) a model called "situational leadership" where leadership reflects the needs of the person being led. The method was widely spread in Sweden during the 1980s and 1990s and is still included in most leadership training. Their classification is based on four different leadership styles, where each style forms a square as shown in Figure 12 below.

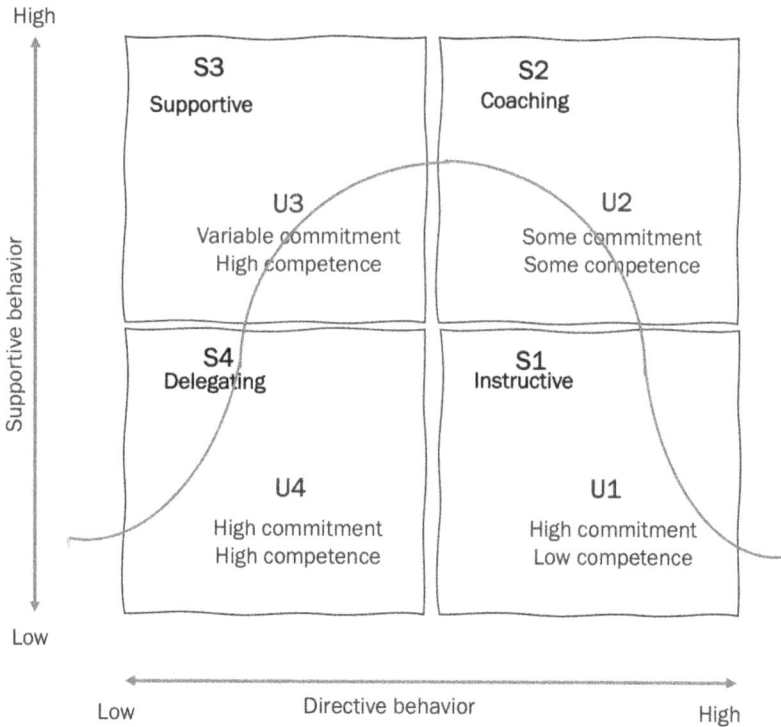

Figure 12. Situational leadership

U = Development level
S = Leadership style

The principle of situational leadership is that the leader uses an instructive leadership style (S1) when the employee is new or when the task is new, and the focus should be on explaining the task (U1). According to the model, the employee has a high degree of commitment but perhaps a lower level of knowledge in the new tasks. When the employee has grown into the role or task and is given more responsibility (U2), the leader should switch to a coaching leadership style (S2) and become more individual-oriented. The commitment has then decreased, and the employee's knowledge has increased a bit. With increased maturity, the individual orientation becomes even higher and then a supportive leadership style is used (S3). The employee's knowledge has increased and, with greater certainty, commitment increases (U3). When the individual is completely autonomous (U4), both task and individual orientation decrease, and the leadership style becomes delegating (S4). The employee has a high level of knowledge, and the commitment is probably higher, as they feel that they can perform the tasks in a simple way.

The model is based on the leader being able to use the four different leadership styles and is also based on a one-to-one relationship between the leader and the employee. The interesting thing about the model is that the leader must act based on what the employee needs to be able to perform the tasks, which may seem good. However, the model is based on a traditional hierarchical approach that the manager should lead the subordinates. What is often shown when analyzing managers and leaders in situational leadership training is that most of them have some leadership style that they are better at; for example, they may be better at instructing than delegating. Here, one can speculate whether this is linked to orientation according to Theory X and Y or based on the current organizational culture. There are other challenges – for example, that the leader does not always have deep enough knowledge to be able to instruct or does not understand the difference between delegating and supporting.

It becomes interesting when applying the principles of situational leadership to a group. A new team member, in many cases with a strong commitment, often needs quite detailed information in order to be productive. In this situation, the group can take joint responsibility and split the onboarding activities among those who can do different parts best. Another situation is about people who have knowledge but perhaps have little commitment and may need coaching from the rest of the group. Those who have fairly high competence but shifting commitment and engagement need to feel support from the group members, while those who are committed with high competence become independent and can act as mentors for others in the group. This is essentially what Centigo has done. New graduates always get a person who guides them into the organization and makes sure they get to know others. This will be like a coach or advisor for the new consultant. When the consultant has worked for a few years and has completed some assignments, he or she is offered a new role as Business Consultant (and receives a new salary model). With this, it becomes natural to receive support from a customer coordinator who is trying to find new assignments. An experienced consultant usually has his or her own customer relationships and can receive an offer to become a partner and is usually a coach to new employees.

What can be learned from the Centigo example is that the team can reflect together on the various tasks to be performed, as well as what support they need to give each other so that the tasks can be performed in the best possible way. This way of working creates organizational learning in the team where it becomes natural to share knowledge and help each other. It also becomes easier to see what support new team members need to be onboarded to the team.

TRANSACTIONAL LEADERSHIP

Leadership as a field has undergone some changes where various trends have dominated during different periods of time.

Transactional leadership came as a modernization of the strict authoritarian leadership that is significant for Command and Control. But it is based on the same, or at least similar, foundations. Originally it was called "rational-legal authority" and was presented in a leadership study by Max Weber in 1947. James MacGregor Burns further developed Weber's work and renamed the concept "transactional leadership" in 1978.

The basic concept is that employees can be motivated by being rewarded for good performance. The leader's task is to follow up and control, as well as correct undesirable behaviors or performance through feedback and by not giving rewards. Punishments can even be given in some cases. The name comes from the fact that there is a transaction between a performance and a reward. This theory is based on an individualistic philosophy that can be linked to Theory X because both the leader and the follower believe they are acting for their own gain.

A large part of today's bonus system is based on this approach. Bonuses are given as a reward when the employee achieves a certain result and can be omitted if the result is not reached. Figure 13 below summarizes the pros and cons of transactional leadership. As can be seen in the figure, the focus is on results and employees adapting to the leader's desired goals and behavior. This can motivate some people and lead to short-term positive results. On the negative side, creativity and innovation are not encouraged, which can lead to a situation where commitment and motivation suffer. It has also been shown that managers who receive a significant bonus as part of their compensation avoid doing things that do not have a positive effect on their bonus, even if these things may be important or critical for the organization.

Pros	Cons
Results and behaviors are rewarded	**Limited creativity**
Those who deliver results are rewarded. Desirable behavior is encouraged.	Strict and rigid system that does not encourage creativity and innovation.
Productivity	**Punishment**
Short-term goals can be achieved quickly. Strengthens high productivity in repetitive processes.	Punishments such as nonreward, demotion, blame, negative criticism, etc. lead to low engagement.
Order and Structure	**Motivation problems**
Instructions, expectations, roles, measurements, and rewards are clear.	Many people are motivated by things other than performance-related rewards.

Figure 13. Pros and cons of transactional leadership

TRANSFORMATIONAL LEADERSHIP

As the world changed, the need for a different type of leadership arose and several theories emerged. One of these theories is transformational leadership, based on the work of James MacGregor Burns from 1973.

In 1985, Bernard Bass extended the work of Burns and defined four different behavioral dimensions of a transformational leader:

1. **Idealized influence** – the leader acts as a moral role model and seeks new challenges and tries to live up to his or her values, which inspires and instils confidence.
2. **Inspirational motivation** – the leader shows optimism and inspires, creates meaning, and communicates an attractive vision that creates a sense of context and connection.
3. **Intellectual stimulation** – the leader encourages employees to question their current beliefs and creates conditions for new ideas. The leader advocates creativity, which leads to increased innovation.
4. **Individualized consideration** – the leader provides individual support and encourages achievement and shows empathy and compassion. The leader coaches every person according to specific needs.

A large part of leadership research highlights the fact that leadership has an impact on employee well-being and health. Many empirical studies show that poor leadership increases employees' stress and can lead to feelings of hopelessness, burnout, increased sick leave, and people leaving. In a study from 2010, Kelloway and Barling theorized that certain leadership styles, such as the transformational style, have positive effects and can reduce mental illness and protect against burnout. Within the frame of our research and during our three decades of working life, we have seen how good leaders create harmonious relationships that also help people whose personality or private life makes them fragile to find a good balance in life through their work. But we have also found far too many cases where people burn out because of constant change and because they feel pressured to get into things that do not come natural to them. Not all people feel good about taking risks or constantly thinking about the next step in their professional development.

Figure 14 below summarizes the pros and cons of transformational leadership.

Pros	Cons
Openness, honesty, and ethics are encouraged	Too much holistic focus
Doing the right thing in the right way and acting in the interest of the company and society.	Miss details, processes, and operational work as the focus is on the future and on change. May lead to lower operational efficiency.
Engagement	Too much change
Employees feel included, respected, and valued. Communication and collaboration are encouraged.	Too many change activities and pressure on employees can lead to burnout and lost focus on achieving goals and vision.
Innovation and Change	Absent from reality
Encourages new ideas, finding new ways, and changing ways of working. Focus on change and improvement.	Too many ideas and initiatives that lead in different directions without being in step with the organization's reality.

Figure 14. Pros and cons of transformational leadership

SERVANT LEADERSHIP

There is a leadership style associated with the agile mindset and agile organizations and practices. This leadership style is called *servant leadership*. Even though this style is mainly associated with agile thinking, the concept was coined by Robert K. Greenleaf in his book *The Servant as Leader* from 1970, long before agile was born.

In short, servant leadership can be defined as a leadership style that is based on an altruistic philosophy where the leader chooses to primarily serve, and then lead as a means of extending service to people and institutions. It is a type of leadership that encourages cooperation and trust.

It is primarily based on four characteristics:

1. It is the opposite of authoritarian leadership where leaders use their power to manipulate others or get others to act according to their wishes
2. It builds on collaboration
3. It emphasizes mentorship and coaching
4. It is forward-looking

The *Scrum Master* role in the agile method Scrum is a typical servant leader where the focus is on removing the obstacles that can stand in the way of the team. It can be simple things such as ensuring that the team has access to certain software or is given priority in a testing laboratory. But it also means protecting the team from disruptions that may stem from some stakeholders being eager, which can potentially start a conflict. A Scrum Master does not plan for the team but helps the team to complete their plans. The team is at the center and there is more focus on the team than on the organization as a whole.

Jayway had practiced servant leadership for a long time but they realized that the leaders became like curling or helicopter parents and it came to a point when it was not possible to recruit for a leadership role because the role meant being the team's running boy. In other organizations in which we have been active, extreme cases of servant leadership have led to organizational conflicts that can be compared to conflicts between parents fighting with each other to protect their children.

The role of Scrum Master is considered a lonely role that becomes difficult to fill, and agile coaches have emerged as a result of the problem. These coaches have the task of supporting the serving leaders/Scrum Masters and also to break the introverted working method and culture that can evolve in these teams. In one of the organizations that we studied, which developed according to this method, servant leadership created a strong team focus and loyalty, which resulted in great difficulty working across functions or even temporarily exchanging people between teams. Team loyalty became so strong that some said they would let the team down if they had to work on another team or project for a few months.

The primary difference between transformational and servant leadership is that the servant leader focuses on developing people, while the transformational leader focuses on inspiring people to work towards a common goal. The transformational leader pays attention to each team member while the servant leader has a stronger focus on the team itself.

There are both proponents and opponents of the servant leadership style, but we can state that there is less and less talk about it. Few companies describe in their company presentation that they practice a servant leadership style, and almost no recruitment ads mention it.

Some advantages and disadvantages are illustrated in Figure 15 below.

Pros	Cons
Listening	**Missing the big picture**
Active listening to the team. Understanding team members and their needs.	Team focus takes over and the organization's goals can be missed.
Teamwork and focus on people	**Decisions can take a long time**
The people in the team are in focus. Collaboration is encouraged and everyone's opinion counts.	Everyone is involved in decision-making, which can take a long time and require a lot of dialogue.
Reflection and learning	**Weakness**
People must develop. The team learns from past mistakes. Reflection is built into way of working.	The leader can be perceived as weak in that they are supposed to support the team. Can lead to parent-child relationship .

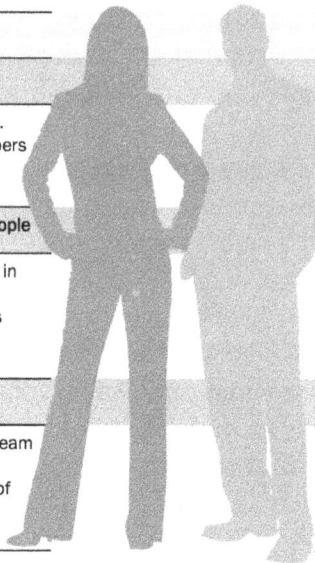

Figure 15. Pros and cons of servant leadership

The different types of leadership, namely situational, transactional, transformational, and servant, have come from different views and ideas about people.

It is about having different focuses, for example in matters regarding what motivates people, what people need, how people are inspired, or the perception that people may need to be "protected." Common to all these leadership styles, however, is that there is a relationship based on the leader having the power and practicing leadership over the subordinates.

LEADERSHIP IN SELF-ORGANIZATION

In parallel with the fact that the above-mentioned leadership styles are becoming more and more inadequate for today's organizations, we see that newer research findings about leadership highlight relationship building between people and a coaching approach.

K2K and the NER group, where NER means "New style of relationships" (*Nuevo estilo de relaciones* in Spanish), suggest that organizations should build a culture that focuses on the relationships between people. When leadership is practiced in relation to other people, it often becomes a mixture of softer aspects and facts.

The new progressive ways of organizing are built on a leadership that is based on the belief that all tasks have equal value. The person sitting at the reception desk is just as important to the organization as the engineer who develops a new product. But different types of knowledge and skills are required to perform different types of work.

Sociocracy and Holacracy are based on each circle organizing work within the scope of its area of responsibility. The team members express which roles or areas of responsibility they want to work with, usually based on their skills or area of expertise. Opposing opinions are resolved through open discussions and through the consent method (see the section on decision-making). The person who takes responsibility for an area leads the area. In this way, it can be said that the leadership is distributed to the team members. The leader's role here is to coordinate and ensure that nothing falls through the cracks and to be aware that overlapping areas of responsibility do not arise. In most cases, the role or responsibility is time limited to, for example, one year. When the time expires, the role/responsibility can pass to someone else, or stay with the same person for another period. Each person can also express which area they want to work with in the future and develop there.

At Buurtzorg, there are different roles that are also rotated within the team. Among the various roles, there are four roles that can be classified as leadership roles and that in some way replace the traditional responsibilities of a manager. These roles are:

A. The **informant**, who is responsible for following up and making the team's productivity visible. The work includes summaries of the services delivered and financial reports.

B. The **developer**, who is responsible for the cooperation within the team and between different teams. Leads the work with sharing new knowledge and insights within and outside the team.

C. The **planner**, who leads the planning of the group's time commitments regarding the customers' needs. Advises the team on any changes and encourages future improvements within planning.

D. The **mentor**, who takes care of new employees and is responsible for their onboarding and coaching.

At Centigo there are no formal managers, but it is very clear that there are leaders. These leaders are responsible for the business area or for customers. The leader responsible for the business area is responsible for planning onboarding, coaching, and the development of the team, while the leader responsible for customers is responsible for handling customer relations and finding the right assignments for individuals who belong to different teams.

The employees are encouraged to have an entrepreneurial spirit where new ideas and innovations are initiated and are led by the one taking the initiative or those who show interest.

The coaching approach that the leader responsible for the business area practices is explicitly based on situational leadership; although not described that way, in practice this is the way it works.

In all the organizations that we have studied, worked in, or in some way been in contact with and that practice a new style of leadership, there are some common denominators. These are that the leader is not responsible for motivating his or her employees, nor for giving feedback and following up alone. In these organizations, there is also not a single leader who owns all questions regarding what work is to be done and how.

The traditional image used in the 1990s, where a leader was like a conductor in a symphony orchestra, no longer applies. Nor does the image of the inverted pyramid where the leader/manager holds the pyramid apply. A leader in systemic organizations is one among all others.

Voice from the field: Andreas Jonsson – principal Holma Folk High School, Höör, Sweden

Andreas Jonsson has a background as a human ecologist and is passionate about holistic solutions where the long-term perspective and ecosystem are in focus. He works today as a permaculture designer and teacher, both on his own farm in Vånga in Skåne and in the folk high school world. Andreas was elected by the staff as principal at Holma Folk High School in Skåne.

In addition to his job as principal at Holma folk high school, he works as a teacher and consultant in Sociocracy and organizational development, including through Sociocracy For All.

Here are my thoughts on leadership:

We face a future that is more uncertain than ever before in human history. This means that we must go into everything we undertake in the future even more consciously and even more collectively. Collaborations, ethics, and a sense of purpose are already absolutely crucial for how we will live on. We need tools that are adapted to the new reality we see.

The old-world tool is called *control*. That tool has its origins in the industrial approach, where we allow a mechanistic structure of thoughts to construct the world as a machine. This way of thinking has its origins in the Enlightenment, the rise of scientism, objectification, and methodology. Things can be taken out of context and observed as entities. It is through this mental representation hat we humans have begun to treat the planet and everything contained in the biosphere through a mechanical belief in linear causal relationships. And only when we choose to see it so simplistically can we see human leadership over nature as something that makes sense, a belief that we can direct cause and effect through control. A need for control that is actually necessary for the planet and nature to spin around.

But there is a fundamental concern with this perspective. Life! The world, people, and nature are not a machine. There are in reality very few purely linear causal relationships around us. However, there are plenty of living systems that interact. Self-organizing systems that cannot be controlled, because we are influenced by an enormous number of sources all the time – at the same time. Living systems want to move in their own directions. They build resilience through increased complexity. We can throw the control perspective out the window. With living systems, we must have a completely open way of working.

We design the systems we see as necessary based on our purposes, we dance with them in the direction we have jointly chosen, and we constantly adjust our movements depending on the input and feedback that comes to us. We give ourselves up in the dance, we feel the sweat on our hands and the tickling nervousness of new dance partners. But we still dance, with the corners of our mouths forming a smile, because it's actually fun. Life.

Social systems are like any other system. Input comes from everywhere, and that's actually good. The change shows possible ways forward. Collaborations change, someone gets sick, another gets nervous, a third is extremely goal-focused, maybe we have a power cut?

Sociocracy is a model for how we can lead ourselves in a group, and then dance with our self-organizing forms of cooperation. A design tool with clarity, transparency, equality, and efficiency as keywords. A collaborative tool with clear paths for how we decide together, how we evaluate the decisions, how we can exchange professional titles and individual performance requirements and control, for collaborative roles that can be improved by everyone, and not least – Sociocracy enables a great confidence in daring to test paths forward together.

In Sociocracy there is no boss – instead there is a leader chosen by the group who reminds everyone involved of their own roles and responsibilities to achieve the goal. Goals, and areas of responsibility that everyone has already participated in and decided on themselves. The leader's role must also be evaluated based on the role description that everyone has agreed to before the role is filled. If it does not work for the group to achieve its goals with a specific leader, then someone else gets the role. Someone else gets to try the role of leading the dance.

It's actually not more difficult than that. The world is open and changing. We don't make perfect decisions that are written in stone. We make decisions that we can later evaluate together. Do we have enough information to dare to go ahead and try? Can we evaluate in a week? Does it feel safer then?

There is no one else but us who can face the world we see in front of us.

It is a conscious responsibility taking for the whole and a self-leadership we need from everyone.

Good enough for now, safe enough to try!

THE DP MODEL: **Leadership**

DECISION-MAKING

Decisions can be made in many different ways, by different people and forums that may involve several people, an entire group, or organization, and they can also be made by a single person.

There are also different types of decisions, for example operational, tactical, and strategic, which we will return to later in this section.

Our research in general, and our experience, shows that decision-making is one of the most difficult and challenging aspects of a cultural journey and in organizations that are not strictly hierarchical. Decentralizing and distributing decision-making requires more time than having a manager who makes all decisions; it also requires knowledge about how to make decisions in a different way. People need to learn and relearn, which can initially take time because most of us have been trained in a Command and Control approach.

Schools, universities, and the vast majority of organizations educate people to follow the leader, and the leader or teacher has the last word and is responsible for decision-making. Decades of this approach cannot be changed overnight, but the journey must begin as soon as possible. The future will consist of organizations that have embraced the new paradigm where power is distributed within the organization.

Before you read on, take a moment to reflect on how decisions are made in your organization.
What is it, or what has it been, like in your family? Yes, there are also structures that govern how families distribute decision-making. Who makes decisions about new purchases for the house, for the children, where and when you will go on holiday?
How does the process work?

DECISION MECHANISMS

In this section, we present the mechanisms used to make decisions in organizations. We begin by presenting a summary of different decision mechanisms in Table 7 below.

Table 7. Different forms of decision-making

Decision-making mechanisms	Authority	Majority	Consensus
How decisions are made	Through authority and power where the power is normally a part of the hierarchy.	By voting or expressing an opinion. Most votes win.	When all participants agree. Through dialogue.
Who decides	Decision made by a manager. Both power and position in the hierarchy matter. Decisions made at higher levels have more weight and override those made further down.	Decisions made by the participants that have the authority to vote or have the opportunity to share their opinion.	Decisions are made by the whole group being a part of the decisionmaking process.
Strengths	Fast and in general quite clear who decides.	It can be fast depending on the process. It is possible to include large groups of people and even a whole organization.	The whole group of people feel participation. The discussions open up for new ideas and different opportunities are considered.
Weaknesses	No inclusion and the decision could be excluded from reality and miss anchoring in the organization.	Group members could feel overrun. Risk of polarization.	Takes time. A lot of discussions and difficulties in coming to a decision.
Based on	*Command and control.* Hierarchies where power are concentrated at the top.	Democracy.	The Swedish management school.
May be called	Tyranny of those in power.	Tyranny of the majority.	Tyranny of the minority.

Consent	Concordance
When there are no more objections to the proposal (see the presentation of Sociocracy in the section about progressive organizational models).	When everyone feels that the decision is consistent or when everyone has their say and then trusts the group's preferences.
Decisions are made by participants of the circles with input from people involved in the advice process.	Decisions are made by a group of people. The method does not define the group constitution but people who have knowledge within the area and people who are affected by the decision shall participate.
Decisions are made by people with knowledge within the area and/or, if possible, those who are affected by the decision. Facts and clear consequences are presented and are the basis for the decision, instead of personal preferences.	Is based on veto, which means that decisions are committed. Facilitates implementation because everyone is committed, and feelings are considered.
Everyone needs to understand the decision-making process and that it is not about personal preferences. Need for trust and prestigelessness in the group of people.	The group of people need to be trained in the method and be able to use "pass" and "veto."
Sociocracy. Also used in Holacracy but with some modifications in the objection round.	The Human Element and psychology.
Controlled by facts.	With heart and brain.

In practice, most organizations and groups use a mix of these decision-making mechanisms, but in most organizations, there is one mechanism that is more common than others. It may depend on the organization's culture and size, and the types of decisions that the organization make regularity.

An example of how a mix of these mechanisms is used in practice could be that a manager or management team decides that Team A should make decisions regarding how the new office should be designed. This means that the first decision, the one about a change to be made in the premises, has been made by authority, namely that the top management made the decision. Through a consensus decision based on dialogue and consideration, the management team can determine that Team A is the most appropriate group to handle the issue. Team A, in turn, can use a majority decision to vote for different types of office layout or, through a consent decision, ensure that there are no objections.

DIFFERENT TYPES OF DECISIONS

There are decisions of different natures, and these require both different forums and different decision-making methods.

Most well-functioning organizations make a clear distinction between operational and strategic decisions. There are also organizations that include a third level, namely the tactical one. The tactical level can also be called the "development level," i.e. questions intended to develop the business, and lies naturally between purely operational questions that concern the here and now and strategic ones that have a longer time perspective. Tactics can be said to be the art of consciously choosing between and coordinating means and methods in a given situation to achieve set goals. This may involve the use of more or less established guidelines.

The distinction between the different levels concerns several aspects:

- distinct forums
- different members/persons
- time to make decisions
- basis or preparation
- planning/time regulations
- communication of decisions
- how long the decision is valid

Different forums for the operational, tactical (development), and strategic work that are separated from each other both enable the focus to be on what is intended and ensure that that is the case. In almost all the organizations we have worked in and studied, operational work has tended to take over. It is natural that this happens because the operational work is usually of an urgent nature and more tangible. It is also the most understandable to most people. The strategic level deals with the future and is often more abstract. An interesting thing is that people who have a lower ability to deliver, or less knowledge of the operational work, prefer to focus on strategic things and avoid conversations that deal with concrete operational issues.

During a time when one of the authors supported a school in Gothenburg as an organizational consultant, it was clear how urgent daily problems took up all the time and how meetings that were intended for pedagogical long-term planning were transformed into dealing with things close in time. This could, for example, be discussing who would be on duty in the schoolyard next week or talking about difficult situations that occurred on an ongoing basis. The reason was that the school was located in a vulnerable area characterized by violence and unrest and the daily situation became very stressful for the teachers, which was evident in the school's everyday life. In such a situation, it is natural that operational things take over; it is what is happening here and now that becomes the focus.

SRS started so-called "focus groups" with the intention of managing development issues that are of a tactical nature. In reality, the focus groups were to a large extent managing operational issues. On the other hand, many of the employees believed that the focus groups were intended for strategic issues. In several other organizations that we have worked in or studied, it is common that there is ambiguity about what is strategic, tactical, and operational. This in turn leads to the fact that different forums and meetings diverge from their purpose even though there are clear agendas and descriptions for what they should deal with. The consequence can be that the meetings do not have the right participants or that the focus is completely wrong.

To avoid this ambiguity, we successfully use in our assignments three different colors for these questions/opinions: yellow for strategic, orange for tactical, and red for operational. When, for example, a tactical or operational question appears in a strategic forum, the question or opinion is written on a card, which is then forwarded to the correct forum.

Within the DP model, we believe it is very important that forums of different natures are separated from each other and have the right members. This is to ensure the principle that the decision is made by those who have knowledge and, if possible, those who are directly affected by it and therefore should be part of the decision.

Operational decisions usually have to be made much faster and are a prerequisite for the work to continue. Strategic decisions, on the other hand, need more preparation, background information, and a longer time for evaluating the situation and its solutions. Tactical ones can often result in improvement initiatives intended to develop the business. Strategic and tactical decision-making meetings need planning, to which, in addition to the permanent forum members, others with relevant knowledge can also be invited. This is very clear at Centigo, which has its partner meetings where strategic and tactical issues are handled. At the time of writing this book, they had 36 co-owners (partners). Their principle is that no one in the partner group owns an issue alone, but everyone must take responsibility if it is a partner issue. However, Centigo realized that it became ineffective when there were 36 people making decisions, so they created engagement groups consisting of six people. Questions are sent for referral to these groups, after which the single representatives from each group meet to make decisions. Each representative has a mandate to represent the engagement group.

Within the DP model, we believe that a good approach is to use clear names for decision-making forums. In Sociocracy, operational and strategic meetings are called *operational* and *policy* meetings, respectively. However, the name policy meetings can be misleading and have associations that are less positively loaded than if they were called by their proper names, i.e. operational and strategic meetings, respectively.

Holacracy calls the operational meetings *tactical* and the strategic meetings for *governance* meetings. This can also be misleading and lead to misunderstandings. Within the agile development method Scrum, different types of decisions are handled in different forums. *Roadmap planning* and *sprint backlog refinement* become the strategic decision forum, *sprint planning* becomes the tactical forum, and *daily stand up* becomes the operational forum. In this way, everyone involved knows what types of issues are handled in the various forums, which are also called "ceremonies."

Within the DP model, the fundamental view is that most operational decisions are made in daily work and not in meetings. We can also conclude that it usually goes faster and has fewer negative consequences if the organization has defined how to make decisions, for example avoiding decisions having to be changed because the right people were not involved in the decision.

CLARITY IN DECISION-MAKING

How decisions are made in an organization can be strongly linked to the organizational culture (see the section on culture). During our years at Ikea, we could see that the inclusive culture that existed in the company led to consensus being the predominantly accepted decision-making model even if some authority decisions were made. In many cases, it took a long time to make a decision, and even worse, already made decisions were discussed again because new people had joined the discussion. This in turn created some kind of disloyalty towards already made decisions, something we call "moving decisions," which in turn gives a sense of ambiguity.

At SRS we could clearly see that there was a lack of clarity regarding decision-making even if they had every ambition to create a good organization where participation in the decisions was encouraged and where the decisions shall be made according to the Sociocracy principle (not stated), that is, by those who have knowledge or are directly concerned. SRS's CEO told us that the principle of making decisions was concordance, while the rest of the employees believed that it was consensus, authority, or majority decision-making that was applied.

A sense of ambiguity is created when there is no stated, anchored, and well-communicated way of making decisions, or when there is no knowledge or understanding of who is responsible for making decisions. This was part of the findings from the SRS case study, where almost everyone felt it was unclear, even on issues that seemed clear. The reason for the general feeling stems from the fact that principles around decision-making were not communicated to everyone in such a way that everyone understood how and where decisions were made (more on communication in the section on transparency and communication). The feeling of ambiguity is one of the most common problems that occurs when organizations move from being a hierarchy of authority to an organization where decision-making is distributed, because people do not know who made decisions in a new way. In a hierarchy of authority, it is known that it is the manager(s) who makes all the decisions. Therefore, a distributed or networked hierarchy requires a different type of communication regarding when, how, and about what decisions are made.

Within Sociocracy there is a main rule that says "Good enough for now and safe enough to try," which means that you don't need to go into depth before a decision is made. You can make a decision and move on as long as you feel safe with what you know and can do at the moment, and with enough facts. The principle also invites a new dialogue if the situation shows that more information is really needed. This is in line with the agile methods where things are done in steps and based on the facts available at the moment, and where you plan and make decisions on the understanding that the plan or decision can be revised.

K2K advocates that the decision should be made by consent, but also uses large gatherings where majority decisions are applied. They distinguish between operational and strategic decisions. Their philosophy is based on trust that people can and should make operational decisions. A basic principle that everyone must follow is that a decision is valid and must be followed until a new decision is made. Anyone in the group has the right to ask for a decision to be revised, and in this way it is ensured that the decisions are followed and that there is flexibility and dynamism in that things can always be revised and changed.

The DP model's recommendation for effective decision-making is to use the consent and advice process as far as possible. However, there are occasions, above all within operational decisions, when the responsible person makes the decision on his or her own. It is important to train everyone in the methods and to have clarity about when different decision methods apply.

PARTICIPATION IN DECISION-MAKING

In addition to having clarity around the mechanisms used to make decisions, it also matters who participates in the decision-making.

In a sociocratic organization consisting of autonomous circles with the right to make decisions within their area of responsibility (domain), it is quite clear who should participate in each decision. This does not mean that people who belong to other areas of responsibility do not have the opportunity to give opinions or make suggestions. Anyone can make decisions they feel comfortable with. However, before making a decision they must ask those who will be affected by the decision and those who are experts on the subject for advice. This is called the advice process and involves four steps:

1. Present or formulate the proposal
2. Collect feedback
3. Respond to any objections
4. Make decisions

This is not a consensus process, but rather a way to get relevant information and develop the proposal so that decisions can be made.

SRS has several cross-functional groups called "focus groups," which are intended to make decisions about operational development and improvements. It is not always obvious that the people participating in the meeting can make decisions. In some cases, this is because they do not have knowledge of the topic being discussed, or because there are dependencies that have not been investigated. The consequence is that many decisions cannot be made without new meetings and discussions. This is experienced as time-consuming and sometimes frustrating. On the other hand, it can lead to more thoughtful decisions that are better anchored in the organization. It is important to have a balance between participation and the time needed to reach a decision. One approach that we advocate in the DP model is to have a dialogue around the criteria for when a decision has been made, so that everyone agrees on what the decision is.

Within the DP model it is also suggested to adopt an approach where it is possible to make a decision at a given time and that this is valid even if it later turns out to be wrong and must be redone. People can consider not following the decision if the decision violates the organization's principles.

At K2K, it is very clear that those who participate in a meeting have their own group's mandate to make decisions and that in the vast majority of cases, they can make decisions in a meeting without having to call for a new meeting. They also use a kind of on-call system, which means that if there is a risk that the group's representative needs to consult others in the group, they are available by phone. This creates speed and safety and is a very efficient way to create participation and anchor decisions that can be executed immediately after the meeting.

In his book *Tear Down the Pyramids!*, Janne Carlzon, former CEO of Scandinavian Airlines, tells a story about when he came back from the USA and there was chaos at the arrivals hall because the monitors that showed where the baggage was to be collected did not work properly. He asked the woman at the information desk why they did not make temporary signs so people could find their luggage. She replied that that was exactly what she thought and she had told the manager, but that the manager did not think it was necessary because the monitors would be fixed soon (it had already been a week). Janne sent a message to the concerned manager suggesting he take his nice desk and move to the arrivals hall so he could see what was happening there and thus gain the required knowledge to make decisions. Alternatively, he could continue to sit in his office but no longer make any decisions regarding the arrivals hall.

This anecdote is a clear example that decentralization and distribution of power is what organizations must use and is the basis for having motivated employees and satisfied customers. K2K's hotline system is not good enough if people always have to ask someone else before they can make a decision. Then they are not the right people to participate in the meeting or serve the customer for that matter. Therefore, we believe that in a meeting where decisions are to be made, all participants must have the authority to both make decisions and ensure that their team will stand behind it. Of course, there are times when decisions must be postponed, for example due to new questions or new facts coming to light during the meeting, and until all ambiguities have been clarified.

If there are any topics on the agenda where not everyone can contribute, or that are somehow not their area, the only right thing to do is to not participate in the decision but still stand behind it. This should not happen with a perfectly constructed agenda and well-defined areas of responsibility. But since the world is not so perfectly constructed, we see that there are many situations when this happens. But just like in all aspects that we present in this book, it is important to use common sense and feel safe in not participating in the decision.

The approach to handling decision-making when everyone who should be involved is not present differs quite significantly in the organizations that we have analyzed. Some choose to go ahead with the meeting but not make the final decision until the person who is absent has his or her say, while others cancel the entire meeting. Some organizations make decisions anyway and, which is what concordance advocates, the absence is interpreted as the person having no preferences and accepting what the meeting decided. K2K's position is that everyone concerned should be given a fair chance to participate. If they do not use this, they cannot be against the decision later. In other words, everyone understands that if you do not participate, you accept the result.

We know that it is very frustrating to go ahead with a meeting that may have to be redone, and furthermore, it is not a good idea to make a decision that is not anchored with those who will be affected by the decision. Therefore, within the DP model, we advocate not going ahead with such a meeting. It is also a way to reduce the stress of those who, for various reasons, cannot participate, and it is also the most efficient approach for everyone. It is not right either to think that the meeting is a good way to use the time because it can be a good discussion so that the decision will be made faster later. We know from experience that everything has to start all over again the next time, and it also creates an imbalance in the exchange of information. If you have been part of the discussion before, you have more knowledge about how the rest of the group thinks and many questions have most likely already been answered and knowledge has been shared among the participants.

DECENTRALIZED DECISION-MAKING

Since each organization is unique and exists in specific contexts that are unique to that organization, it is not about following a ready-made template to implement decision-making. Instead, it is important to first understand to what extent the teams are autonomous in relation to decision-making in the organization, as well as the influence there is between different teams.

The rule is that decisions should be made in as decentralized a manner as possible and be as centralized as necessary. Regardless of how autonomous the teams are, there are decisions that, by their very nature, must be made in a centralized manner.

Even in an organization like Buurtzorg, there are central decisions that affect, for example, finances and investments in new regions. Having principles that support decision-making is a prerequisite and these must also regulate how to handle deviations from the principles when the situation requires it.

ETHICAL PRINCIPLES AROUND DECISION-MAKING

Decision-making in an organization that follows the DP model must follow the basic principles and have a stance on ethics.

K2K has the following ethical principles that must always be met when decisions are to be made:

1. Those who will be affected by the decision must be the ones who decide.
2. The decision must be transferable to other groups, making a decision that only applies to a few or certain groups not acceptable.
3. The decision is completely transparent, i.e. if it is not possible to inform and make it visible to everyone, then there is something in the decision that is not okay and therefore it should not be made.

We know that there are times when decisions have to be made by groups other than those who will be affected, and in such cases we recommend a round of gathering information where, if possible, those who will be affected can give their views, both before and after the decision has been taken. This mainly concerns strategic decisions such as expanding into new markets, discontinuing a product line, company mergers, closing down, etc. The principle in such cases must be that information is given to those concerned as early as possible. There may be laws, regulations, processes, etc. that govern when information can be given, but if information is given as early as possible, people's peace of mind and security in the fact that no "game" is going on beyond their knowledge will increase, which will also lead to people's engagement and trust in others within the organization being higher.

Voice from the field: Maximilian Tropé – founder and CEO of Me-Maximilian, Malmö, Sweden

Maximilian Tropé has over 25 years of experience in organizational and leadership development, internationally and nationally. Maximilian is co-author of *For Full Potential: Exploring the Possible, Achieving the Extraordinary* and *The Human Element @ Work*. He has a bachelor's degree in business administration with a focus on organizational studies and leadership from Lund University and a master's degree in political science with a focus on negotiation and conflict management theory as well as a certificate as Master Facilitator The Human Element.

The way decisions are made can be crucial for the organization and I am often asked which decision model is preferable.

First, in my opinion, there is no optimal decision model for all situations. Which model to choose depends on the purpose and how extensive the decision is, i.e. how much of the system is affected by the decision. What is obvious is that in today's increasingly fast-moving world, we can no longer relate to linear processes where we have an analysis phase, a decision phase, and an implementation phase. We need to move to more circular processes that allow us to act into the future by setting up various hypotheses that we then test, observe, analyze, and develop. This iterative way of working creates a system that constantly creates a space to change decisions and chosen strategies towards the desired goal.

This agile and more hypothesis-testing way of managing today's organizations in a new reality requires a different way of relating to decision-making. My experience with these processes makes visible a number of different decisions that must be made and that require different forms of decision models. The fundamental decisions about where we are going and what design (methodology) we are going to use to get there are extremely important to create the clear ownership that will be required to deal with all the blockages and inertia that we will encounter as we try to transform our system. But in order for us not to drown in various ego-driven locks that prevent us from making a decision, the perspective and interests of the individuals need to be set against the needs of the business (customers and users). By making visible why we exist and what gives us a justification for existence, it is easier to separate the internal human blockages from the external operational ones.

Processes such as consensus, which require us to use logical arguments to convince each other of which is the right decision, are far too slow in relation to most issues in today's fast-moving world. If we wait until we have all the facts on the table, we will be irrelevant before we have time to make the decision. It is also the case that we will make many wrong decisions when we have to explore the possible in a world that we do not know or of which we have no experience. *Fail fast, learn fast.*

The exciting thing in my world is that the thoughts in a decision model like concordance focus more on dealing with the internal blockages in a decision process that prevent us from handling or acting adequately in a situation that we cannot handle or control 100%. This model constantly makes visible why we are unable to make a decision and what the cost of this blockage is. It has its clear similarities with consensus in that everyone has a veto but differs in that concordance focuses not only on taking a position based on factual arguments and previous experience, but also on ensuring that we stand behind the decision with all of ourselves, that is, intellectually, emotionally, and physically. Concordance also has a clear structure based on the FIRO theory, i.e. who will participate (those who are best suited and those most affected, however, participation is always based on me actively wanting to be involved), control (distribution of power, everyone has a veto), and openness (everyone has a responsibility to be open and honest with their thoughts, feelings, and experiences in relation to the decision-making process).

The strengths of consent are that the method ensures participation in a structured way without compromising the speed of the process. The risk with a decision-making process that only stops the decision if there are strong objections is that the collective ownership will not be as strong and that certain decisions that should never have been made will be let through. The decision model is suitable for fast iterative processes where the consequences of a wrong decision do not lead to major negative consequences. The model also does not have the same positive impact as concordance on the group's development in terms of openness and responsibility.

The strengths of a decision model such as concordance are that it develops openness and responsibility in the group and thus the group's trust and psychological safety, factors that have proven to be absolutely crucial for a team's effectiveness and ability to handle today's increasingly uncertain, complex world with increased interdependence. The disadvantage is that it is far too slow and risks stalling unless the people are both very knowledgeable on the subject and very psychologically mature. The model is usually suitable for decisions that have fatal consequences if they go wrong and are not as easy to change if they turn out to be wrong.

Consent, consensus, and concordance are all connected but have different focuses. Consent is based on the principle *Good enough for now and safe enough to try*. In consensus, everyone is convinced that this is our decision or agreement. Concordance is an even more extreme form of consensus that focuses even more on ensuring that there is no objection left at all.

My view is that today's fast-moving companies use some form of consent without necessarily knowing about this themselves or defining it as consent.

TRANSPARENCY AND COMMUNICATION

Transparency and good communication are prerequisites for a well-functioning relationship in all kinds of relationships. Transparency is also strongly linked to various aspects of trust. One of these aspects is trust that the receiver can receive information and handle it in a correct way.

In hierarchies of authority and political organizations, there is usually a perception that the receiver may feel bad about information, and that it might be spread in a way that may cause harm, or that people will not understand the meaning. This actually occurs in a parent-to-child relationship where the parent wants to protect the child. There is also a tendency to keep information secret and carefully plan for the occasion when to share it, mainly based on the sender's beliefs and preferences. Most of the time, information is shared in a filtered way as a cascade down through the hierarchy, thus running the risk of being beautified or distorted.

Another aspect is people's trust in the information they have access to and that has been communicated to them. If people do not trust that there is an openness in the organization, they do not trust that information is accurate or complete, and it can lead to suspicion that certain information is withheld. Instead, people talk to others in the organization whom they trust in order to figure out what is missing or has been withheld. This often leads to speculation, and it is in this way that rumors and conspiracy theories arise.

Therefore, it is important that the management communicates the whole truth and involves the people at an early stage in discussions regarding the business, not least when it comes to finding solutions to problems or other challenges. Getting information when everything has already been decided is not a good way to create an environment characterized by trust. In addition, people's contributions are lost if they are not involved before the decision is made.

Information also has a best-before date. Delaying the process is very common in many organizations, but as a part of the DP model, we advocate total transparency even during the time that information is being put together, meaning openness also before everything is completed.

TRANSPARENCY

In most of the organizations that we have worked with, participated in, or studied, people say that there is a transparency in communication. However, this is often far from the truth. In reality, only a few organizations, or parts of organizations, apply transparency to a wider extent. Most organizations are transparent with certain information or in selected areas, for example presentation of sales figures or market shares. They are usually more secretive when it comes to reorganizing or phasing out product areas.

K2K advocates radical transparency, meaning transparency with all information, including future strategy and plans. In an organization where all roles and people are equally valuable, it must be ensured that everyone has the knowledge to understand all information. It is not transparency if numbers, strategies, or plans are presented in such a way that the common employee cannot take in this information due to, for example, complexity or a lack of background to fully understand it. Unfortunately, this is more the rule than the exception in most workplaces.

A unit manager from a pharmaceutical company put it this way: ... *I don't understand, all the financial information is available, budget, strategies, and plans, and yet they [the employees] do not seem to understand. Nor can they ask relevant questions.* For the manager, transparency was equal to availability, and for him, there was transparency if the information was available.

Have you ever thought this way? Or have you heard someone express themselves in similar terms? You get information but you do not really understand it. Reflect about what can be done to avoid such situations.

One of the first activities that K2K carries out in the cultural journeys that they support is to train everyone, absolutely everyone, so that they understand the content of what is presented or distributed. K2K also trains the people who produce information to do this in such a way that the information is easy to interpret and receive.

Within the DP model, we strongly suggest that decision-making should be facts-based, and that these facts must be understandable, and that, in addition, everyone must have the opportunity to acquire basic competence to analyze the data. When graphs, numbers, charts, results, and plans are presented, employees must have the knowledge to understand what those mean, otherwise it is not real transparency. This could be compared to news broadcasts on the television. Complicated data must be presented in a way that viewers understand and can interpret it. The focus is that the receiver can take in the information in a way that makes them interested and engaged.

Within Sociocracy, Holacracy, and S3 there is a mechanism known as a "double link," which is, among other things, a way to ensure transparency. A double link means that a circle (organizational unit within these models) is always represented by two people, who are both members of the circle's parent circle. One of these representatives is the leader of the circle, the other one is called the "delegate" and is chosen by the team members. The quality of spreading information increases by having two representatives, who also complement each other and have different perspectives. Most often, the delegate has deeper domain knowledge, while the leader usually focuses on the long term.

This combination provides both depth and a holistic perspective, which in itself increases the quality of information sharing.

Within the framework of our research, we have searched for various radical implementations of transparency. We found, among others, Bridgewater (one of the companies studied for the emergence of the DDO model), which is a very successful Wall Street firm founded in 1975 and which describes itself as an independent and employee-driven organization. They have implemented what they call "radical transparency" and "radical truth."

On their website (www.bridgewater.com) they introduce themselves like this: *By fostering a culture of openness, transparency, and inclusion, we strive to unlock the most complex questions in investment strategy, management, and corporate culture.*

In their implementation of radical transparency, they have gone so far that they record every conversation that takes place inside a room, as well as all meetings. Some conference rooms also have cameras recording the meetings. Everyone in the organization has access to the recorded material. If your name has been mentioned, you will receive a message with information about which recording it is about. In this way, they have ensured that there is nothing that can be considered a conversation "behind closed doors" or that is confidential and stays "between us." Their founder, Ray Dalio, claims that this radical transparency encourages open and honest dialogue and enables the best ideas to thrive and win. There is a lot written about both Bridgewater and Ray Dalio's leadership, which has also been noticed in a couple of TED Talks and praised by both Bill Gates and Bloomberg.

We think that in an atmosphere where there is trust, it should not be necessary to record and have an algorithm that notifies people that their name has been mentioned in a conversation. We believe that there is a risk that a lot of energy is spent listening to what has been said in various meetings and what has been said about each other. It can also lead to people who are never mentioned and therefore never receive a notification, feel less important, and thus less valuable to the organization.

Introducing such a method can, in our opinion, only occur in a culture that has an inherent "radical" suspicion. Such technical solutions are not needed in organizations where people trust each other and trust that they receive information at the right time, and where there is a culture of constructive feedback. This example raises questions about DDO. On the one hand, the theory advocates that it is important to create an atmosphere and culture where people can be themselves, that there is trust, and that no one should have to use energy to think about what others think. But this example shows the opposite, a lack of trust.

In its culture journey, SRS has distributed decision-making and responsibility to different kind of groups where the majority of employees participate. At the same time, transparency and information sharing have increased. They also removed the management team and the hierarchy of authority that they previously had. This led to the fact that there was no longer "secret" information and that the management team controlled how information was to be distributed to the people in the organization. In addition, they introduced new digital platforms for sharing information and a weekly meeting, which they called the "beehive." The purpose of the beehive was to be able to "buzz" about everything that happened and what you wanted to spread information about. In our employee survey at SRS, we saw that information sharing and transparency were the areas that the employees thought had improved the most.

An interesting question to ask is whether all information in the company must be shared. The DP model states that all information should be available to everyone, but there may be some information that cannot be shared, or at least you must choose the timing. There might, for example, be occasions when a person wants to tell their closest colleagues something personal that may affect work. It could be that you have gone through some tragic event in the family, which means that you are not performing as usual. This type of information is personal and the person telling it must be able to decide whom to share it with and when. In addition, there are legal requirements that can govern how information is spread. In most countries there are specific rules for how personal information may be shared, which, of course, must be respected. If it is a listed company, it must comply with applicable legislation, otherwise there is a risk of being accused of spreading "insider" information. There may also be other types of information that are governed by different regulations. If the ambition is to go for full transparency, it becomes important to also discuss, define, and communicate the type of information that may not always be available to everyone.

FEEDBACK

Feedback is one of the foundations of an organizational culture based on openness where it is possible to make mistakes (as long as we learn from these) and where there is space for new ideas and innovations.

In traditional organizations based on Command and Control, it is implicitly understood that it is always the manager who gives feedback to his subordinates. If it is a project, it can be the project manager who gives feedback to the project members. It can be about achievements, actions, behaviors, or preferences. The purpose of feedback is to return to a person with something that can be positive and be given in the form of praise or negative feedback with the expectation of a change. At Patagonia, there are managers who ask for feedback from the rest of the group instead of giving feedback to the employees.

Research in general indicates that critical and nonmotivating feedback leads to disengaged employees. A 2016 Gallup survey on workplace feedback found that only 10.4% of employees whose manager had given negative feedback were engaged. This means that after negative feedback, 89.6% were disengaged and had negative feelings such as feeling disappointed, unmotivated, or depressed. Furthermore, the survey said that four out of five employees who received negative feedback were considering changing jobs or were actively looking for a new job.

It is difficult to understand why there are still leadership and management training programs that promote critical feedback as a way to improve performance. It is dialogue and a focus on how we create positive work results that create better performance.

Have you been in situations where you have received or given feedback in the form of criticism and the result was expected to lead to improvement?

We look at feedback in a broader way where everyone can give feedback to everyone in the form of dialogue, including to managers/leaders or owners. Within the framework of the DP model, feedback is about creating dynamics and a space for new ideas and constructive dialogues.

There are several different theories and concepts regarding feedback, and most leaders who have attended leadership training have encountered at least some of these.

Below are some of the best-known feedback methods with both advantages and disadvantages.

THE SANDWICH METHOD

This method consists of negative feedback being delivered like the filling in a sandwich where the bread symbolizes the positive things. It starts with delivering a positive message, then a negative or critical message, and it ends with something positive again. An example from our observations is when we heard a project manager say the following to a team member:

"Maria, you are so great at helping your colleagues, which is really appreciated (bread). But your ability to deliver reports on time is not so good. It happens every single time that we must wait for you (the filling). But your choice of language and images in the documents are always much appreciated (bread)."

The method involves trying to be nice, and the idea is that Maria should not react negatively when she receives criticism for her late deliveries. In addition, the idea is that she should be encouraged and feel appreciated despite this. The biggest risk is that the message may be lost, that what the project manager wanted to say and see changed, namely that Maria should not deliver late, does not come through because it is hidden in the filling. In addition to this, Maria may perceive the conversation as dishonest, as if the project manager does not dare to be open.

THE COACHING FEEDBACK METHOD

In this method, the person giving feedback takes a coaching approach, and instead of delivering the message, he or she asks questions and lets the person share their point of view. The positive thing about this method is that it invites dialogue and reflection. However, there is a risk that the person perceives the conversation as unclear or that there is something hidden in the questions and therefore does not answer in a sincere way. It can also happen that they have completely different views and that the dialogue does not lead to a concrete solution. In some cases, it can also happen that the person starts to rattle off everything that does not work or says that other people are the cause, and the conversation turns into a "complaint conversation" instead.

Many of those we have spoken to experience this feedback method as "only getting questions back when they actually want to have a discussion." Furthermore, they indicate that, after the feedback, they want to move forward in a discussion that leads to concrete proposals emerging, and not receive even more "coaching questions."

THE SELF-MESSAGE METHOD

This method is based on the meeting focusing on what the person who is giving feedback feels or how he or she is affected by the recipient's behavior. "You always deliver the reports late and it makes me feel stressed and I cannot do my job well." The positive thing about this method is that it is the act or the behavior being considered undesirable that is in focus and that it becomes clear what the consequences are. The risk of the recipient going on the defensive is reduced, but there is a risk that the meeting will be perceived as egocentric if it does not go right.

NEW WAYS TO GIVE AND RECEIVE FEEDBACK

Below are some new ways or methods of giving and receiving feedback.

FEEDFORWARD

One of the big problems with feedback is that it is often about things that have happened, about things that are in the past. The focus lies back in time and sometimes quite far back. The more time that has passed between the event and the meeting, the more difficult it becomes.

In addition, the word "feedback" usually evokes unpleasant feelings.

Imagine that a work colleague calls and asks you to make an appointment for a feedback meeting. What feelings and thoughts do you get? Will you think "What fun, we'll do that right away!"?

Most people want to focus forward and not backward.

The feedforward conversation is based on focusing on the future, on what can be changed and be done differently. The positive thing about this method is that the conversation "is easier" for both parties and that it is a solution-oriented conversation where there is no guilt.

The meeting begins with a finding or a future need that requires a change in behavior, after which a number of questions are asked.

In the case of Maria, it could go something like this:

The project manager: "Maria, we have an important customer activity at the end of the month and your delivery is an important part. Since you have previously delivered your reports late, we will now see together if there is anything we can do to ensure delivery on time."

Maria: "I don't know, I'm doing the best I can."

The project manager: "Think about whether there is anything that you would like to do differently or stop doing, and that could make it easier for you and help you deliver on time. What can we do together or with the help of someone else?"

Maria: "Perhaps I should not participate in all salespeople's information meetings. It always takes so much time. It would save time for me if I read the minutes instead. It could give me more time."

The project manager: "Is there anything else that could free up time or make it easier?"

Maria: "Perhaps reduce the number of images in the report because they are time-consuming."

The project manager: "I will find out which of the salespeople's meetings will focus on your area so that you can prioritize attending them. You can read the minutes for the remaining meetings. Reach out if there is anything you would like more information about. The team can also help provide input on which are the most important images."

The method contains much of the coaching feedback method, but the difference is that questions are asked with a focus on finding a solution, which is positive. Looking at Spotify, a principle called 70–20–10 is used there. This means that 70% of the feedback shall be related to the future or is about activities that lie in the future, 20% in the present and only 10% backwards in time.

The shortcoming of this method is that there is no reflection on, or analysis of, what works and what does not work; mistakes can be repeated, and important lessons can be overlooked. This can lead to an eagerness to do things in a different way without knowing why or reflecting on the consequences.

In order to avoid such a risk, we have developed within the DP model a method called R&F (Retrospective & Feedforward) where the meeting starts with a retrospective part without any element of feedback, after which it switches to feedforward. R&F is also based on the REPI methodology. Both methods are described in the chapter "The way forward."

RADICAL CANDOR

Radical Candor is a fairly new method and approach that was created by Kim Scott, who is the author of *Radical Candor: Be a Kick-Ass Boss Without Losing Your Humanity* and cofounder of the company Radical Candor.

The method is based on a classification of different focuses that the person giving feedback may have. If the focus is on the person receiving feedback, there are two outcomes. The first is that you are so empathetic that you are afraid to tell the truth, which can even lead to lies because you do not want to hurt the other person (1 in Figure 16). The second outcome is wanting to create a change that develops the other person by daring to say what needs to be said even if it is difficult, and that it is done in an effective way (2 in Figure 16).

If, however, the focus is on the one giving feedback, the sender, there are two other possible outcomes. The first thing is to be afraid to say how it is. This is not because of fear of hurting the receiver, but instead because of fear that the receiver will not like you and that he or she may criticize you or affect your reputation negatively (3 in Figure 16). The other possible outcome is to be so strongly convinced in that the sender's view is correct that the message becomes aggressive (4 in Figure 16).

Depending on how strong the focus is and what approach is used, it will produce different results for the receiver. If you are kind and empathetic and therefore do not say it as it is, or say that things are good even when that is not the case, this usually leads to no change taking place and the person remaining unaware of what needs to be changed. It will also lead to unconsciousness on the part of the receiver. Acting by not saying how it is or lying to manipulate the other, and getting them to like you, is just manipulation and leads to mistrust.

If the message is delivered in a direct manner with an aggressive tone, where the most important thing is to be right, it leads to little change and to the receiver going on the defensive. If, on the other hand, there is a genuine interest in the receiver and the message is delivered in a direct manner but with respect and consideration, it will lead to a real, profound change and personal development for the receiver.

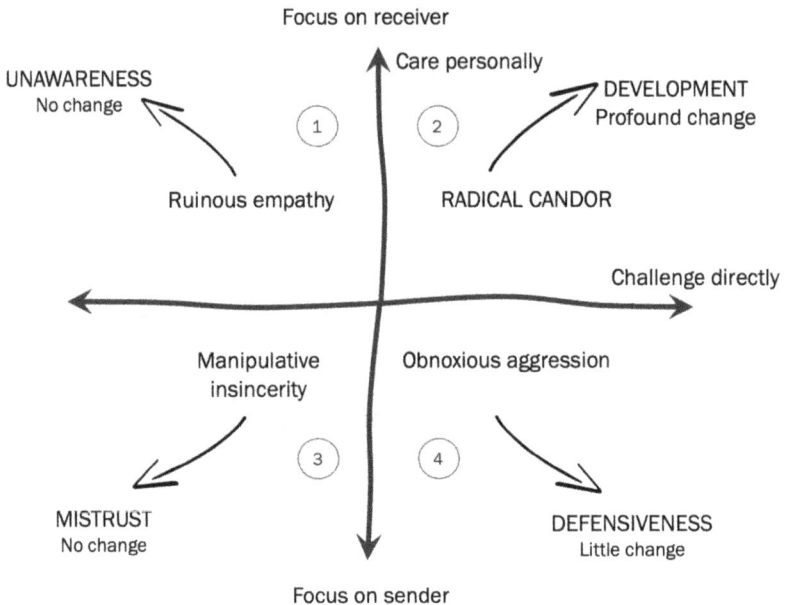

Figure 16. Radical Candor (updated from Scott 2019)

COMMUNICATION

Creating a culture where communication is open and where it is possible to express everyone's thoughts and feelings without leading to negative consequences is a prerequisite for a good organization.

Amy Edmondson highlighted the concept of "psychological safety" after a research project at Google where she defined psychological safety as an atmosphere or organizational culture where people can express everything and show themselves as they are without fearing that what is said will affect them in a negative way. In an atmosphere of psychological safety, all ideas and positions can be expressed without anyone saying anything negative about it. This means that communication is open and that there is a collegial way of exchanging both information and thoughts. More on psychological safety can be found in the section on people.

Marshall B. Rosenberg, who created a framework called Nonviolent Communication (NVC), has this to say about the power of words: "Human beings have enormous power to enrich life. We can use words to contribute to people's enjoyment, their wisdom. We can use words that can make life miserable for people. So, our words are very powerful. We can touch people in ways that give great pleasure, great nurturing, support. We are powerhouses, and there's nothing we enjoy doing more than to use that power we have to enrich lives. So, isn't it wonderful that we have this power and the joy it brings when we use it? That's to be celebrated. Wow! And the more we celebrate that, the less we will be willing to do anything else" (Rosenberg, 2003, p. 13).

Sociocracy, Holacracy, and Teal, which we present in the section on progressive organizational models, advocate NVC as an approach to communicating and collaborating with each other.

NVC is based on the following four basic principles:

1. **Mindfulness:** A set of principles for living a life of compassion, cooperation, courage, and authenticity.
2. **Language:** Understanding how words contribute to closeness or distance – the power of words.
3. **Communication skills:** Knowing how to ask for what you want, how to listen to others even if you disagree.
4. **Influence:** Sharing "power with others" rather than using "power over others."

NVC is an approach based on inclusion, genuine interest, and acceptance of other people. Communication according to NVC is based on a process that takes place in four steps to create closeness to others by 1) understanding what others observe, 2) getting into what others feel, 3) sensing what others need, 4) listening to their needs and discovering what would enrich their lives. Communication that takes place in that way invites empathy, compassion, and cooperation. Table 8 below summarizes what NVC is and is not.

Table 8. Nonviolent Communication (NVC)

It is	It is not
A way of dealing with conflicts without the use of force and punishment	Passive communication
Constructive, rather than destructive	Turn the other cheek
Non-judgmental and non-blaming	Having a laissez-faire attitude
Considers needs of self and others	
Encourages empathy and co-operation	

Voice from the field: Mette Aagaard, Partner, Agora, Denmark

Mette Aagaard has been driving organizational change and development in both big private and public organizations for more than 30 years. She is a frontrunner in developing and integrating teal and shared leadership in Denmark and has participated in several projects exploring how teal looks like in practice, among others, as head of development in a mid-sized Danish municipality. She is the author of the book *Shared Leadership: When the Team Is the Boss*.

Transparency as an organizational principle is a prerequisite for the teal organization and for shared leadership, for qualified decision-making as well as for building trust. But there is also a flipside to it, which I will touch upon at the end of this article. But first, let me share a story from real life.

Although they saw it coming, nobody was happy about the message. The part time position as day-time cleaning assistant didn't survive the cost saving that the Blomstergården nursing home had to implement as part of its general efforts to cut costs due to severe financial problems in the whole municipality. Apart from having to say goodbye to a good colleague, the employees now had to absorb the task on top of everything else that was part of their job in taking care of the 50 elderly people at the home.

"In the old days, I don't even think anyone would have asked us... 'What do you need? How many vacuum cleaners? How many carts? How would you like it to be organized?' Instead someone ... and to be honest I don't even know who ... would have made a desktop decision, without knowing about the daily practicalities. This time, we did it ourselves. Together we managed to gather all the information we needed, find out what the budget was, what regulations we had to comply with, and made a plan. My colleagues accepted it and started implementing right away. And we did all that in one week! That's pretty crazy."

That is Mette speaking, not the author of this article. Mette is a common name in Denmark. This Mette is a social and health assistant at a home for the elderly. Having integrated shared leadership at the nursing home (inspired by sociocracy) a year before, they placed the task of finding out how to get the daytime cleaning done in a co-led circle with the participation of the employees who would be impacted by the situation, including Mette. They were trusted with the full mandate to come up with a solution that would work for them and their colleagues. Within budget. Fast. And in compliance of course.

This everyday life example is one small example. But it is illustrative of the fact that full and easy access to all relevant information is at the core of decision-making, collaboration, and effectiveness in a teal organization. Think of all the facts they needed to collect and get right to develop a solution that would work: a budget, legal and formal agreement requirements, equipment and vendors, OHS (occupational health and safety) issues such as how to handle chemicals— and not least, access to information about daily routines at Blomstergården that would be needed to develop a solution that would integrate well with the daily rhythm of both employees and residents. It is hard to see how they would have managed if without full transparency on all related matters.

When people are transforming their workplace towards shared leadership, applying transparency is inevitable. Financial transparency is an essential go-to and one of the first steps to take when applying full transparency for at least two reasons: one related to circles and the other to the whole organization.

First, financial transparency is a precondition for making autonomous teams (circles) effective. Eventually, you will have to provide circles with the mandate to make decisions that have budget implications—within clearly described boundaries of course. Financial transparency is necessary to administer that mandate, as the above example illustrated well. I often see how an unclear or even missing financial mandate creates confusion, is perceived as lack of trust from those delegating the mandate, and how that hinders circle effectiveness.

Second, financial transparency for the entire organization, not only the circle, is a precondition for allowing people to demonstrate responsibility and build trust with one another. Understanding the full picture gives people a fair chance to contribute with ideas as well as action when/if needed. "Understanding" is a key word here. We cannot expect everybody to understand budget interdependencies, drivers, market impact, shortage of supply impact, and timing issues, among others, in finance. Making the numbers available on the intranet does not equal "transparency." Pushing the information alongside training and dialogue does.

Financial transparency for the entire entity includes sharing the good as well as the bad news. "If the house is on fire, we tell people that the house is on fire. How else are they going to help put it out?" as a senior leader in a teal organization asked me rhetorically the other day. There are two sides to this coin. One is that it builds trust and a healthy power balance when communication about critical matters is shared openly. It demonstrates respect. It invites inclusion. It enables trust. It allows people to act responsively. But the other side of the coin is that it bears with it a risk of people getting concerned, even worried. I do not consider people getting worried to be a bad sign, but I have worked for decades in big organizations that consider worried employees to be something negative, something that pulls the average engagement score down, and something that requires an action plan and has to be fixed.

But in a teal organization, we shouldn't mind that people get worried. When there is lack of transparency, people are worried because of what they don't know—and then they speculate. Due to transparency, there is probably a good reason why people are worried. And that concern can enable action. While we do not strive to worry people, we do not shy away from it either, because it would mean not sharing. When offered transparency, you will be empowered AND you will run the risk of becoming worried.

SALARY MODEL AND PROFIT SHARING

The new paradigm "away from hierarchies of authority and Command and Control" also means a new way of looking at salaries, remunerations, benefits, bonuses, compensation, and profit sharing. This perspective must be part of the change journey, otherwise we believe that the journey that the organization takes is not about a new paradigm, but rather an improvement in the way an organization is managed, but no more than that.

Two of the most important values that we presented in the section on people in the DP model are "people first" and "everyone's equal value" and these must of course be reflected in salaries and compensation.

The new way of organizing that we are promoting in the DP model requires a new transparent method for the salary model, the salary review process, benefits, compensation, and profit sharing. Financial compensations must also be harmonized in the same way as power must be distributed to avoid it staying among managers.

This is in line with what both Teal and Sociocracy advocate and is one of the most important pillars of K2K's approach and methodology.

THE SALARY MODEL: THE TRADITIONAL WAY

The traditional way of managing salaries is based on the view that managers are worth more than the rest of the organization, that a department manager should earn more than a team manager, a division manager more than the department manager, and so on. A higher position in the hierarchy means a higher salary and more monetary privileges. This is explained by the fact that salary comes with responsibility and that senior managers have more responsibility than managers who are lower down the hierarchy, and above all that managers generally have more responsibility than other employees. This has led to the fact that making a career has been the prevailing and normal way to develop. Many have entered a managerial role with the aim of climbing up the hierarchy where power, prestige, and money reside. Once people have started to climb up, it is difficult to go down or to the side, because they can lose power and prestige and risk lower salary. This could be called the "salary trap." If a person wants to change position or job, he or she does not want a lower salary. This can lead to people ending up in positions they do not want but feel they cannot leave because it might lead to a lower salary.

We have walked along the career path ourselves, from system developers to technical experts/architects, to project managers, line managers, department heads, and heads of global functions. This was before our souls and minds revolted against this ancient way of "evolving" and we became freelance consultants and academic researchers.

During the 1990s, there was a trend to find solutions where people could continue to work with what they really loved and did well instead of climbing onto the managerial ladder. The solution was to talk about "alternative career paths." Yes, what a name! Companies that were considered progressive and modern introduced these alternative career paths. People would not have to go into management roles or change jobs to get a higher salary or to be able to develop and make a career.

This trend has continued since then and nowadays there are expert or specialist careers in many professional fields, professions, and industries. One example is that in Sweden 2013, on behalf of the Swedish Parliament, something called the "career path reform" was introduced in Swedish primary and secondary schools. With this, a position called "first teacher" was introduced. How did they come up with such a job title? Did they think that there are first and second kinds of teachers? Financed by state grants, first teachers received, in addition to a nicer title, a salary increase of approximately SEK5000 per month. The first teachers would also carry out pedagogical development work (we may think that this is something that is within the scope of all teaching jobs). The government was actually looking for a way to raise teacher salaries, but there might be other ways than creating the title of a first teacher. It is good that there is a focus on educational development in school, a natural part of schoolwork, but with the career path reform an unnecessary hierarchy of authority was created. When the reform was to be implemented in 2014, one of us authors had an assignment as an organizational consultant at a school in Gothenburg and could see from the inside what conflicts, frustrations, and rivalries the reform brought.

In Sweden in 2017, the Swedish National Audit Office made an evaluation of the reform and drew the following conclusion: "Teachers' general salary level and relative salaries in relation to comparable professions have increased since the reform [...] But the reform has also met with strong criticism and negatively affected cooperation among teachers. It is perceived to have too clear a division between 'first,' 'second,' and 'third' teachers, where the third teachers have not benefitted from any government grant (RiR, 2017:18, p. 75).

This reform was an unnecessary hierarchical division based on power, prestige, and salary.

Traditionally, the salary is based on a limited number of facts and with the support of a series of subjective assessments. In the vast majority of cases, the salary is set by the direct manager (within the frames of the decided space for distribution of salary increases). Even though the word "direct" indicates that the distance is short, it happens far too often that the manager who sets the salary does not know what the people do and/or how they perform their tasks. Often it happens that conflicts and frustration pop up in connection with the salary audit and that the process as such creates mistrust in the organization.

These types of salary models intensify competition and increase the desire to be better than others, or at least to be able to perform better to get more.

Think back to the workplaces where you have worked and think about whether there has been someone or indeed a few who have "made themselves better" when the manager is around or when the manager comes into the room, just to be able to show them-selves in a better light in an attempt to raise their sala-ry or get a better career.
Reflect on your own situation. Have you been satisfied with the salary reviews you have been part of? What have your feelings been?

In the traditional way of managing salaries, a sense of unfair-ness is created and, moreover, many rumors about how much others earn. Transparency and insight are the cornerstones of the DP model, but we know that salary can be a very sensitive subject. It is easier to decide from the start to openly share how much everyone earns than to go from a closed and secretive process to total transparency. One example is Jayway where the Swedish organization has introduced the idea that all managers know what other managers and all employees earn. Because of some internal resistance, the employees do not know what other employees earn. On the other hand, Devoteam in Norway, of which Jayway is a part, introduced completely transparent salaries from the start.

THE SALARY MODEL: THE "MODERN" UNCERTAIN WAY

However, the traditional way for most employees does not apply to many consulting companies.

In recent decades, many consulting companies in Sweden have changed their traditional salary model, which used to consist of a good market-based salary PLUS a variable part based on how much the consultant invoiced the customers. Instead, many consulting companies have now developed a salary model that consists of a minimum level that is fixed and can be a quarter of the market-based salary level, while the remaining part of the salary is variable.

We have found a specific case with a consulting company where the fixed part also disappears if the consultant does not have an assignment for three months, which leads to the consultant being employed without a salary until he or she receives a new assignment. During the period when the consultant is without a salary, he or she is expected to work with internal routines, administrative work as well as marketing and sales. Fixed costs such as telephone and computer, which should normally be covered by the consultant's revenues, are paid by the company during the period when the consultant does not have an assignment, but those costs will be a debt that the consultant must pay back later. The most ironic thing is that the company markets itself as Teal, and on their website and in recruitment ads they write "With us you set your own salary," but they do not say that the salary can be zero!

This is an extreme variant of a model that is growing increasingly stronger with, above all, IT consulting companies and some management consulting companies. The model assumes that the company keeps 30% of the consultant's revenues and the consultant receives 70%. The consultant's 70% includes salary, payroll tax, holidays, various types of insurance (for example, provisions for pension and health insurance), computer, telephone, training, etc. The company's 30% includes premises, joint activities, and in some cases sales activities. The consultant can earn quite well when the market is good, but in bad times with no assignments, the consultant earns a very low amount. It is also a model that does not provide security in case of illness and parental leave.

In the models mentioned above, the company takes very little risk but can make a lot of money. We think these models are quite cynical and far from the values of both the DP model and Teal. Some salary models and payment methods that have come with the so-called "new economy" and the "gig economy" are of the same nature.

THE SALARY MODEL: NEW WAYS

The entry salary level can vary a lot since it is based on subjective parameters such as estimated market value, how good the person is at presenting him/herself, the need right now, and more. This level is also the basis for how the salary develops, and later it can be difficult to significantly adjust the salary levels. The result is differences in salary for the same work and equivalent performance, which is unfair.

This was the prerequisite for SRS when they were to develop a new salary model as part of their cultural journey. To develop a new salary model a group of people from different functions was appointed and a consultant with expertise in the area was contracted. The process was very long and they did not dare go the whole hog and create a transparent and open model where everyone knows what everyone else earns. Instead, they developed a salary process based on different parameters. The purpose of the new model was actually to reduce the salary gap and increase participation but not to be transparent. This can be compared with the reasoning around innovation in the section on culture, where there is an opportunity to create something completely new, which in some cases can be radical innovation, or just improve what already exists. SRS did not dare change the entire salary and compensation model; instead they tried to create more justice. The following example shows the challenge of taking the full step of being open and transparent with salaries.

The process involves an employee choosing two colleagues to give feedback. Since SRS has some departments with managers and some without, it is either the manager and a colleague or two colleagues. The employee and the two colleagues conduct an assessment of the employee based on the same criteria (see Figure 17), followed by a feedback meeting where the results are discussed. The combined result then becomes input to salary calibration for the individual employee, where they also consider where in the company's salary range the person is. Those who are lower in the range receive a larger share than those who are higher. In this way, differences in salary will gradually decrease. In connection with the feedback meeting, development activities are also discussed in order for the employee to increase his or her salary. After six months, there is a follow-up of the activities.

Criteria		Participates / Performs (participates / performs without commitment)	Carry out / Complete (but not completely independent)	Knowledgeable (independent / shares skills, takes own initiative)	Skilled (skilled, driven and proactive)	Outstanding (creates something beyond, outstanding results, lifts competence in the organization)
Sustainable profitability (activities/actions that contribute to increasing revenues and/or lowering costs with a focus on short- and long-term sustainability)						
	Own responsibility					
	Collaboration					
	Openess					
My role (my contribution in the form of competence / profession in the teams / work I participate in)						

Figure 17. SRS salary model simplified
Source: SRS

SRS's salary model was a compromise, and it can be said that they are cautiously taking small steps forward.

It is a challenge to go from a salary model with large salary gaps to an open and transparent model with small salary gaps. It also takes time to harmonize salaries; you have to count on several years.

K2K, which leads and supports organizations in their cultural journeys towards a new type of relationship such as the one SRS is undergoing, begins by openly presenting everyone's salary. They describe it as taking an X-ray about how equal and fair the company is. They also explain to all employees from the beginning that they are not there to fix the history but to create a better future. The goal is that the salary gap should be between 2.1 and 2.5 times between the lowest and highest salary. From experience, K2K knows that it can take up to nine years before they have reached that state. This is mainly because they also ensure that no one is fired or bought out, which can explain why equalization of salary takes a long time. Sometimes equalization only happens when people who receive a very high salary with a huge gap to the salaries of others doing the same type of job retire.

K2K uses a method to handle active owners where they can decrease their salary level and instead let them have a share of the financial result. It usually looks better and feels good for all parties. In addition to salaries, the goal is that 30% of the profit should be shared with the employees or reinvested in the company. A part of the profit sharing can be used to "correct" the salary gaps that already exist.

Figure 18 below is from a company K2K has worked with that has changed from a classic hierarchy of authority with power concentrated in the nodes of the hierarchy, and with large salary gaps, to the new paradigm. The data is from 2015 and the graph presents the "X-ray picture" regarding the salaries of the 82 employees where each point on the graph represents an employee. First, the employees were divided into four different groups based on type of tasks and job category. What was calculated was only gross salary because in Spain there are specific supplements based on the number of years the person has been employed by the company. These supplements can vary depending on which collective agreement is applied and, in many cases, these provide around 3% in supplements after five years. In addition to the gross salary, some people may have other supplements that they have received several years in a row. If this has been the case, these supplements are included in the gross salary. The reason for this is that there are cases where the employees have been able to negotiate extra salary increases for specific tasks or areas of responsibility, even though they belong to the same job category as the rest of their group.

The first principle for creating what they call the "balance" around salaries is that the company must be competitive. This means that everyone cannot end up at unreasonable salary levels because that would mean higher production costs than the competition.

The second principle is that no one will be worse off as salaries are not reduced; indeed, many will be better off. K2K believes that it is about creating a different way of looking at justice where it is necessary to create a more equal organization without anyone being negatively affected. Therefore, salaries are not reduced in order to create equality.

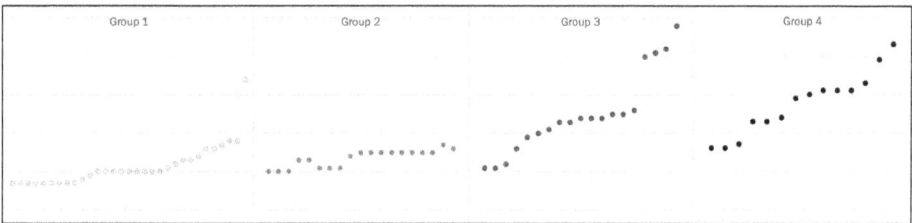

Figure 18. Example of salary graph from a K2K assignment

In the graph in Figure 18, we see that there is a person who has a very high salary level within the first group, which is quite common in many of the companies they work with. In this specific case, it is a person who could no longer be part of the high-tech group (third cluster in the figure) due to a technology shift that led to the person being moved to production. The person was about to retire, and apart from the principle of not firing or buying anyone out, the Spanish system states that the employer must pay a compensation equivalent to 45 days per year worked in connection with dismissal, which can be very expensive.

In total, 36 of the 82 employees were below the recommended salary level. These 36 could not be fully adjusted in the first year because the company was not doing well financially. However, this group received an extra 2.4% (€53,940) increase in 2016. This is in addition to the annual increase that follows the inflation index.

Another example is Freitag. They have around 250 employees at the headquarters in Zurich and since September 2016 have been organized according to Holacracy, which, like Sociocracy, organizes itself in circles (see the section on organization). In 2019, they introduced a new salary and compensation model, which is currently based on four salary levels. They started the work by mapping all activities and working steps. Then these were divided into different jobs (roles), which are not the same as titles or positions. The level at which most of an employee's job is performed determines the person's salary level. The four levels differ depending on a number of different aspects, such as complexity, area of responsibility, and whether the work is operational or strategic. There are also different sublevels within the four levels based on experience, expertise, and how well the work is done, but the company's highest salary is roughly four times the lowest salary. The model also includes everyone knowing how much everyone else earns; there is absolute transparency. The model and levels are quite like K2K and the NER group. What differs is the salary process, as Freitag uses feedback from the group as a basis for the salary revision.

The salary revision takes place in the following way:

1. Each person writes down on a post-it note for each role/job in the circle how important they think the role is and how much energy the person doing the job puts into it. This on a scale from 1 to 3.
2. In the next step, the so-called "feedback market," everyone writes their feedback about other people's work on post-it notes.
3. Then, one at a time, they look at the feedback they have received and reflect on it.

4. Now it is time for a round where each person gets at least two comments from the circle and reflects on them.
5. At the end, everyone reflects openly on how the session went.

Another example is from Meridium, an IT company with offices in Kalmar and Stockholm, Sweden that delivers various types of web solutions. They use a salary model, which has the following steps:

1. Proposal and motivation. In this first step in the process, people write a proposal for their own new salary level together with a motivation in Meridium's salary portal.
2. Once everyone has completed Step 1, they provide anonymous feedback on each other's salary claims.
3. The feedback from Step 2 is gathered and compiled by a salary committee, which then conveys the feedback that has been received.
4. When all employees have received their feedback, they can update their salary claims in the salary portal. If needed, there is also the option to provide additional feedback.
5. After these feedback rounds, a final check takes place where everyone gets the opportunity to say if they think someone's salary is not fair. In such cases, it is the CEO who decides on the final salary.
6. Now it is time for the final budget control. The teams work to analyze their own revenue budgets, and a budget forum with representatives from all teams work to ensure that the total budget is balanced.
7. The board has the formal responsibility to approve the budget, and when it is approved, the salary revision is completed.

Since 2018 Meridium has been part of Tietoevry, a large consultancy company, and has changed its name to Tietoevry Customer Experience, but the team continues to use the same salary model.

Centigo, which is a management consulting firm, has a different salary model. The interesting thing is that the model is open to everyone but what each consultant earns is not open to the other consultants. However, you can, in most cases, guess the salary levels with the open model. Guessing is not openness and transparency, but a step on the way. As mentioned in the section on leadership, new graduates receive a fixed salary that is competitive in the market and equal for all new graduates. They have a fixed salary for two to three years, after which they receive an offer of a new position (also called an NRO (new role offer)). If the consultant chooses to switch to the new position, as Business Consultant, then he or she moves into a new salary system where the basic salary is lower but with a percentage that is variable. This percentage is known to everyone, and because of that, one can guess what people earn.

A business unit coordinator and customer coordinator can earn quite a lot as they have a bonus on customer contracts. This has led to a system where the difference between the highest and the lowest salary can be up to ten times. In the Centigo case, one can see that their liberal values come through in the salary and compensation model. This is because it is up to the person to choose assignments and how much they will work and in this way control how much they earn. In addition, all costs are transparent to the person, who can choose more expensive equipment at their own expense.

There are many different variants of new salary models that are more or less suitable depending on the type of organization. The most important thing is to work on reducing the gap between those who earn most and those who earn the least, where the goal must also be total transparency regarding people's salaries.

COMPENSATION AND PROFIT SHARING: THE TRADITIONAL WAY

In most organizations, there are many salary levels, and in some cases there can be a difference of a factor of 30 between the one who earns most and the one who earns the least. In addition to these salary gaps, there are differences in other kinds of compensation. These compensations can be company cars, opportunities to participate in exclusive training, extra occupational pension savings, more vacation days, better equipment (even though the work does not require it), bonuses, and shares in the company. Even organizations that award bonuses to all employees often make a distinction between what managers and other employees receive.

For the most part, a holistic perspective is missing around compensation, which is instead usually linked to isolated key figures and goals, which do not always have a connection to the organization's goals. Sometimes bonuses are linked to a certain part of the organization making a profit at the expense of another part. We have seen this phenomenon at several different companies, with the most noteworthy being one of Sweden's largest companies, which invoiced internally among different subsidiaries. The amazing thing here was that one subsidiary (where the authors worked) billed another with very high nonmarket rates. Because they were part of the same group, the subsidiary that bought the services had no choice but to buy from the other. And because bonuses were, among other things, linked to profitability, several managers received rather high bonuses. This is an example of the risk that bonuses lead to suboptimization.

It also happens that bonuses are awarded even though the company is making a loss. We both experienced this when we worked at Ericsson during the crisis that occurred in 2001. In 2001, Ericsson had a large negative cash flow; the company was bleeding. All bonus systems were reworked overnight and based entirely on the cash flow of the business unit. One of the authors had a variable part of the salary of 25%, which was therefore completely tied to the business unit's cash flow. However, the spectacular thing was that this particular business unit had a positive cash flow, for which reason a large bonus was paid out. This was despite the fact that Ericsson as a company was bleeding worse than ever.

In most cases, individual compensation systems lead to suboptimization where people and teams try to achieve their goals even if they do not always correspond to the organization's goals; therefore we advocate within the DP model these systems being removed.

Think about whether you have been involved in a compensation system that you felt was unfair or focused on the wrong things.
Also consider other types of compensation that you think help the organization move forward and create better cohesion. Share it with us; you will find the contact details at the end of the book.

COMPENSATION AND PROFIT SHARING: PROGRESSIVE WAYS

Jayway is a good example where the company's basic principle from the beginning was not to share profit in the form of bonuses or variable monthly salary, even though they are a consulting company. Their position is based on the fact that, for a company where competence and competence development are central, this type of financial compensation would defeat the purpose. Instead, all employees get is 12 days of competence development per year. In addition to the 12 days that they get, the company makes investments in competence development during those days. The people can use the days to participate in conferences, buy in expensive lecturers, work with completely new technology, and more. The company does not just give the time, they make sure that it is quality time where the people decide what they want to do with this time.

In our search for good examples and concrete evidence, we find that K2K, and all companies that are part of the NER group, are exemplary. With them, the basic principle is that 30% of the profit should go back to the employees. Of course, they can temporarily deviate from this in cases where this is not possible, for example due to the company's financial situation, or if there is a real need to reinvest, or if it is crucial for the company's survival. The goal is for 30% to be shared among the employees and there are different ways to do it. The decision is made at a general meeting where all employees participate. At this general meeting, it can be decided to share equally between everyone regardless of salary, position, or length of employment, or to share percentages based on monthly salary. The decision to share the same amount among everyone is more common the further the company has come in its cultural journey towards a new paradigm.

At Freitag, a portion of the profit is shared. If the operating profit is above a certain predefined amount, which is well communicated to everyone, 20% of the profit is shared among the employees. Seventy percent of the total amount is shared based on the basic salary that each employee receives, and 20% is a fixed amount that is divided equally between everyone. The remaining 10% is shared according to a joint decision where everyone participates and where the employees decide what it will be used for, or if they want to donate a part or all to a charitable cause.

One of the largest banks in Sweden, Handelsbanken, started in 1973 a profit-sharing foundation named Oktogonen. SEK10 million (about €1 million) was initially set aside for the foundation. In 2019, the foundation managed approximately SEK20 billion (about €2 billion) and 90% of this was reinvested in the bank, which means that the foundation owned 10% of the bank and was the single largest shareholder. All employees, regardless of position, receive the same allocation. The principle for provisions is that if Handelsbanken, compared to other commercial banks, shows a better result than the average, the bank must make a provision to Oktogonen. The rationale behind it is that if Handelsbanken has achieved better results than the average, this is thanks to the employees having done a better job than the average, and therefore part of the profit should go to them. When the employees reach the age of 60, they can choose to withdraw their share as a one-time payment or spread it over 2–20 years. Depending on the length of employment, the employees can receive many millions.

Unfortunately, in 2020, Handelsbanken decided not to invest in Oktogonen any longer. Many emphasize that this is the best profit-sharing system ever in Sweden.

Voice from the field: Dunia Reverter – K2K and NER Group, Lisbon, Portugal

Dunia Reverter holds a bachelor's degree in Mechanical Engineering and a master's degree in Manufacturing Engineering. Dunia has over 25 years of experience in large international companies as CEO, COO, and change leader. Today, she leads change and transformation work in collaboration with K2K Emocionando and the NER group.

When it comes to salaries, who is the boss?

I was talking recently to the founder of a very progressive Swedish consultancy and we were reflecting on the relevance of "democratizing" the salary setting process in a self-managed or "boss-less" organization. He said: "So long as someone has control over your private economy, you have a boss." That remark left me thinking... if it is not one person who should decide, who should it be? Should the team collectively decide our salary, or should we be free to decide for ourselves?

Recently, in collaboration with K2K Emocionando, I have been involved in coordinating a few transformations of organizations, taking them from hierarchical structures with bosses to self-managed teams that choose their representatives and no longer have someone telling them what they should do or how they should do it. One of the areas we always review in those transformations is the salary structure. We normally propose an equilibrium that is fully transparent and more balanced (raising salaries to reduce the gap between who earns more and who earns less). This means that typically we will start a transformation with a significant salary increase to the many employees who are at the "bottom of the pyramid." No matter how caring, fair, and democratic I think it is to be telling a lot of people their salary is about to increase significantly, if I, as the coordinator of the transformation, decide the salaries of the whole organization, I have become their boss. Of course, this happens only at the beginning, in order to provide a starting point to the self-managed teams, but it is somewhat contradictory to the ethos and values of freedom, trust, and responsibility that are prevalent in our work. There has to be a more coherent way to provide a starting point to an organization that is avoiding traditional hierarchy. Same reason why you can't find peace using violence or conscientious citizenry within extreme poverty, you can't have a boss-less organization if someone decides the salaries.

In the next transformation that came my way I was determined to do it differently. Each employee should decide what their salary is, and after hearing what their colleagues think, each person should have the final say on what they should be earning. If we believe people should be trusted, and given freedom and responsibility, then this is how it should be. And I couldn't have picked a more challenging place to experiment this new approach. A small clothing factory of 30 employees... in the Dominican Republic!

As with every aspect of a transition to self-management, in order to remove bosses and hierarchy, we provide a structure to prevent chaos. So first we looked at the different teams and came up with a few job families based on the self-managed teams that had been agreed previously and the qualifications needed for the job. In this particular case we had four families (I have given names to each family for the reader to more easily understand the nature of each of them.):

1. The *artisans*: cutting/sawing/finishing
2. The *forgers*: ironing (very tough artisan work)
3. The *technicians*: designers & support functions
4. The *ambassadors*: coordination, commercial & external representation of the company

As an example, a starting position for a technician would be higher than that of a forger or an artisan, and so forth.

Then we proposed three levels of expertise for each family. Level 1 is that of a person with limited experience, focused mainly on learning and mastering their main responsibility. Level 2 is that of a person with a few years of relevant experience, who is completely proficient at their job and can perform other roles/functions within the team – someone who can support teammates in their jobs and who can positively influence the "team spirit." Level 3 is that of an expert with many years of experience, who is fully proficient at many functions while displaying great ability to adapt and be flexible, who is in a position to represent the team at different company forums, and who can positively influence the overall "organizational context."

So, we ended up having four families and three levels for each family, which overall represented nine salary bands. Finally, we agreed the overall amount we were ready to allocate to increasing salaries (18–20 % of the overall salary base) and that the top band could not be more than three times higher than the bottom band (Ambassador Level 3 cannot be more than three times the salary of an Artisan Level 1).

Band	Artisans	Forgers	Technicians	Ambassadors
1	Level 1			
2	Level 2	Level 1		
3	Level 3	Level 2		
4		Level 3	Level 1	
5			Level 2	
6			Level 3	
7				Level 1
8				Level 2
9				Level 3

And then the fun began. We held meetings with each of the

teams where we asked each person to proclaim themselves at a level within their category and listen to what the colleagues and the coordinator had to say about that. Then, they would decide if they wanted to change their initial proposal or stay as they wanted to be. Additionally, we suggested a few guiding principles in regard to the conversations we were about to have: honesty, better to confront than to stay quiet; talking with care and compassion; curiosity and being open to hearing what others have to say; and if tomorrow we regret something and want to talk more, we can.

We had a few people that lowered their nomination after hearing what others said and we had some that raised it. We had many that courageously decided to stay at a higher level than what the coordinator had suggested, but we had no one staying at a level that most of the team members did not agree with. We ended up with fewer "ones" and more "threes" than what we would have had if the coordinator or I myself had done the exercise... No one likes to be at the bottom, but we also ended up with strong commitments and meaningful words of appreciation.

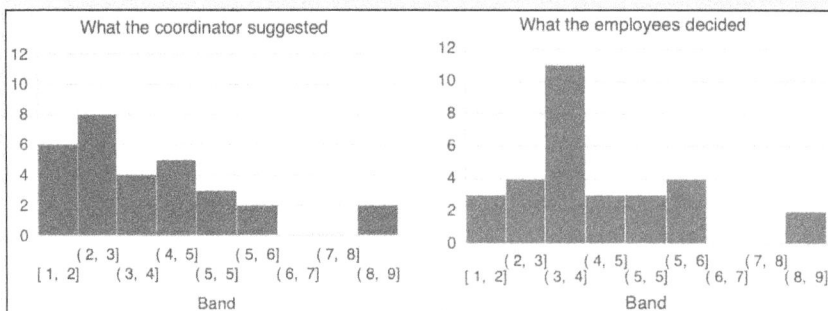

Financially, the fact that the distribution was more skewed towards Level 3 did not matter, because only when this calibration was finished did we attribute a value to each level, to reach the overall target of an 18–20 % increase. Once we had assigned values to the bands (increasing each band in the same proportion), we presented the proposal at a general assembly to all employees. One team objected as they felt a few colleagues had made the wrong decision, therefore we decided to have a second round with that team to recalibrate them and then the proposal was agreed by the whole organization.

After an intense week, I left the Dominican Republic with a feeling of satisfaction and curiosity about what the future will bring to this organization. I felt that everyone realized we were really living the values we discussed at the beginning of this transformation process. We were acting with full transparency, with freedom and responsibility, with trust, with generosity... and with no bosses!

DIGITAL TOOLS AND TECHNOLOGY

Digital tools enable an organization to work with transparency, collaboration, participation, co-creation, and development in a much better way. One of the reasons why there is an on-going global change in organizing is that there are different types of digital support that facilitate the work of spreading information, documenting, making decisions, and more.

The way of working has changed a lot in recent decades. Globalization has led to a situation where people who belong to the same organization are no longer at the same workplace. In addition, interactions between organizations and customers have increased and do not always take place via physical meetings. The Covid-19 pandemic has accelerated the degree of digitization and has resulted in many organizations moving to full or partial online working for office work.

This does not mean that an organization that does not have access to digital tools and technical solutions cannot become self-organized, sociocratic, or Teal, but it is becoming more difficult because roles that are traditionally responsible for sharing information, documenting, making decisions, etc. no longer exist.

DIGITAL TOOLS

Common to all the organizations we have studied and that have succeeded in transitioning to the new organizational paradigm is the fact that they have digital and IT solutions that support the new way of working. With the help of these tools, they have been able to create a culture where there is transparency, openness, cooperation, and independence in work.

An ecosystem means that customers also get a voice. It can be about design teams that take in the customers' views and wishes, which are used for developing new products or for feedback on products, services, or the company.

IT solutions for collaborative work, such as pharmaceutical research and software development, have existed for a long time. What is new is that there are tools that both support and enable self-organizing or other kinds of progressive organizing for all types of organizations, and for different roles.

In the section on transparency and communication, we emphasized how important it is that information is made easily accessible in an understandable way for all people in the organization. In addition, it is important to consider the time at which the information is made available. The more distributed or the larger an organization is, the more important it becomes to have digital tools that enable the information to be published, shared, and made available to everyone as soon as it is created. Added to this is the need to gather people's opinions and knowledge before certain decisions are made. With the help of digital solutions, questions can be sent for review and everyone has the opportunity to provide input, ask questions, and clarify.

SRS experienced a big change around both engagement and acceptance for their cultural journey when digital tools were made available to everyone. In addition to Returrum, which is their intranet solution, they use PLAYipp for information sharing, and Teams, Skype, and Workplace for collaboration and remote work. The digital tools became enablers to be transparent and open with information, which was one of the areas that the employees felt had improved the most during the cultural journey.

Centigo uses Teams for collaboration and communication along with SharePoint and Outlook for e-mail. They also have a digital solution to match client assignments with consultants' availability. Another way Centigo spreads information is by recording many of the digital meetings in order to pass on information to those who were not at the meeting. They also work with film and have their own studio where they produce a lot of information material. Centigo is managerless and focuses on horizontal communication, i.e. spreading information among teams. They also want a lot of interactivities and avoid one-way communication. For this, they avoid having too many online meetings and instead meet physically, which is also a way for the consultants to meet, as many spend much of their time with clients.

There are several different areas where digital tools are needed that enable collaboration and self-organization. These include:

- Information on how the work is to be performed
- Communication
- Document management
- Task management
- Content management
- Brainstorming and activities for idea generation
- Chatting and messaging
- Collaborative writing/creation
- Discussion rounds and decision-making
- Project management
- Shared calendars for groups
- Customer feedback and collaboration
- Searching for and mapping competence
- Recruitment and onboarding

There are a range of solutions and products to suit different sizes of organizations and also different wallets, where some are even free of charge. These solutions can both enable and slow down the transition to self-organizing. The reason for that is that most solutions are not designed for progressive or self-organized teams. Even at the time of introduction, when users are to be registered in the system, a hierarchical structure with department affiliation, managers who must approve access to information, etc. may be required. All this works against autonomy and transparency because the systems lack support for self-organization.

Technological development is fast and new solutions are constantly being launched. When the book is read, there will surely be new digital tools that are even better than when the book was written. For example, new solutions based on virtual reality (VR) are starting to appear that can make communication and collaboration at a distance even more realistic.

Among the digital tools that have grown in popularity during the pandemic are: Slack, which is a communication and work-flow solution designed for teams; Teams, which can be seen as a hub for managing teamwork in Microsoft 365; and Flock, which is a collaboration software that ensures support for easy communication. Two other digital tools that are growing are Google Workspace (formerly G Suite), which is a collaboration software that provides cloud-based file sharing, web conferencing, and scheduling solutions to increase team performance, and Zoom, which provides video telephony and online chat services and is used for digital conferencing, distance learning, and social relationships.

In order to have democratic decision-making, tools such as Loomio can be used. When the discussions develop into initiating a proposal, the group can give feedback in the tool, which is presented via an updatable pie chart. The tool is excellent for use in the "advice process" that we described in the section on decision-making. The members of the group can either accept the proposal, make objections, or refrain from commenting.

Another tool is Mural, which is a collaboration and co-creation tool that enables teams to think and collaborate visually to solve or discuss problems. The strength of Mural lies in its speed and ease of use when it comes to creating diagrams and facilitating more efficient meetings and workshops.

One of the digital solutions launched in 2021 enabling a move to the new self-organizing paradigm is HEP (Highly Engaged People), which is an evidence-based framework for managing competence that separates task from role. In the Holma case, we talked about how the school's principal belonged to different circles where he had other duties and roles that had nothing to do with his role as principal. An organization that takes the position that there are tasks that must be performed and that these should be done by the people who are most suitable and currently have the opportunity is based on the principle "the right person for the right task regardless of role."

In self-organizing, Sociocracy, Holacracy, DDO, and organizations with an agile approach, people have their own responsibility both for carrying out tasks and for taking on tasks that they are competent to do and in which they are interested. For this to be possible, there must be digital tools that create transparency regarding the competence that exists in the organization and around the tasks.

HEP enables this collaboration among different teams through an easy way to search for people who have a specific knowledge that you can then collaborate or consult with. The tool also provides support for describing what knowledge and what abilities and skills are needed for the working task. This is not only based on the task itself as it also considers context and organizational culture. Furthermore, HEP makes hidden talents visible by making competence transparent and giving all people in the organization ownership of their own competence journey. HEP is based on our research in competence and learning, and the background is described in the section on competence and learning.

More information is available at: https://www.hep-online.se/

Most of the tools we mention above are used for collaboration and transparency within organizations or between different organizations, for example with suppliers or customers.

Reflect on which tools you use in your work and what advantages and disadvantages they have.
Are there areas where you would like digital support that do not exist today?

TECHNOLOGY AND ORGANIZING

Above we presented different types of digital tools for collaboration and transparency within an organization and between organizations, which also include customers and suppliers. In addition to development around these types of tools, a strong technological development is taking place in the world. Much of the new technology becoming available in recent years deals with data management, that is, the ability to collect, analyze, and intelligently use large amounts of data. An example of a relatively new technology for collecting data is the Internet of Things (IoT), where different types of devices that are connected to the Internet exchange information among themselves and can send data to the user. Big Data Analytics is a way of analyzing large volumes of data to, for example, create an understanding of the environment in which the organization operates. Finally, an intelligent way of using data can be, for example, Artificial Intelligence (AI) or Machine Learning where applications can use data to learn, develop themselves and make decisions.

These technologies have been discussed for a long time, but one reason they come into focus right now is that economic growth cannot continue without something new. Specifically with regard to AI, several projects are underway. Unfortunately, many of these lack any real plan or purpose, and people are looking for useful applications. There will be more and more investment in AI solutions to support decision-making and business intelligence, which to some extent can already be seen today. One example is the city of Malmö in Sweden, which uses the robot Tengai for recruitment interviews, which affects organizations because the people who are hired have been selected by a system that always has the same preferences and which only takes into account selected parts of the people's competence and personality.

Avatar technology is also used in recruitment, where candidates experience work-related scenarios that test their abilities. This could be dealing with an irritated customer or the accuracy with which one verifies a medical form.

There is also another aspect of AI that needs to be highlighted, and that is that AI systems learn from past data, which can limit the ability to predict future needs and changes. Another weakness is that the intelligence in the system can be copied. We describe it with the following example: Recruitments made with the help of a robot can be "hacked," that is, companies will appear that offer services such as writing your CV in a way that matches the robot's preferences.

Since the original version of this book, several new AI applications have been launched. The most mentioned is ChatGPT, a language model developed by OpenAI that is based on the GPT (Generative Pre-training Transformer) architecture, which is a type of neural network designed for natural language processing tasks. The number of AI applications that will support organizing will increase significantly in the near future.

Another technology that has been around for a long time and has not been so well known, but is now on the rise, is augmented reality (AR), which is a development of virtual reality (VR). With the help of this technology, there are opportunities to get more information about things you are looking at, for example in video meetings and similar. Many may remember the enormous spread of the mobile game Pokémon GO, where you could experience a digital game in a real environment.

How does technological development affect progressive ways of organizing and the DP model?

These types of technologies are one of the reasons why people work more with their brains and hearts than with their hands and legs. Repetitive work and analysis of data is automated, and people in organizations work instead with information and knowledge produced by technological innovations. This has contributed to the fact that the organizational models developed during industrialization are now inadequate. If you take an example such as Ikea, the organization is increasingly working on developing digital solutions that make it easier for the customer to shop. This could be automating payments for the customer in order to scan and pay without going through the checkout, finding products through digital solutions such as virtual and augmented reality, combining shopping in the store with buying online the products not available in the store, etc. With this, the role of the employees in the stores changes to having more knowledge about Ikea's products and supporting customers in choosing the right product.

Automation of processes will transform the labor market as more and more tasks disappear. In some cases, there are only a few legal jobs left, which leads to more pointless tasks as David Graeber described in the book *Bullshit Jobs*. His point is that the machines will be responsible for creation, decision-making, and managing varying tasks that require more of a thinking process, and many of the tasks that will remain are checking that the machines have not missed anything.

The technological development also means that the organizational structure must be more flexible and able to change quickly based on the change in the surroundings. Organizational forms such as Sociocracy and Holacracy have a flexible way of creating new circles, closing those that are not needed, changing areas of responsibility, etcetera. On the other hand, in a hierarchy of authority with centralized power and a greater share of political games, changes are made more slowly, often in the form of transformation programs, which happens less often in progressive organizations based on self-organizing.

As the need for learning new things increases, people also need to be more transparent about what knowledge they have as well as needing to collaborate more. Here, a tool such as HEP offers great support because it enables and stimulates these very things.

We previously indicated in the section on culture that cultural aspects both influence and are dependent on technological development. Since technology and digitization lead to many people being able to work when and where they want, it becomes even more important to work with culture and the cultural journey. One of SRS's goals in their cultural journey was that they would be more transparent and open with information. They worked hard on this and insisted that all parts of the organization would be part of the journey.

Since SRS is a diversified organization and contains all the parts of a producing organization, transparency becomes more difficult to achieve than, for example, in Jayway where most people have the same background. Centigo has another challenge as their consultants work most of their time with different clients. For them, communication has been adapted to compensate for a lack of presence in the office or collaborative tasks.

Digital and technical solutions are not only enablers but a prerequisite for self-organizing to work and not create chaos. It is important to choose tools that are designed for self-organizing and that do not require a traditional organizational structure when implemented.

PROS AND CONS OF DIGITAL ACCESSIBILITY

Freedom and flexibility are created through digital and technical solutions that enable us to work at any time and from different locations. It is easy to access information, documents, and digital tools remotely and via different devices. In the section on workplaces and working hours, we reasoned that the flexibility of being able to work when you want and where you want is based on digital support.

This accessibility not only has positive effects, but it can be felt that way, as an employee of a large Swedish retail company operating in the global market told us: *It is like a tap where water flows all the time, there is always a lot to do and I always have access to what is needed to be able to work. Only I can turn off the tap and think that I also have a life and a family.*

As previously mentioned, many organizations have changed to more remote work during the Covid-19 pandemic. We have addressed the pros and cons of remote work from a business perspective. But it is also important to maintain social contacts when working remotely. Many organizations have started with digital meetings for lunches, coffee breaks, training sessions, after work, entertainment, and more. Now when the pandemic is over, we can see an increased demand and willingness among people and organizations to work remotely, in whole or in part.

Many people prefer what is called "hybrid work," meaning working some time from home and spending some time in the office. Hybrid work can also combine the freedom with being remote with continuing to have social contacts with colleagues.

In self-organized teams, where there are no managers responsible for reviewing the workload, there is a greater risk than in traditional companies that the work-life balance will be disturbed. We have found evidence that, in several of the companies we have studied, it has happened that employees have been overworked and on sick leave, and no one had noticed that it was about to happen.

At Beetroot, this gets a lot of attention. The owners are aware that the employees experience the company as a kind of oasis and as a place where their children are also welcome. There they can be themselves and walk around in their indoor slippers, which means they can work as much as they want. To promote awareness of life in balance, Beetroot often offers open lectures on mental health, which are called "Beetrootyourself."

The same digital tools that enable freedom in where and when we work mean that we leave "digital traces" in the form of information about, for example, the number of minutes we have been inactive or whether we are logged in or not. Unfortunately, there are organizations where this information is used to control employees. We have seen this phenomenon on several occasions during the pandemic, where managers and even other employees demand an immediate response to a chat message or where people are even afraid to go to the toilet or make coffee. Since such behavior cannot occur in Teal, self-organized, or good organizations, we do not delve into this. This type of behavior mainly occurs in hierarchies of authority in which unfortunately some of our larger universities must be counted, as many students have experienced during the pandemic.

Another aspect that should be considered with digital tools is that of privacy issues and data security.

A balance between work and other activities is required in an organization based on systemic thinking. Digital availability must be a support in the balance and not lead to demands where the employees feel stress and pressure to be constantly available.

Voice from the field: Madelon van Tilburg – Project Officer at Buurtzorg International, The Hague, the Netherlands

Madelon began her career as a professional photographer. Inspired by several assignments in the healthcare sector, she decided to obtain a bachelor's degree in healthcare. After an internship in home care, it was clear to Madelon that this was where her heart belonged. Madelon started at Buurtzorg in 2011 as a home care nurse within a self-organizing team.

The global interest in Buurtzorg caught her interest, and she got the opportunity to contribute to this. Inspiring, coordinating, and networking all over the world is now part of her daily work.

For many years, care professionals have adapted to computers and other appliances with which they had to register and account for their work. Management was predominantly occupied with implementing all sorts of control and registration systems. Little attention was paid to usability and applicability in nurses' daily work. The option of having colleagues exchange information amongst themselves through the intranet was hardly used.

This was also the situation I had to deal with in my previous jobs in the healthcare sector. It took me days of training to get an understanding of the different IT programs, and still I was struggling. It felt more like a burden than an added value for the day-to-day practice. An additional difficulty was the fact that all the different systems I needed were separated, meaning duplication of information, which was very time-consuming. There was less time for clients and more and more time was spent sitting behind a desk busy with administrative tasks. Several times I put this topic on the agenda for a meeting with the manager, but she made it clear that this was necessary. End of discussion.

This way of working made me and a lot of other care

professionals unhappy in their work. This is not what we are trained for as nurses. Our heart is in taking care of our clients, not feeding a monstrous IT system...

So, this and other reasons made me decide to quit and apply for a job at Buurtzorg. Didn't know that much at the beginning, but I read a lot about this new way of working. When I signed my working contract I received a token to get access to the IT system, the Buurtzorgweb. Curious as I am, I started to explore this new online environment. It is web based so accessible from any computer, laptop, phone, iPad, etc.

In my first week working in the team, one of my colleagues showed me the different layers of this Buurtzorg web. Wow, this is really amazing. With one single sign in, you can log on to the system 24/7, and really helpfully, everything is connected. Step by step in an intuitive way, I got a better understanding of all the different possibilities and options. I realized this is supporting the care professionals instead of an extra hurdle.

The simple organizational structure of Buurtzorg is reflected in the IT solution. The web offers a place for my necessary registration but I can also share knowledge, respond to colleagues' questions, to the managing director's blog called "Jos the Blog," and to back office announcements and questions.

Being autonomous, but in connection with all the other team members, is very valuable. A professional network is created and maintained by all of us. It is transparent and contains a management information system simplified to team level. It is more like a tool for the teams to enhance their reflection on the team activities, and which gives input for continuous improvement.

This approach reflects trust and stimulates self-organizing. Only do what is necessary and minimize bureaucracy as much as possible. As we like to say at Buurtzorg, "keep it small, keep it simple." The different dimensions make the web the backbone of the organization. "Reinventing your own wheel," looking for solutions, and feeling supported are key in self-organizing and make you grow as a team and as a professional. Another helpful element of the Buurtzorgweb is the learning environment, which offers a big range of different topics and subjects – ready to use if you need it at your own pace. By using IT intensively, Buurtzorg succeeds in considerably decreasing teams' administrative burden. For many like myself, the computer has changed from a necessary evil into a form of real support.

When Buurtzorg started at the end of 2006 it was clear that a smart IT system should be part of the organization. The approach of "Let nurses lead the way" is reflected overall in the vision of the organization and also in the IT.

Every time there is a possible new module, pilot teams are asked if this is helpful in their work. If not, the IT company goes back to draft a new version. When Buurtzorg started it was not as advanced and comprehensive as it is today. It started small and grew organically with the growth of Buurtzorg.

Also crucial in my view is support on a daily basis. An "always friendly" helpdesk center offers help in any possible way to me and all my other 14,000 colleagues. To follow new innovations and insights in healthcare and society, Buurtzorg is always looking for improvement. A new element has been added to the Buurtzorgweb: Clients can have access to their personal file and care plan. This stimulates the self-reliance of our clients and the involvement of informal carers – two very important pillars of the Buurtzorg vision.

It shows that the starting point of Buurtzorg is, and will always be, the relationship between care professionals and clients. This is the heartbeat of our organization. Every day we are looking for the most practical solutions in day-to-day practice and try to avoid unnecessary things.

Often other organizations (from abroad) envy this IT system and see this as THE solution. I believe the beginning should be the mindset of providing holistic care, building up relationships, creating networks, and offering support. The Buurtzorg web is a very user-friendly and pragmatic tool aligned to this vision of the organization.

COMPETENCE AND LEARNING

As previously mentioned, work is becoming more and more knowledge-intensive as the world changes, i.e. people have to learn new things more and more often. Parallel to this, there is an increasing availability of knowledge, not least through digitization and being able to find information and knowledge via the Internet.

WHAT IS COMPETENCE?

Competence is basically a person's ability to be able to use his or her knowledge and proficiencies to achieve a result. Knowledge is what you can and have learned, for example being able to sell, program, English grammar, and more – often called "hard skills." Without knowledge, it is not possible to perform a job. It is important to make the distinction that knowledge is not information or facts. Knowledge is gained *through* information and facts.

Different types of abilities and proficiencies are applied in order to use knowledge. There are many kinds of abilities – for example, you can be good at listening, presenting, finding solutions to complex problems, being thorough, learning new areas, or seeing opportunities. Our research shows that different people could have the same level of knowledge, but this can be used in different ways depending on the people's abilities. If, for example, two people have a deep knowledge of English, but one has strong social abilities while the other has a strong ability to express himself or herself in writing, the knowledge is used in different ways. People with high social ability comes into their own when they communicate in speech, while people with a strong ability to express themself in writing uses their knowledge in the best way in writing documents or other texts.

> *Think about what your strengths are. What knowledge do you think you have and what are your strongest abilities or proficiencies?*
> *Do you use these in your work, and if so, in what way?*

Digging deeper into the difference between knowledge and ability, we state that knowledge is connected to the brain while ability belongs to the heart. Does this sound strange? After all, knowledge is what people know and what people can learn through books, courses, training, etc. However, knowledge is used in different ways because people have different abilities and levels to be able to use it. Often, one's ability is controlled by feelings – for example, how one feels right now, self-confidence, a sense of safety, or how cooperation with other people works. All people have talent and are good at something. When people do something really well, it is often said that they do it with their heart, which actually has to do with attitude towards, and engagement in, what they are doing. Based on this reasoning, competence is when a person uses both the brain and the heart together in the best possible way.

The basic definition of competence that we use also assumes a connection to achieving results. Will people achieve the same results regardless of the context in which they are using their knowledge and abilities? Our many years of research in the field have shown that context plays a big role. We discussed how culture affects our behaviors in the section on organizational culture. This also applies to how we use our knowledge and abilities. In an organizational culture dominated by a fear of failure and introversion, people with low self-confidence are likely to be inhibited and then perform less well than they would have done in an organizational culture characterized by trust and openness. Thus, the organizational culture becomes very important for how people can use their knowledge and abilities to achieve good, and over time sustainable, results.

There are also other contextual parameters that are influential – for example, if the organization is geographically scattered, its size, its financial situation, if the market moves quickly, or if different languages are used. The effect of context is such that if a person does a good job in one environment, the result will probably be different in another, either better or worse. Therefore, the weakness of a CV is that this often describes what a person has done in a specific environment in the past and what knowledge the person has. It does not indicate what that person can do in another environment or what abilities are significant for the person.

Because we believe that competence is a key factor in an organization's ability to succeed, we developed, based on our previous research on competence, a framework and a digital service called "HEP." HEP stands for "Highly Engaged People" (*www.hep-online.com*) and it is based on the principle "Right person in the right place" by using fact-based decision-making. Other things, such as finding hidden talents and making knowledge visible for others, are a part of the framework. If a person has some knowledge that no one in the organization knows about, and is also passionate about this subject, it is a hidden talent and knowledge. In addition, people become more engaged if they are allowed to do what they are passionate about and can use their strengths. And as we discussed in the introduction, productivity increases a lot when a person feels engaged in his or her work.

HEP is based, among other things, on the research within competence management that we have previously conducted, and which led to a doctoral thesis, a book, many academic publications, and presentations at several major academic management conferences. Part of this research resulted in a new competence concept and model called "The Competence Lemon" (see Figure 19).

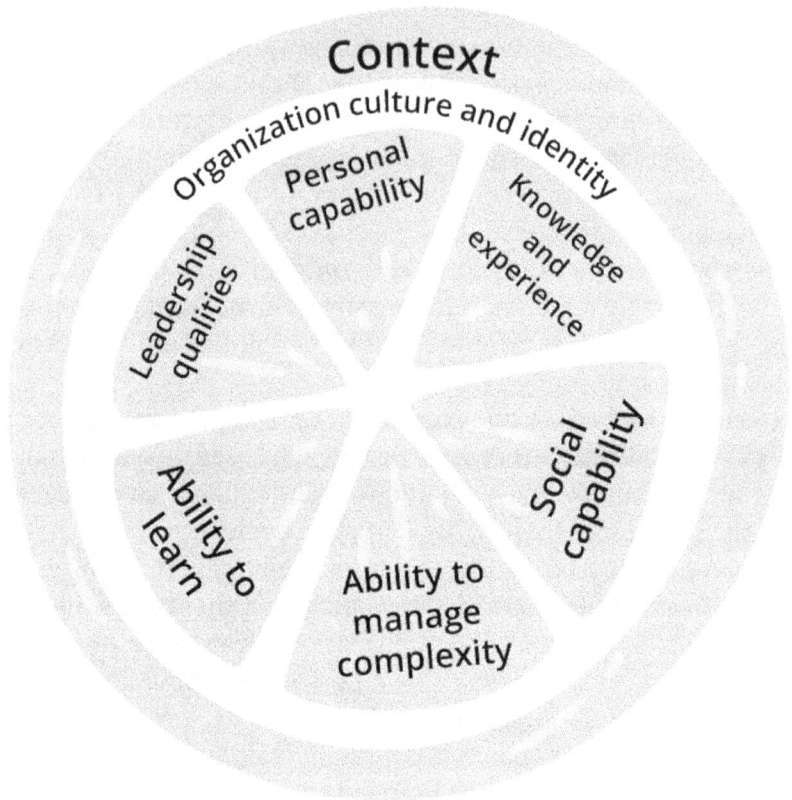

Figure 19. The Competence Lemon

Source: Managing Project Competence – The Lemon and the Loop

The basis of this competence model is knowledge and five different perspectives on abilities. The five perspectives are personal capabilities, social capabilities, leadership qualities, the ability to learn, and the ability to manage complexity. Most previous models consider personal and social abilities and, in many cases, leadership qualities as well. The difference between The Competence Lemon and other models regarding leadership qualities is that our model considers leadership as inclusive. A leader ensures that others can do their work as well as possible. The abilities to learn and manage complexity are new perspectives on competence that become increasingly important the more knowledge-intensive the business becomes. A person needs to learn new things within his or her usual working area but also in other areas. In addition, complexity increases as more and more information and knowledge become available, and also with the number of interactions with different stakeholders. The Competence Lemon also takes into account the context of organizations in terms of size, globality, market situation, and so on. In addition, it considers the culture of the organization. Context and culture influence how people can use their skills. For example, tasks are performed in different ways if the culture is rigid and top-down or if it is permissive and inclusive. This affects the way we collaborate, dare to make mistakes, handle information, and much more.

Think about whether you yourself have been influenced by different types of culture and context when you have worked in different organizations.
For example, was it possible to ask whatever you wanted? Was it okay to make mistakes? Did people cooperate with each other?

ROLES AND JOB DESCRIPTIONS

In the past, when organizations were seen as machines, clear descriptions were developed about what the various "machine parts," i.e. the people, were supposed to do. Since the workers were not considered to be able to think for themselves, they were instructed so that they could perform their repetitive tasks in the best possible way. As this happened during industrialization, tasks did not change very often. Activities were estimated in terms of time, and efforts were made to optimize the activities as much as possible. The supervisor was the one who understood the operation and developed job descriptions and instructions. In our increasingly knowledge-intensive world, it has become difficult to describe what is included in a person's tasks. In reality, a job description becomes counterproductive because it describes something that is likely to change, if this has not already happened by the time the job description is completed. The consequence is that if the job description is not fully followed, it becomes limiting. It can also create contradictions or cause tasks to fall through the cracks.

A job description is usually linked to a role. The more roles an organization has, the more detailed the job or role descriptions need to be. A role can be linked to a person even though several people can have the same role. A person can also have several roles that, for example, vary with the season or production cycles. However, roles tend to become permanent and difficult to change. Tasks that arise must be assigned to different roles and this whole process creates work that does not add value.

Within the scope of the DP model, we recommend minimizing the number of roles and placing the responsibility for tasks, as far as possible, at team level. A team has a defined area of responsibility and a purpose. Within Sociocracy, S3, Holacracy, and agile methods, there are what are called "domains" or areas of responsibility that are distributed or assigned to different teams. Within these responsibilities, the team can distribute the tasks among themselves, and the best way is if the team members can choose which tasks to work with. However, the common agreement must be that all tasks have to be accomplished by the team. K2K ensures this through what they call *el compromiso*, which means *commitment* in English. It is based on the team themselves determining the scope of their deliverables in terms of quantity, quality, and delivery date. It is then the team that plans and finds the best way to fulfill the commitment. Javier Salcedo of K2K explains it with the following metaphor:

When a group of parents get together to take turns dropping off and picking up their children at school, it is a commitment that everyone agrees on. For example, if it is my day to pick up the kids and my car breaks down, it's up to me to fix the problem. I can rent a car, take a taxi, ask someone else, or somehow find a solution. This means that it may also be me who must bear the extra costs finding the solution.

The same applies to the working groups in a company, they may have to work extra, bring their friends or neighbors there. Then it is not the roles or job descriptions that rule, instead everyone in the team has to do everything in their power to achieve the agreed commitment.

The metaphor may feel foreign in a non-Spanish environment, as it is not that common everywhere for a group of parents to manage together dropping off and picking up the children, but it shows K2K's view of agreed commitment in a team with a common goal.

The DP model suggests moving away from detailed job descriptions and role descriptions to focus more on what the team is supposed to accomplish. This is in line with agile development methods such as Scrum, which have emerged within, above all, product development. The agile team has few roles and distributes work based on skills and workload with the aim of reaching the next goal.

Teal goes even further: People will use their unique qualities and special talents when there are no detailed job descriptions and no manager saying how the work should be done.

> **Think for a moment about whether you have experienced a situation where role or job descriptions have limited the tasks people have carried out.**

Roles have a connection to organizing, which in most organizations is based on old structures and paradigms. This means that organizations to a fairly large extent follow an old-fashioned way of managing competences, and that tasks are linked to roles that belong to a specific organizational unit or group. Within Sociocracy, work is organized in circles and people can belong to several circles and perform tasks that require different knowledge and proficiencies. It is a way to make use of the entire human competence.

We see within the DP model that the future way of managing competence is that tasks are disconnected from roles. There is cooperation among different organizational units regardless of whether they are departments, nodes in a network, or circles in a sociocratic structure.

BRIEFLY ABOUT THE ROLE OF EXPERT

In the same way as role descriptions and job descriptions can inhibit both competence utilization and competence development among employees, experts can also be an obstacle. Where there are experts, there is a tendency to be a hierarchy of power based on a few people being allowed to decide without dialogue or reflection. Those who do not possess the expertise are excluded from the decision-making and the discussions, and the experts have the floor. There are many examples from working life where the IT experts alone make important decisions that affect the company and the future of the employees, while no one else has insight because the experts have the "power of knowledge." The same can apply, for example, to security experts.

Axis Communications has a different view on experts and has introduced an expert ladder where people can go from step one to step five. But you need to help others to grow to get to the top steps. This has resulted in more people learning things within the subject area and counteracting the power hierarchies of experts.

UTILIZE THE TALENTS IN THE ORGANIZATION

We mentioned earlier that there are many hidden talents in an organization. In many cases, you do not know what your colleagues or employees are really capable of or passionate about. In the introduction to this section, competence was described as the ability to use knowledge. The question is: What is the easiest to learn, abilities or knowledge? The answer is that it is much easier to learn new knowledge than to develop one's abilities, as the latter simply take longer to develop. Then the follow-up question is: How do you know people's abilities so that resilience can be created in the organization in a way that people do not have to be replaced?

It has become common to exchange competence by dismissing employees and recruiting new people with other kinds of competence. Companies doing so express it in terms of the world is changing and new competence is needed. But in reality, it is new knowledge they need, for example in new technology. If leaders in the organization do not know what knowledge people already have and, above all, what abilities they have to learn such knowledge, it leads to unnecessary changes and disturbance. In today's organizations, one of the most important things is knowing what competence exists in the organization in order to be able to ensure that people and business develop in the right direction. No exchange of competence is usually needed if the focus is people's learning.

The motto of the DP model is that people's potential and abilities should become visible, and also to allow them to try new things, which leads to increased commitment, better results, and more innovations. Jayway is a company where competence is always central, and all employees have the chance to show and share newly acquired knowledge and proficiencies during the so-called "competence days."

Many organizations still work with annual development talks while at the same time they have difficulty connecting where the organization is going with people's wishes and abilities. Many of the organizations that we have analyzed and that have notified staff have had well-established methods and digital support for competence development. Why do they have to dismiss staff because there is a need for exchange of competence? The answer is not simple, but most of the time it is because the organization has not worked with competence development in the right way.

As a part of the DP model, we advocate a continuous dialogue regarding the organization's and people's development and goals. These are connected and are the basis for the success of both the organization and the individual person.

In the move to a more knowledge-intensive work environment, competence development becomes a core process that includes continuous learning. Learning activities can be trying new things, coaching, courses, group learning, simulation tools, and much more. Working tasks will continuously change, which means that the people who perform the working tasks must also change. Or conversely, if people learn new things, they can perform new types of tasks that add value to the organization, which is also innovation. Here again, it can be stated that detailed role descriptions prevent innovation, competence development, and teamwork. If the role descriptions detail what one person is supposed to do, the team cannot distribute the work in the same way as if the team has an area of responsibility where everyone is involved.

The traditional way of organizing is to create an organization in a top-to-bottom structure. Roles with different competence requirements are created in this hierarchy that are to be filled with people. Another approach to utilizing talent in the organization is to map what knowledge and abilities exist in the organization and see opportunities. What can be done with the current competence? Such an approach can result in new innovations and new ways of carrying out work. This was what happened at Studsvik when Tõive stepped into his role as CEO. Instead of dismantling the company, which was the task he had been given by the board, he set in motion an innovative process where the employees used their competence to develop products and services that could generate profit. As a result, the long-term trend of losses was turned into profit in just a few months.

RECRUITMENT

When we look at recruitment within the DP model, the focus is on what the candidate can bring to the organization, i.e. a person's potential. Of course, recruitment is a mutual process with two parties: the recruiting organization and the candidate. This means that both parties need to understand each other. The candidate needs to understand how the organization and its culture work, what is expected of an employee, how the team works, the organization's purpose, etc. The recruiting organization needs to know the person's view of work, his or her abilities, proficiencies, and knowledge, but also how the person fits into the organization.

Traditionally, the recruitment process has focused on previous experience. The interesting thing is that competence is more dependent on context and organizational culture than on previous experience. Just because a person has done a job in one way in one environment does not mean that he or she will do the same in the next environment. Experience is a parameter, but the focus must be on abilities and basic knowledge in the field. Of course, there are professions, for example doctors, where it takes longer to acquire knowledge.

The traditional recruitment process also focuses to a large extent on finding the knowledge and experience that the candidate does not have. This becomes counterproductive as one misses the person's potential. The fear of hiring wrong people leads to being afraid to people who do not have an experience that meets the role 100%, and therefore the process focuses on finding the lack of experience. The reason why people want to change jobs is usually that they want to work with something that is not exactly the same as what they have done before. In addition, the candidate risks being considered "overqualified" if the match is too good. This way of recruiting increases the probability of a bad hire, and of recruiting people who cannot develop themselves in the organization they end up in. There can also be nepotism and clientelism, which means that in many cases the recruiting manager prefers to recruit people who are loyal to him or her and who maybe do not have the best interests of the organization in mind.

As we said in the section about decision-making, decisions must be made by those who know the area, as well as, if possible, by those who are affected. This also applies to recruitment. If an individual is to be recruited to a team, representatives from the team should meet with the candidates or preferably manage the recruitment process. Both representatives from the organization and the candidate should feel that both parties fit together regarding the organization's purpose, culture, and approach to work.

Who should initiate the recruitment process? Self-organized and Teal organizations do not recruit people based on predetermined numbers of people who should be a part of the team. New recruitments are based on the need for competence – for example, current or future needs. At Buurtzorg, each team decides when a new person will be recruited. This is based on the demand for services in the particular geographical area where the team offers its services. The team is supported by the central staff in terms of managing contracts, etc., but the entire recruitment is handled by the team, and who in the team manages the recruitment varies from time to time.

Centigo initiates new recruitments based on what the customer coordinator sees as being needed in the market. Because the recruitment is for the company and not for the team, people from different areas are involved in the process. As culture is important, recruitment has focused strongly on finding people who fit into the organization and culture. However, it has been realized that there is a weakness in this approach as it can lead to recruiting people who have the same profile and preferences as those who are managing the recruitment. In order to increase diversity and balance, Centigo started to use an external firm in order to not only look inward but also to have other perspectives. This is a good example of how the company focuses on continuous renewal and learning in its way of managing recruitment.

Just like in the case of Centigo, many companies with a strong culture want to recruit people who fit into the culture. This is the right approach because the culture is the basis of a good and healthy organization. However, most of the culture is behind the surface, in the values people have. The values are the basis for the organization's principles, i.e. the rules that the people in the organization have agreed on and which should guide behavior. If you look too much at how a candidate should fit into the culture, it is easy to see the cultural perspective above the surface, for example how you look, dress, express yourself, or where you have studied. Diversity can be broadened if instead the focus is on the organization's purpose and principles. Another perspective on recruitment is that the organization should not only select a person for a role.

The candidate must also be able to choose where to work. Then purpose and principles also become important and the basis for the agreement that the recruiting organization and the candidate make when he or she becomes part of the company. We have seen far too many recruitments where representatives of the recruiting organization only focus on what the candidates have done in the past and have not spent any time explaining "this is how it works with us" in terms of which behaviors are accepted and which are not. Behaviors create principles and principles guide behaviors. Recruitment is an agreement between two parties, and then it is even more important that the parties understand each other from the start.

EXTERNAL COMPETENCE

Many organizations are dependent on external expertise or contingent workers. This can be consultants, temporary staff, suppliers, partners, customers, or others who are part of what the organization delivers.

In most cases, when external competence is brought in in the form of consultants and temporary personnel, the focus is almost exclusively on knowledge and very little on how the people fit into the organization. These people are seen as replaceable, even though they are hired to add value in the form of knowledge and proficiency that the organization needs. As they will work in different teams, these should be considered in the same way as when hiring for employment. Since the DP model advocates an open and equal culture, external competence must be considered equivalent to internal, meaning that all people are considered to have equal value and must be able to feel a part of the business. This is an important position. This means that people who work in the organization but do not have direct employment must also be covered by feedback and development activities. The same applies to communication and transparency: There is hardly any reason not to be completely transparent with people who are not employed. But for some reason, most traditional organizations differentiate between employees and nonemployees, even though everyone contributes to, and participates in, the organization.

Other external competence can be in the form of suppliers and partners who deliver products or services to the organization. In many cases, there is a need to work closely together to achieve the best possible results. Choosing a supplier or partner happens in most cases because they possess some kind of know-how that the organization needs. In an organization that follows the DP model and thus has a purpose and an open and positive culture, efforts must be made to choose suppliers or partners that have a similar culture to the organization. This facilitates collaboration and also supports the DP model's philosophy of a holistic and systemic approach, and responsibility throughout the value chain.

Another perspective on external competence is to increase the organization's knowledge as external people bring new knowledge and new ways of thinking. Knowledge sharing and organizational learning are increased with increased transparency and participation. In most of the companies we have studied, external expertise in the form of temporary staff, consultants, and suppliers is used only by allowing them to perform the tasks for which they have been hired. It is not considered what they really know or what the people can contribute in terms of the organization's development and learning.

In many cases, a contingent worker or a consultant performs tasks that are "slightly below" his or her level of competence. This is because it is expected that the person comes in with expert knowledge and will be able to perform the tasks directly. With the basic view of the DP model, everyone has equal value, and the external people are also part of the whole in a systemic thinking. Therefore, they should not be treated differently from employees. Some processes only concern employees, for example the payroll process, but in general there are no other differences. Hiring external competence should also follow the same way of thinking as when recruiting: making sure that the external people agree with and accept the principles and behaviors of the organization.

COMPETENCE DEVELOPMENT AND LEARNING

Traditionally, competence development is mostly connected to courses and training. As a part of the DP model, the focus is on learning and that work itself involves learning. The most important things for learning are attitude and willingness, reflection, being able to work together with others, seeking new knowledge and information, trying new things, and being allowed to make mistakes. Many organizations fail here, and an investment in this type of organizational culture can bring fantastic results. Looking a little deeper into this, there is a clear philosophy in that learning is something that goes on continuously. The traditional courses are enablers and an inspiration for continued learning, and passive learning turns into active learning when people practice what they have gone through during the course.

Attitude and willingness to learn new things come from within oneself and create motivation to learn. Reflection is looking back, thinking about why things turned out the way they did: Can you connect things that happened and use this to look forward? Working together with others and sharing knowledge together increase group learning. It is also possible to practice different things in the team. One must go outside the daily work and seek new knowledge and information in order to increase learning. This can happen in different ways – for example, by participating in networks, searching the Internet, reading books and magazines, or discussing topics with other people. Being able to try new things and sometimes fail is linked to the organizational culture.

We reasoned earlier that it is easier to learn new knowledge than to develop one's abilities. It takes a longer time to develop abilities because in many cases they can be linked to behaviors. Being able to practice and reflect becomes even more important when developing abilities than when learning new knowledge. For example, a person who feels uncomfortable speaking in front of other people could try to make a presentation in front of a small group that they know, and on a subject that they are very familiar with. Afterwards, they can reflect on how it went and preferably discuss it with someone in the group and continue to practice again. This procedure is part of a methodology that we developed in the early 2000s and that we call "REPI" (see more in the chapter "The way forward"), and this approach to learning is one of the cornerstones of a modern and forward-looking organization.

Do you have an example of when you yourself or someone else have/has taken a big competence leap? What made you or the person take this leap?

FLEXIBILITY

One reason why most progressive organizational theories and methods suggest that role descriptions and having many roles should be avoided is that they reduce flexibility. Through our research and our years in the field, we know that it also creates limitations when people have to relate to tasks that need to be done but that are not part of the job description. When moving away from the view of humans as machines, there is no reason to suggest (and expect) that everyone who has the same job must do exactly the same type of activities. There are of course some tasks that form the basis and must be included in the job, but others can be performed by those who are most suitable based on time, knowledge, and interest.

We visited a bakery with two bakers in the south of Sweden. One had a great interest in, and knowledge about, locally produced and organic ingredients, while the other had a passion for the aesthetic, how the bread and pastries should be presented and shown to the customers. In addition to baking, they had tasks that suited their knowledge and interest, and they split the tasks based on this.

The optimal flexibility and competence utilization in an organization is achieved when the tasks can be done by those who have the competence, interest, and availability at the time the task must be carried out. Competence must in this case be made visible to the entire organization. In addition, the organizational unit that the people are a part of should only be seen as a placeholder and not as a belonging, meaning they have to do all the work as a part of the unit. This becomes very clear in Sociocracy where people belong to several circles and these circles can be at different levels and belong to different domains. The organization at Holma is based on the principles of Sociocracy and the staff are divided into different circles. Each employee belongs to several circles depending on competence and interest. It becomes a natural way to collaborate and work across organizational boundaries.

The school's principal, Andreas Jonsson, who is also one of the biggest experts in Sociocracy in Sweden, is, for example, a part of seven different circles. In some he is a leader and in some a member, depending on the purpose of the circle. The role of rector is also a formal position in relation to the outside world as folk high schools' operations are based on the Schools Act.

In agile teams, competence utilization at the organizational level does not always work so well because there is a tendency for team members to become loyal to "their" team and not to participate in, or contribute to, the work carried out in other teams. Some organizations have developed a process for job rotation in order to avoid stagnation and increase understanding between teams. This means that, for a limited time, you can work in a different organizational unit than the one you belong to. This is a good thing in itself but is not always the ultimate solution as flexibility is limited if there is a formal process governing it. Teams that work together for too long tend to stagnate if inspiration or a focus on the learning process is not brought in. Working in several teams can bring new influences that people can bring into other teams and thus contribute to continuous improvement. Heterogeneous teams based on different knowledge, background, abilities, etc. develop more. However, it can take time before this type of team achieves good cooperation.

Voice from the field: Gustav Henman – co-founder Beetroot, Stockholm, Sweden

Gustav Henman is one of the founders of the Swedish-Ukrainian IT company Beetroot and the education company Beetroot Academy. Since the start in 2012, he has focused on the development of new ways of working based on self-leadership. Gustav has a master's degree from Chalmers in Gothenburg, Sweden and a degree in medical technology from Moscow State Technical University, Russia.

Personal development

My experience so far shows that managing oneself requires significantly more from each individual than what is the case in a traditional organization. This means that everyone must be prepared to act, reason, and stay informed at the same level as a traditional manager. The reward is a more limitless opportunity to grow with your responsibilities and shape your own role based on your own drives and interests. This evolution takes place in dialogue with colleagues, as long as it is in line with other adjacent roles and the commonly defined direction for the organization. We do not separate professional and personal development but talk about it as a single phenomenon, as an important part of always being yourself.

At Beetroot there is no ladder to climb or conventional promotion, but you "roll" forward in your role and get new responsibilities dynamically. By developing your own way of performing your role and managing your responsibilities, with the opportunity to discover and develop new abilities, natural competence development takes place as part of the daily work. In some cases, this evolution involves external or internal courses and training, sometimes with the support of someone more experienced within the organization, some-times a coach or trainer, and sometimes self-study.

We encourage a person's own initiatives for the development of the organization, oneself, and one's team. A defined way of contributing is that, in step with increased seniority in the role, you share your experience and become a coach. This means that in quite organized forms, you package and share experiences with your colleagues.

We regularly organize training in attitude and mindset where the core is learning to relate to each other as adult, responsible, and capable persons. These behaviors are absolutely necessary for us to continue to build and develop strong relationships, high trust, and a healthy feedback environment. I also feel that it contributes to people not putting sticks in each other's wheels or disrupting or limiting each other's opportunity for development.

Recruitment

It is clear to me that what shapes an organization more than anything else is the sum of all the people in it, something that is even more clear in a self-organized environment. This means that the recruitment and integration of new individuals into the organization becomes one of the most important activities and absolutely crucial for what happens to the organization as it grows.

We recruit above all based on attitude, mindset, openness, etc. Of course, relevant experience and background are also important, but every recruitment is handled as a long-term decision, and what determines whether someone long-term fits a role is usually the ability to learn new things and the way the person relates to his or her colleagues. Whether all previous experience and abilities are on the CV or not is secondary. This means that our recruitment processes are often long with many interview steps where more or less all the people the candidate will interact with are represented.

Beetroot Academy

As an effect of social drivers and the desire to achieve positive change, we started in 2014 the Beetroot Academy project to help people enter and get their first job in IT. We have since then developed the project into a separate company and a relatively large organization, which, together with other parts of our business, forms a kind of ecosystem.

The effects and synergies we experience from conducting training ourselves in areas that are directly connected to the other kind of business are enormous. In addition to being a recruitment channel and marketing platform, it positions us as a developer of knowledge and competence within the industry. Thanks to our position, we can tailor training courses according to needs and adapt to the demand for different skills.

My conclusion is that regardless of the type of business, there is great benefit in conducting training in one's area of expertise, either as a parallel business or as an integrated part of the main business. Being able to offer your employees a variety of courses and training combined with unleashing each individual person to find their own way becomes a very powerful combination!

WORKPLACE AND WORKING HOURS

Our workplaces have changed over time, both where operational work is carried out, such as factories, hospitals, shops, etc., and the work in our offices. In this section we will focus on how what traditionally is called "office work" is conducted in relation to the different areas of the DP model.

Historically, work has been divided between white- and blue-collar workers, where mainly the former have performed office work while the latter have worked with production and the like. Today, this division feels outdated, especially when we say that a good organization relies on openness, trust, and equality. There is no reason to divide people into white- and blue-collar workers as we all contribute to the whole.

At the time of writing, we are in the middle of the Covid-19 pandemic, which has a major impact on the workplace because most people who work in various offices, but also other professional categories, must work from home instead of being in the usual premises.

Before we move on, we would like to ask you to reflect for a moment and write down how much of your work requires you to be at your workplace and why. What do you have to do at your workplace and what can you do elsewhere? Save your notes because we will use them later.
When you are done, we would like to ask you to think about where you work best. What is your favorite workplace? Is it perhaps the kitchen table, the balcony, or the office? Maybe you like to alternate between different places depending on what you are going to do?

For many years, we have done this exercise in several of the organizations in which we have been, and a majority say that their favorite place is somewhere else than the office or workplace. Even in occupations that require the work to be carried out in the workplace, such as doctors, there is a certain percentage of tasks that can be performed anywhere, and most respondents prefer to perform these tasks at home or in the coffee room.

We argue that there is a lot of work that can be done in different places depending on how you as a person want to do your work. We are all individuals and have different preferences for how and when we best do our job. Things such as writing documents, analyzing materials, planning, following up on outcomes, preparing meetings, etc. can be done advantageously outside the normal workplace.

Now you can look at the note you wrote earlier and reflect on the part of the work that you thought could be done outside the workplace and think about how much of it you actually did outside your workplace (think of the time before the pandemic or specific restrictions). If you carried out no work at all outside the workplace, write down why. Was it because you could not do it, you did not dare do it, you were not sure if it would be appreciated by others, it was based on old habit, you actually wanted to do it at your workplace, or for other reasons?

Now look at the part where you wrote about what was not possible to carry out outside the workplace and challenge it. Why is it not possible? What would it take for that part to increase?

THE WORKPLACE, WORKING HOURS, AND TRUST

For more than 100 years, the time at the workplace has been what has set the salary, and for proof that work really has been carried out, we count hours and minutes at the workplace. During the 1920s, a new salary system was introduced by H.L. Gantt, who was a disciple of Taylor, which changed wage systems and made the time spent in the workplace important. He introduced performance pay for the talented and hourly pay for the less talented. The stamp clock became the way to ensure that hourly wages were paid correctly. Workers were no longer paid for what they had produced, instead they were compensated based on how much time they had worked. The time worked became money regardless of how much they had produced during that time.

Since the prevailing view of the workers was that they were lazy and would not work if they were not controlled, the stamp clock was combined with supervision in the form of foremen or supervisors. These made sure that the workers did not talk to each other and that they were working and not just standing still. This view gave rise to what was called Theory X and Theory Y, developed by McGregor in the 1950s–1960s. We have described McGregor's theories in the section on leadership. In short, according to Theory X, human beings are described as lazy, usually unintelligent, and as working to get enough income to live. Thus, workers must be instructed, supervised, and controlled. This was how production lines were set up in the early twentieth century, where workers performed the work and were instructed and supervised by management.

According to Theory Y, people are driven by internal motivation and want to do a good job and take responsibility for this. With that, a different kind of leadership is required where the leader instead supports and helps the individual to do a good job. However, there is still a focus on productivity and efficiency, as well as following procedures and policies. Theory X and Theory Y are the basis for later theories regarding what motivates people.

It has been 100 years since Gantt's wage system based on time was introduced, but still the lack of trust and the view that people are inherently lazy remain in many organizations. Even if the stamp clock has now been removed from many workplaces around the world, it still remains in many countries, just like 100 years ago.

Before Buurtzorg had introduced self-managing and autonomous teams, the home care market in Holland was characterized by a system where every activity was timed and followed up by a planning department. The amount of time it took to give a patient a treatment, injection, follow-up visit, or similar was carefully time stamped. The planning department planned each nurse's day and which patients were to be visited. They even placed barcodes on customers' houses that the nurses scanned when they went in and out. This led to dissatisfaction among staff, patients, and their relatives, and to poor profitability. There was no time for social interaction with the patients.

In response to this situation, Jos de Blok co-founded Buurtzorg and introduced self-managed and autonomous teams where most of the common central units, such as the planning department, were removed. Instead, each team was given control over how to organize its work. All teams eliminated the definition and tracking of time-stamped activities. Instead, the nurses themselves had to decide how to handle their patients. The nurses spent time with their patients (who became healthier and happier), involved relatives, and in the long run were able to handle more clients per nurse. Buurtzorg became increasingly attractive as an employer, took market shares, and became very profitable. In addition, they had very satisfied customers, not least the family members who saw that their relatives were doing much better. Here it is clear that too much time management and control lead to inefficiency, customer and employee dissatisfaction, and poor profitability.

If we go back to the 1980s in Sweden, there was a big change for teachers as they became able to plan a significant part of their time themselves. A working time regulation was introduced where the employer no longer monitored actual time worked; instead the employees regulate their time based on what the task requires. Many teachers today have 40% scheduled teaching time and 60% of what is called "trust time." As the term suggests, the teachers are trusted to manage this time themselves, which is used for planning, correcting tests, and more. This way of trusting people has since been followed by several other professions within the public sector.

Within nonpublic organizations, there has also been a change in recent decades leading to more flexible working hours. This does not automatically mean that trust in the employees has increased. We have encountered many cases that show that there are employers or managers who do not trust that the employees work when they are not at the workplace and use different control mechanisms that go against the company's policies on leadership, which usually talks about trust and confidence in the employees. This creates the nonfunctional culture that we describe in the section on culture.

It is still time that normally frames both work and payment in the world. An eight-hour working day was introduced in Sweden in 1919 (then there was a six-day working week). That number of hours is what is still considered full-time. Working hours should be between 06:00 and 18:00 from Monday to Friday to be considered normal. Time that falls outside these hours and days is considered inconvenient working time. What a name! Working more than 40 hours a week means overtime and is financially compensated with higher hourly pay. It is also legislated how many hours of overtime a person can work and the union monitors compliance with this.

As this way of managing working hours is incredibly inflexible, many companies have introduced other types of contracts where overtime and inconvenient working hours are exchanged for an extra week of holiday. Many have also introduced so-called "flexitime" and a "flex bank" (where hours are saved and can be used later), which means that employees can work more than eight hours a day, which enables them to work less on another day. In traditional hierarchical organizations, this is applied with time control to those at the bottom of the hierarchy, while there is usually a greater trust in managers who are paid to "do their job and deliver" regardless of working hours or workload.

An important question is: Do we have to work 40 hours a week and why?

In 1930, Lord John Maynard Keynes, a very famous English economist, predicted that technological progress would enable us to work 15 hours per week. It has been 90 years since his statement but we are still far from that scenario, although the technological advances that mankind has made since then are enormous.

In several countries the 40-hour working week has been a political issue. Belgium has introduced the right to work four days per week, New Zealand and many countries in Europe are testing the same, and different companies are also trying out fewer working hours per week. Some countries and companies are trying a six-hour working day with the approach that there is no difference in productivity if a person works six or eight hours per day. In the UK, there is a new legislation that, if it is possible, gives workers the right to request flexible working arrangements from day one of their employment.

Despite these examples, in the near future we do not see that there is any collective approach that can change the view of time and work; it is difficult to move away from time as the measurement of work.

Within the DP model, we believe that the work that people do should not be based on time units but on what is accomplished, which creates added value for the organization.

NEW PARADIGMS AROUND WORKPLACE DESIGN

In the 1980s and 1990s, many organizations went from having their own offices to having so-called "open landscapes" where many people sit in large open rooms. These rooms can have long desks where people sit next to each other in long rows or small desks with screens between them. We had the opportunity to experience two companies in Sweden, ABB and Volvo IT, that early on rebuilt their offices in that way. These environments were not particularly appreciated by the employees and the noise level was very high. Although no one was apparently talking, there was always the kind of "buzz" that occurs when many people sit in a large room.

The reason why these environments were created and became popular during these two decades was almost solely to do with financial savings. Premises became more expensive during this time and organizations wanted to reduce their fixed costs, and premises were considered necessary but not important to have.

Reflect: Do you work, or have you worked, in an open office landscape? What did you think of the work environment? Were you able to concentrate, talk on the phone, discuss with colleagues?
In what way did the workplace affect you, positively or negatively?

A new workplace design took off in the twenty-first century for other reasons. It was triggered by the fact that different environments are better suited to different types of activities. There are, for example, tasks where you need to be by yourself without noise or other disturbances. Other tasks are of such a nature that it is good to be together with others and be able to talk to others while sitting in front of your computer. Maybe it is preferable to sit on a sofa or armchairs near a window when having a dialogue between two or three people. This type of environment promotes dialogue and closeness as opposed to being in a conference room with a table between the people. A room is needed for conference calls or long phone calls in which these can take place undisturbed and without disturbing others. Who wants to listen to a phone call when the focus is on finishing a document? There are also conversations that are of such a nature that they must take place in privacy. This actually turns the concept around and suggests that the workplace should be designed according to the activities that people will perform rather than that people should adapt the work to the workplace that is offered, and also that we are all different and have different preferences.

Research has increasingly come to highlight the impact that the physical work environment has on creativity, collaboration, and well-being among employees. The research also says that productivity increases when you can do your work in an environment that is adapted to the activity itself, which is obvious according to common sense. This has also led to large open office landscapes being split up, islands with social meeting places being introduced, and smaller rooms being available for undisturbed work.

Another aspect is that digitization means that we can work differently; we can do many tasks anytime and anywhere using the mobile phone and the computer as tools. This brings us back to the pandemic when we suddenly had to do a lot more work remotely.

Did you work a lot at home during Covid-19, and if so, how did it feel? What was better about working remotely? Did you experience anything worse?

The way of designing the workplace according to the activities to be carried out has given rise to what is referred to as "activity-based workplaces and working methods" (ABW – Activity-Based Working) where office work is no longer carried out at a separate desk.

Unfortunately, there are many cases where ABW is implemented in an inadequate way because everyone needs to learn to use the different possibilities of the activity-based workplace in an appropriate way. Managers and project managers who are used to seeing their team together on site often find that they lose control of their team. People need to show consideration to others, not always use the places that are considered the best, clean up when leaving a place, and similar things. The environments must be adapted to the tasks carried out in the specific workplace and not just be a copy of another workplace. The nature of the work must be adapted – for example, you cannot depend on large amounts of written documentation that must be moved around or special equipment that cannot be moved. On the other hand, the workplace must also be adapted for activities that need specific equipment. Factors such as ergonomics, the function of the furniture, sound, light, temperature, and air quality are also of great importance for health, well-being, and acceptance of ABW.

If there is not enough support and training while introducing ABW, the workplace is more or less transformed into an open office landscape, and both the purpose and the potential are lost.

On the other hand, a properly designed ABW workplace gives the people the opportunity to plan where to work and thus have both control and flexibility. This became very clear at SRS and their cultural journey towards self-organizing as a way of organizing work. When they introduced ABW, cooperation among different teams increased, social relations among employees improved, and people experienced a higher degree of understanding of each other's tasks.

In the south of Sweden, we found the company My Workspaces, which is niched in supporting organizations to develop sustainable ABW workplaces. They apply a holistic approach in connection with the design of the physical workplace where they also work with changing culture and leadership and with relearning and learning new things about how to use the new environments. As each workplace is unique, each solution is also unique. My Workspaces has many years of knowledge in the design of work environments but also use previous and current research in the field. Based on this, they can measure the impact of the work environment on productivity, job satisfaction, increased collaboration, and cost savings.

THE FLEXIBLE WORKPLACE OF THE FUTURE

It takes time to break assumptions, and new paradigms are not created overnight. We still "go to work," we do not just "do the job." The Covid-19 pandemic has accelerated the possibility of working without being "at work." We are convinced that it is a change that is here to stay, and, in the future, we will be able to see a hybrid between being at the workplace sometimes and working remotely sometimes. Working from home some days will become a reality for more people than before. A question to ask is whether the distinction between work and leisure is becoming increasingly blurry.

How do you manage the difference between work and leisure?
Is it a problem, and if so, in what way?

Although people have the opportunity to be more flexible with when and where they do their job, there is much more to do to make it work well. What is it that makes us always book a meeting room when we have a meeting with a person? Instead, we could take a walk in the park, or just around the block, and have the meeting there. Why does the "one premises–one business" relationship still prevail?

Many people think that we have flexible work environments when the flexibility consists of choosing where in the office we can sit, or because we have the opportunity to work from home from time to time. But there are several dimensions of flexibility. Two of these dimensions are "indoors-outdoors" and "transformation." The latter means that physical premises can be used for different types of activities depending on the time.

A two-year study has been conducted with five administrations within the city of Malmö, together with Malmö University in Sweden, in order to evaluate how parts of the work that is usually carried out indoors could be carried out outdoors. The results show simple, cheap, sustainable, and efficient ways to work outdoors. Having a conversation with a colleague while walking is an example that stimulates the mind, opens up a positive and creative dialogue, increases closeness, and thus reduces the hierarchy as our relationships become more equal when we are outdoors. Documenting can be done by, for example, using a mobile phone to record a summary, a tablet to write on, or simply with paper and pen. Flipcharts to draw on can be brought in if the surroundings allow. The challenge is to feel that it is permissible to go out and still be aware that we are working. In addition, there are positive effects for health because we sleep better when we have daylight, fatigue is reduced when we are outdoors, and we strengthen both the body and the immune system when we move.

Working outdoors and even creating outdoor offices is a trend, albeit a slow one.

Cookfox Architects is an architectural firm in Manhattan that, if they undertake work, requires green outdoor environments to be included in an office building.

There are other examples that also indicate that we are on our way out of the office. Corporate Rebels, a consultancy firm from the Netherlands, acquired something they call the mobile office. They bought a camper and furnished it so that six people can work and sleep in it. In this way, they created much more flexibility where they can go to different places and work. For example, they can be at the beach during the summer and work at the same time, they can follow the wind to practice kite flying, or they can be at a music festival. This shows that there are many, almost unlimited, variations and possibilities that we have not yet tried.

Today's rate of utilizing workplaces in the rich world is in general not sustainable because these are not converted into different activities based on the time of day or the calendar. Most buildings are completely unused in the evenings, on weekends, and during public holidays. Compare this with production facilities where you try to have a high-capacity utilization. Outside normal office hours, there is a great need for meeting places for various activities such as association activities, birthdays, celebrations, etc. There are also many professions that could perform jobs and services if they had a pop-up location at a reasonable price or at no cost. Why not use empty conference rooms as massage rooms or therapy rooms on Saturdays and Sundays? Or hold a weekend exhibition? Maybe organize a cooking class in the dining room?

Think about what the office could be used for during holidays, especially if we have an activity-based office without our own seats. Here, our companies have an opportunity to give back to society by giving youth associations a place, supporting cultural events, connecting society with the company and culture, or organizing youth activities.

You can actually reflect on what it is that stops us from using the buildings when the regular business is not running. Is it that we have access to more resources and consider it unnecessary, or less trust, or is it our way of looking at property that is based on an old paradigm?

However, there are examples all around us and these are related to the view of work and people. When we worked at Jayway, our daughter celebrated her eighth birthday at the office on a Saturday. The conference room, with space for 30 people, was converted into a party room for 20 children!

When was the last time you celebrated a children's party at a workplace or in a training room? Have you witnessed a workplace being used for something other than what it is normally used for?
Think about what your premises could be used for apart from regular work.

Many of us must do most of our work in a particular location. If you work in production, are a doctor, teach, work in a store or similar, you must spend a lot of time there, although perhaps not all the time. Many can, in reality, be very flexible with where and when they do certain tasks. The important thing is that together in the working group, we agree on common standards for when we meet, how we communicate with each other, how we notify when we are not available, etc. The difference between sitting together for eight hours a day and working in different places is significant, which leads to the importance of us having clear and open communication with clear standards. Saying that now I have to concentrate on something for the whole afternoon must be acceptable. "Please, only bother me if it's really necessary." Some other days I work remotely. "Feel free to bother me, I'm on the chat." Communicating such small things to each other allows us to do the work where we do it best. The important thing is what we do not just spending time.

As an example, below we show the principles from an agile development team at Ikea.

- We are present and on time for ceremonies* and meetings
- We work in the office on Mondays, Tuesdays, and Thursdays from 9:30 to 16:00
- We are transparent and share knowledge with each other
- We have fun together
- We share responsibility and everyone's voice has equal value
- When we are not in the office, we are available on Slack from 9:30 to 14:00
- We respond on Slack within 20 minutes when working remotely (Wednesdays and Fridays)
- When we work remotely and are at lunch, we change the status to "at lunch"
- We communicate to the team via Slack if we are sick or absent for another reason
- We tell others if we have problems, and we ask for help

Ceremonies involve recurring activities that require the presence of the team.

The team spent much time working together, and with the help of their common and fairly simple rules, they knew what was expected in order to work effectively together. You can see that they dealt with working hours, communication, openness, equality, and attitude. If you have a communication platform such as Slack, you can agree on which statuses you can use to signal to others how available you are right now. Our reflection is that the response time requirement on Slack is too short if you want to work in a concentrated manner.

Feel free to think about which principles you would like to have in your workplace so that work would be a bit smoother.

Voice from the field: Charlotte Petersson Troije – Mälardalen University, Västerås, Sweden

Charlotte Petersson Troije is a PhD student in occupational science at Mälardalen University and has taught leadership and organization at Malmö University for many years. Since 2010, she has developed the idea of StickUt ("Go out!" in English), which is about integrating urban outdoor environments into daily working life to see how this can contribute to a more innovative and more sustainable working life. With her background from various industries and areas, she is passionate about questions related to how we can become wiser together. In addition, she is a board member of SIRA (Swedish Interactive Research Association).

Interview with Charlotte

What do you think of today's way of working with offices?

In today's working life, many of us spend large parts of the day sitting still in front of our computers, something that is neither good for the body nor for our mental capacity. It's actually quite strange. When it comes to our children, we emphasize how important it is for them to get out and play in order to learn, feel good, and develop their social relationships. But somewhere along the way, this kind of need seems to disappear and is replaced by requirements such as being able to sit still indoors for long periods of time. We are expected to be able to concentrate and perform well in this way. This norm follows us into working life, leading to us losing many good opportunities for variation as well as inspiration, daylight, air, and new energy, and not least unexpected events.

You are researching working in an outdoor environment and have managed a research project together with the city of Malmö (StickUt Malmö). What gains did you see there and what gains do you see in general?

There are many research results that link spending time outdoors and contact with nature to positive effects on health and well-being, not least on recovery from stress, but also to other aspects of central importance for working life, such as strengthened cognitive functions and deepened learning and creativity.

StickUt Malmö was about seeing how this potential could be utilized in working life – by exploring possible forms and conditions for bringing work usually carried out indoors, in office workplaces, into the urban neighborhood. Many of the participants were doubtful that it would work at the beginning of the project, partly because of the weather/our climate and partly because they needed access to various things (especially the computers) in their offices. But after a year and a half of practical testing and follow-up, it turned out that many types of activities worked well outdoors – although not in all situations. The most common were outdoor meetings of various kinds, preferably walking. Taking a *"walk and talk"* provided variation for the body and also contributed to better, more relaxed, and open conversations.

Another popular form was walking alone to think – to reflect, solve problems, plan, and develop ideas. In addition, there were many who simply went out and sat down for a while, to read, sketch, or write. Working outdoors was perceived positively in several ways. It gave energy, but also a sense of calm. The participants experienced it as an opportunity to "breathe" and think better ... but they also felt a little guilty, as if they were slipping away from work, even though they were doing exactly the same thing they would have been doing indoors – and maybe even being more productive.

What does it take to be able to work outside?

First of all, a culture and a leadership are needed that both allow and encourage work in different places. The outdoor environment can be a valuable addition to the office, but it assumes that it is permitted to work in different places and that is not a given. Not everyone is blessed with that flexibility and the capability of self-control, and in addition, we as individual persons have variations in health and function. At the same time, it has become clear that some of the obstacles to taking care of the positive effects that spending time outdoors during the working day can have lie elsewhere. When I first got the idea for StickUt, I thought it was about quite practical things and about the physical environment, but afterwards it turned out that it is largely about our view of work. During the project, we could see that it made a big difference if the managers sometimes suggested outdoor meetings because then it became a legitimate alternative.

To get going with outdoor work, it's a good idea to start by writing down what you do during a typical work week and then think about what tasks could be done outdoors. And then it is important to give it a chance – to test and find your favorite shapes and not least explore the outdoor environment, where there are good places and trails nearby. There is technology that solves most practical things, so it's mainly about making small adjustments in our habits, like recording or simply having a pen and paper in your pocket! One of the most important things is whether there is sufficient trust and openness both from managers and from colleagues. At the same time, it should be pointed out that a major obstacle lies in our own ideas – in our view of work. We say it is important to have fun at work, but can we really be productive while sitting and enjoying the sun?

How do you see the workplaces of the future?

What I wish to see going forwards is more courage and less imitation when it comes to developing different solutions based on the unique needs of each business and individual person. Given the great potential out there, hopefully we will consider the outdoor environment as a natural part of the workplace, but I suspect it will take some time. There is an endless number of ideas and theories about different ways to organize and lead successfully, but unfortunately there is no single "right way" that works in all situations, as it is always dependent on us individuals who make up the organizations.

On the one hand, there is a clear trend towards more flexible working conditions, where people have more freedom to shape their working day based on their needs, but at the same time there are trends in terms of rationalization and bureaucratization that go in the opposite direction. It is easy to be seduced by the opportunities for control and steering that increasing digitization provides.

Personally, I do not see any contradiction in good and clear procedures for follow-up versus autonomy and personal freedom. But it is extremely important that we reflect on what it is that should be measured and valued and to what extent it actually creates good conditions for taking care of and developing ourselves as human beings, in all our magnificent diversity. I see it as a matter of fate that we succeed in this in order to contribute to more innovative organizations, and to a democratic and sustainable social development.

SOCIAL RESPONSIBILITY AND SUSTAINABILITY

There is a trend where companies have become aware of how important it is to work with sustainability. In some cases, it is because the market demands it and in other cases because there is an increased awareness of environmental destruction. We see that there is a very strong connection between sustainability and the social responsibility that organizations must have.

This is because sustainability consists of many aspects and not just the environment. How the company manages its employees, produces, and distributes its products, and does business affects both people and the environment.

SOCIAL RESPONSIBILITY

We have previously argued that an organization should have a purpose. A purpose is about an outside-in view that explains why you exist. If you exist for someone else, you have a responsibility towards them. However, every organization should lift their gaze and look at their own social responsibility in the world, especially if they have a systemic approach. Social responsibility can be seen from several different perspectives. An example is the environmental responsibility where we tear the earth's environment in different ways and where different types of materials affecting the environment are used. We address the use of the earth's resources below, under the circular economy.

Globalization increased during the latter part of the twentieth century. The easiness of moving capital and converting currencies spread across the world based on Milton Friedman's idea that markets would take care of themselves without government intervention. In parallel, new technological innovations made financial transactions much faster. This, along with the fall of the Soviet Union and the end of the Cold War, was one of the reasons why globalization took off. Globalization meant that products became available and cheaper in rich countries and consumption increased rapidly. The term "low-cost countries" was created. Low-cost countries were those countries where production was cheap, usually in Eastern Europe and Asia. But there was a downside to being able to produce at low cost: that wages were lower, working hours longer, and the working environment and other working conditions worse. The value chains were extended in parallel with this change, meaning that production was outsourced to suppliers, who in turn outsourced certain parts to their suppliers, and so on.

This also applied to services such as the development of IT systems, analyses, and similar. The longer the chain becomes, the more difficult it is to ensure that the production of goods or services is done in a socially responsible way. The socially acceptable level was often broken.

A much-discussed example is the Taiwanese company Foxconn, which, among other things, manufactures the iPhone for Apple. Foxconn was known for poor working conditions, and in 2010, 14 people committed suicide at their factory in China. Foxconn's response was to make workers sign a contract promising not to kill themselves, which the company later withdrew.

In recent years, consumers have become increasingly aware of, and interested in, how a product or service is produced. This is facilitated by the fact that more information is available through the Internet. If the organization is part of a larger cycle or ecosystem, it must take responsibility for how the products and services are created. This trend will increase and become natural for organizations that want to work in a systemic way supported by the DP model. It is not possible to contract suppliers who have a different view of social responsibility or sustainability than the contracting organization. For example, Foxconn used to be known for very long working hours, short holidays, a lot of overtime, stress, and surveillance. Whoever is responsible for the product that Foxconn manufactures on their behalf must take responsibility for how the product has been produced.

Within the EU, work is underway to develop a legal package with strict requirements for improved traceability, sustainability, and recycling for electronic products such as mobile phones.

Patagonia, which sells clothing and products for nature and outdoor life, is a company that invests heavily in social responsibility. Patagonia's policy is to pay fairly, have generous healthcare and flexible working hours, and to be able to carry out environmental work during paid working hours. However, they do not manufacture anything and do not own any factories themselves, and this is a big challenge, especially in the production of clothing. When choosing a supplier, social responsibility and environmental responsibility weigh as much as quality, financial stability, capacity, and fair pricing. In addition, Patagonia has a special social/environmental responsibility team that has a veto right in discussions about partnering with a new factory. Their Supply Chain team also has training in responsible procurement to avoid negative impacts on workers and the environment.

Think for a moment about how important it is to you that a product or service is produced in a socially responsible way. How much do you consider this when making your choice?

Chobani also considers itself to have a high focus on social responsibility. The company recruits, for example, refugees and people who find themselves in socially vulnerable situations. In addition, they have introduced a minimum wage that is above the statutory and the prevailing one. The goal is that everyone will get a monthly salary that they can live on, even if they are a factory worker or have another role that is normally very low paid. All permanent employees receive three months of paid parental leave, which is far above the norm in the United States. The company's efforts and donations during the pandemic have been noticed in the media and also show that the company values social responsibility highly.

As we discussed in the section on the salary model, there should be a limit to how big the difference is between the one who earns the least and the one who earns the most in the organization. This is also part of the social responsibility: not to create large gaps between people, which also counteract the view of equality.

According to the DP model, an organization's social responsibility includes the employees, suppliers, customers, society, etc. This means that employees are not seen as replaceable parts in a machine and with an aspiration for people to be able to make a living from their work, and that even people with different prerequisites get a chance. Furthermore, social responsibility covers the entire value chain.

CIRCULAR ECONOMY

A circular economy is about keeping the earth's resources constant in a profitable way and is based on the principles of eliminating waste and pollution, reusing products and materials, and maintaining or developing natural ecosystems. This leads to a systemic approach for the business as well as organizing work.

During industrialization at the beginning of the twentieth century, production was developed as a linear process, from raw materials to final product and waste. These principles have guided Supply Chain Management until now. The way of organizing the work has also been in the same linear direction based on a supply chain. Functions organized in a matrix were created to run the supply chain. In the last 20 years, many organizations have tried to increase their environmental responsibility by taking care of their waste, which is good but only one step towards a holistic view of the cycle.

In the circular economy, the organization becomes part of a larger cycle where production should not affect the earth's total assets or the environment. The driving forces behind this approach are the understanding that the earth's resources are limited, climate change is increasing dramatically, digitization gives access to more information, etc.

That the organization's resources must be taken care of and be part of the whole will be the guiding principle for the way of organizing in the circular industry. This means that the organization should not wear out its employees, they should support new innovative ideas about how products can be created from recycled materials and develop natural systems, secure the full circle, and much more. SRS works in a circular economy, as its CEO, Anna Elgh, describes in the voice from the field below.

Above we discuss manufacturing organizations, but this is equally important for service organizations. Even if these do not produce physical products, they become part of a larger ecosystem.

Holma is a natural part of a circular economy, especially as their education deals with permaculture, which specifically applies to sustainable cultivation where every plant has a purpose. In addition, Holma has designed its physical environment in different groups that they call "circles" where everything is connected in a cycle. The organization at Holma is based on Sociocracy, which we presented in the introduction chapter, which is designed as different circles where each circle has a clear purpose and area of responsibility, and where all circles are connected in a network. The circles at Holma have, in addition to a definite purpose, a direct connection to the physical design. They also see themselves as part of society and have the goal that none of the employees should work more than 75% of a full-time job. The reason for this is that everyone who works at the school should have time to get involved in other activities. In this way, the signal is given that the organization is part of society.

We analyzed a larger manufacturing company that operates in a global environment and that invests heavily to be able to fulfill the principles of a circular economy. The company tries, for example, to use only new ecological materials or recycled materials. In addition, they are looking for different ways to ensure that the products can be reused and become new products again, with everything in a cycle. This is run as part of the business.

While this part of the organization works according to a circular approach, a large proportion of the company's central staff travel continuously around the world. Many people travel far for short meetings, including many weekly commutes to different offices located in different parts of Europe, regardless of whether it is needed or not, and the proportion of expatriate contracts is large and advantageous. The latter applies among different countries in the world, almost as if you exchange personnel between countries without it being necessary. It is as if the global part of the organization has a culture of traveling.

In this example, the overall view of a circular economy is lacking. One part of the company cannot work in a circular fashion while the other wears out the earth's resources. The interesting thing about this company is that during the Covid-19 pandemic, all business travel was stopped, offices were closed, and everyone worked from home. Then it was discovered that it was possible to meet without traveling around the world. In addition, the work became more efficient because about 25% of those who worked in the global organization were constantly on the move. Traveling is quite inefficient even if we sometimes have to see each other face to face.

In a systemic approach, the earth's resources should not be wasted. Instead, the quest for a circular approach should be encouraged and include the entire organization.

Since the world has passed the point where it could be enough to talk about preserving the environment, we now need to think about designing regenerative organizations, meaning that one of the purposes is to restore and regenerate degraded living ecosystems.

THE ORGANIZATION AS PART OF A WHOLE

We have previously reasoned that in a systemic approach the organization is part of a whole, an entirety. An important parameter if a private company wants to make a cultural journey according to the DP model is that the company's board must be on board on this journey. The company's board is usually appointed by the company's owners and in different ways, depending on whether the company is on the stock market or a private ownership. In the section on culture, we discussed identity. If the organization develops a culture and identity as a progressive organization that is ethical and works with social and sustainable responsibility, ownership should also be in line with this, just as we mention in the section on finances.

An example of a company that lacks in its holistic thinking is the Swedish food company Oatly, which claims that they sell a lifestyle and not food, and that sustainability and climate are two pillars of the company. One of Oatly's major owners is the Chinese state through the company China Resources, which also has two people on the board of directors. In addition, 10% of the shares were bought by venture capital firm Blackstone when Oatly was in need of more capital. The dilemma for Oatly is that Blackstone has also invested in, among other things, the destruction of the Amazon rainforest and has been criticized by UN representatives because their housing deals are in violation of international human rights standards. Blackstone also has a representative on Oatly's board of directors. Oatly claims that this will not affect their strategy and that they want to influence Blackstone to act in a more sustainable way. The latter can be interpreted as an explanation for why they accepted Blackstone's capital.

Oatly is an example that highlights that the organization must be seen as a whole, including the board – especially, as in this case, when the profit from a company (Oatly) that emphasizes that its pillars are sustainability and climate ends up with someone who devastates the rainforest in the Amazon (Blackstone).

Another perspective on the organization as part of a whole, and which is directly linked to social responsibility, is what purpose it has with its products and services. Who will use the product or service and for what purpose will it be produced? This can be a difficult question if, for example, the company manufactures advanced surveillance systems that can be used to save people's lives but also to monitor people in a dictatorship. This becomes an ethical dilemma – where to draw the line? It becomes important for the organization to find its ethical boundaries. It is also important that the employees know the purpose of the products and services, so that they can decide whether they want to belong to the organization or not. As we reasoned in the section on culture, people should be able to share values and norms with the organization they work in. This also increases openness and transparency. The organization may still violate its own or the individuals' ethical principles even if it does not violate any laws.

An area adjacent to this is corruption. In most countries corruption is illegal, at least corruption involving money. The organization must also consider its ethical principles in this case. Corruption can also take place without money being involved. It could be, for example, doing someone a favor that requires a favor in return, receiving gifts, etc. Even in these cases, the organization's principles must guide people's behaviors so that everyone understands that this is also corruption.

The organization's principles must include ethical principles, and these must reflect social and sustainable responsibility. These state what behaviors are allowed and not allowed.

MAXIMIZE PROFIT FOR SHAREHOLDERS OR FOR SOCIETY

Traditionally, limited companies want to maximize profit for shareholders. This means that making money becomes a company's primary goal and purpose. Because ownership of shares generally has an increasingly short-term goal, the financial goals are also becoming more and more short-term. Some years ago, financial departments and investors started to focus on quarterly goals. Financial goals with a short-time horizon lead in turn to investments with the same time perspective and often to an avoidance of risks. It becomes difficult to combine a higher purpose, social responsibility, and sustainability with short-term financial goals. As we reason in the finance section, the purpose of the organization should be combined with a model that makes the organization profitable over time, otherwise the organization will disappear. Shareholders who invest capital in companies to get a return should get a return, but a too short-term horizon easily leads to the company not creating long-term perseverance.

In systemic thinking, an organization is part of something bigger, namely our society and our planet. An organization is dependent on its surroundings and does not only exist by itself. A healthy organization must have a purpose for its existence and the ability to develop together with its surroundings, and thus contribute to the development of society. The people in the organization are also a part of the society and contribute to this. This leads us into how to maximize profit for society, which Hamdi Ulukaya, Chobani's CEO, among others, in his TED Talks and published interviews says is their driving force (see further in the section on the book's protagonists). The long-term investments become more natural if the purpose of an organization is higher than just maximizing profit for shareholders and focuses instead on maximizing profit for society.

There is also a similar approach in nonprofit organizations and public services. These types of organizations must focus on not wasting the organization's resources because these are funded by donors, who are the taxpayers for public organizations. A public organization has a natural purpose to be part of society, and, in the same way as a private company, it must be financially healthy over time to be sustainable.

THE PEOPLE AS PART OF A WHOLE

In an ecosystem, everyone is part of the whole and there is an interdependence between the parts. As we have reasoned before, an organization does not live by itself, it is part of something bigger. The people who work in the organization also work in society and are affected by what happens there.

Jayway in Malmö, Sweden initiated Talent Without Borders a few years ago, which became a nonprofit association. It was founded together with other actors in the region such as Cybercom, Malmö University, Lund University, Minc (incubator organization), Qlik, and Softhouse.

The explanation for why it was started was as follows: "It was started based on the realization that a large number of talented people chose to consider Sweden as their home. Some found a career, others found a partner, and many refugees found sanctuary. Yet many talents currently face unnecessary obstacles to achieving their ambitions. Therefore, we – practitioners, employers, and enthusiasts – have come together to identify and pursue creative ways to handle this unsustainable situation." The aim of the initiative was to help new citizens find employments where they could use their talents or other activities that would lead to employment.

In addition, Jayway's employees have for some time participated as volunteers in Coder Dojo, which is an association of volunteers who teach programming to children and teenagers. They exist in 113 countries and comprise around 1,200 volunteers. By being a part of Coder Dojo, Jayway gave back to the community and also became part of a large global association.

K2K has a principle that they have introduced in all companies within the NER group, which is that employees should also contribute to society during their nonworking time and in this way be part of the ecosystem. The goal is that the companies also contribute with 2.5% of the result and 2% of the working time to social and/or sustainability projects.

All employees of any company that is part of the NER group can propose activities and projects that have social improvements as their purpose. These are analyzed and selected based on, among other things, the interest in participating and are then financed by the common pot to which all companies have contributed. The activities and projects are then staffed by participants who take part in their free time but also with the help of the allocated time provided by the companies.

Patagonia is also a company that gives back to the community. Since 1985, they have donated 1% of the company's annual revenue to organizations who are trying to improve the environment. In 2018, the company also donated ten million dollars to "organizations that work to preserve the air, forest, and water and to find solutions to the climate crisis." These ten million dollars came from the corporate tax cuts introduced by Donald Trump in 2017 and which Patagonia's management did not think were fair. Instead, they decided that the money would be used for the climate crisis. Patagonia also gives a certain amount to selected supplier factories for their employees to select and run social and sustainability projects. This could be, for example, building a school, digging a well in the village, or starting a club for outdoor activities.

The organization must stimulate and make it easier for the employees to be able to carry out social activities and get involved in society.
It is important to point out that this is not about philanthropy or greenwashing. Time and energy are among the most valuable resources that people have and therefore they are also the finest things that one can give. Social involvement from the people in the organization also leads to the development and enrichment of the organization.

Voice from the field: Anna Elgh – CEO of Svenska Retursystem AB and board member of Green Cargo, Stockholm, Sweden

Anna Elgh has a civil engineering degree from KTH and over 30 years of experience in leading changes in many different logistics-oriented businesses, including Statoil, Scandinavian Airlines, and Lantmännen. Anna has a great commitment to driving sustainability issues in all its dimensions and a passion for organizational forms that put people at the center.

My parents were born in the 1920s. At that time, it was completely natural to economize on resources. People mended and patched and basically had a more circular economy than now, albeit relatively local. A circular economy was just normal behavior and not an established concept that was talked about. During the twentieth century, consumption became the engine of the entire economy and society. Access to cheap fossil energy became the lubricant of our time. Globalization gained momentum and developed towards today's economy where all people on earth are completely dependent on each other. The UN's 17 global sustainability goals clearly show how sustainability cannot be isolated to one issue, for example the climate, but rather how the fight against poverty and injustice and biodiversity is fundamental for us to also be able to fight our climate crisis.

We are currently living in a period of high uncertainty, where poverty is about to increase, where polarization drives gaps between people and nationalism reaps success. This is bad news for sustainability work. At the same time, technological development is moving forward in a way that shapes completely new opportunities. Digitization enables large-scale sharing services and transparency in information flows, which lay the foundation for new collaborations and major development steps in poor countries. Transformation of the energy and transport system towards renewable forms of energy is progressing rapidly and the hierarchical way of organizing activities is being questioned and changed. This is good news for sustainability work.

I am proud to lead one of Sweden's most circular companies, Svenska Retursystem. The food industry was forward-looking when, in the 1990s, it decided to change from disposable packaging with corrugated cardboard and wood to pallets and boxes that can be used over and over again. The whole industry cooperated and many producers had to make tough decisions to make the necessary investments in new production lines, adapted to the new return system.

The basis for a circular business model is long-termism, transparency, and cooperation. A product or service must be designed for a long lifetime, be easy to repair, and ultimately be recyclable when it can no longer be repaired. In the sharing economy, information must be available to everyone who shares a product or service. Cooperation, trust, and responsibility are fundamental for the entire chain to work. In a carpool, it doesn't work if no one feels responsible for leaving a refueled and complete car to the person who booked the car next time. In the same way, we at Svenska Retursystem must be able to trust that users of our system follow our regulations and ensure that the boxes are also returned to us so that we can wash and possibly repair them before any other customer in the system can use them again.

Just as the circular macro-perspective needs to be based on certain principles, the micro-perspective needs to work in the same way. A company that wants to operate in the circular economy must be built on a sound and sustainable value base where trust, openness, and cooperation permeate thier own culture. In the same way as a brand must be built from within, the circular business must be supported by its own culture and live based on the circular principles of cooperation, openness, and trust. This is the basis for the cultural journey we at Svenska Retursystem are walking, where we are moving towards a flatter and more cross-functional way of organizing ourselves, and with a high degree of autonomy.

In our company, it is natural for every decision to be evaluated based on social as well as environmental and financial aspects. Employees with us often describe this with sustainability as "our DNA." It can show up in big and small ways and here are some examples that might inspire you who are reading this:

- In our systematic improvement work, we are constantly working to reduce waste. It can be about everything from energy, detergent, and plastic to water. At our facility in Mölnlycke, a number of employees tackled the water issue after they reacted to the risk of slipping in a production area where water is added to make boxes pass through a machine part. At the same time, they had received information from Härryda municipality about a possible impending water shortage in the municipality. An improvement team was created, and the goal was to find a solution that would completely avoid the use of water in this area. After much experimentation, the team concluded that the design of the machine part was incorrect and, together with some external help, was able to produce a redesigned machine part. The result was a reduced annual water consumption of 7.5 million liters, while the working environment in the area was improved.

- Our business model is based on our boxes having a deposit that the customers pay to us upon delivery, and which then follows the box all the way back to us. The deposit on boxes that are out in the system and circulating amounts to close to half a billion SEK (equal to €50 million). This amount is now placed in a fund that actively invests in companies and businesses that drive sustainability work forward and create real change. When we raised the issue of sustainable investments about six years ago, we were met with great skepticism from our bank. Today they thank us for helping us lay the foundation for them to be able to start this fund both monetarily and with tough requirements based on our sustainability expertise.

· Food poverty is increasing in Sweden and more and more people cannot afford to eat their fill. At the same time, close to 30% of all the food produced is thrown away – an incredible waste of resources and a big problem. Inspired by this, a group of employees took the initiative to start a collaboration with Stadsmissionen (a Swedish organization helping homeless people) where we now support their operations – the Food Mission – both monetarily and with our logistics expertise. The goal of the Food Mission's activities is to enable a larger amount of surplus food to be redistributed to those in need instead of being thrown away or going to biogas production. The Food Mission's operations also offer job training to people who have difficulty entering the labor market.

These were some examples from our everyday life. I would like to thank the authors for giving me the opportunity to share my thoughts and our experiences at Svenska Retursystem in this section on social responsibility and sustainability. I feel that despite the coronavirus pandemic, there are many positive winds blowing, and if we all make some change, it will inspire more and ultimately lead to big changes in the right direction.

FINANCES

The financial aspects should not be forgotten in systemic organizations or ecosystems where everything is connected and where all parts must be taken care of. Self-managed organizations and models have been discussed for several decades without becoming the dominant way of organizing.

We believe that a contributing factor is that leading researchers and thinkers in the subject have largely come from the psychological domain where much focus has been on the human perspective, while the financial perspective has not been given space. In the introduction, we talked about how important it is for organizations to have a purpose and, above all, as Frederic Laloux says, there is a higher purpose whereby, according to him, the profit then comes by itself. Even if it is true that people who enjoy, who are engaged, and who have autonomy create value and innovations, today this is unfortunately not enough for many decision-makers to want to walk that path. Bringing in the financial perspective is one of the unique aspects that the DP model offers and what is missing from other theories and models. Because regardless of the purpose of the company, for example Centigo (*Centigo exists to inspire and lead people to create resilient and prosperous companies and organizations. This applies to our customers, and it applies to ourselves*), there is also the purpose of generating profit for the owners. Profit should not be the focus or the only purpose, but it must be there.

Even organizations that are not companies in the sense that they generate profit, such as the public service organization, must manage their finances in order to exist and survive. To believe otherwise is naive.

However, we believe that organizations should focus less on serving their owners and more on serving their employees and society. The financial aspects must reflect this principle, otherwise it's just empty words or a slogan that does not match reality.

We discuss this further in the section on social responsibility and sustainability.

A financial model is a natural part of systemic organizations and must also focus on serving employees and society, not just the owners.

CAPITAL AND OWNERSHIP

Capital and financing are important parts of all organizations. Many start-up companies begin their journey with an idea and with entrepreneurs who believe in what they are doing, and who put all their energy into it, whereby the organization by default becomes quite self-organized. The vast majority of start-ups need external capital to be able to grow and, in many cases, to be able to establish themselves. For the founders of the company, who want to have a higher purpose for their company but must look for external capital, there is a dilemma: What do they have to give away in order to get investors? The traditional way is that investors get shares and/or are part of the board of directors, and thus also have power, which is one of the reasons why many companies that started as being self-organized often fall into traditional hierarchies of authority.

Therefore, there are many aspects that must be considered before bringing in capital:

- How the culture and values of the company and the investor fit together
- How quickly investors want their return on investment
- Should there be active or passive owners?
- If they are to be active, what role and power will they have in the company?
- If they are to be passive, how do they want to have control?

What is preferred are active owners who fully share the company's purpose and where there is a good match in culture and values, especially in small and medium-sized companies. If the investor becomes a passive owner, the focus must be on creating trust to minimize control.

Another aspect that applies to all businesses, whether they are start-ups or established, is where the capital comes from. It doesn't matter that the company has good purpose and values, works with the well-being and commitment of the employees, with sustainability, etc. if the capital comes from dictatorships or from venture capital that makes money from overexploiting the planet or has employees who work in slave-like forms. Then the company becomes part of something that cannot be considered systemic, Teal, people-centric, or planet-friendly.

Seeing the financial aspects and ownership as part of the system is a prerequisite to get balance in the system. Ownership can be seen as a continuum where on one side there is a single strong owner and on the other side there is a cooperative where all employees have the same share of the company. Between these two extremes there are many different variants. Publicly traded companies usually lie between these two extremes and have shareholders to consider, which in many cases is what makes a company focus on maximizing dividends to its owners and putting employees and reinvestment second.

Many of the companies that K2K works with are family businesses within the manufacturing industry. These companies have one or more family members as owners, who are also active in the company. The majority of these companies were formed at the beginning of the twentieth century and the shares have been inherited within the founders' families. In such companies, it is important to find a financial model that balances the ownership and the actual work that these owners perform in the company – above all, when there is a striving for balance regarding salaries. In most cases, the solution has been that the owners' salaries are handled in the same way as those of others in the organization, and that the owners receive a return on invested capital via dividends. The latter is done after meeting the requirement that 30% of profits go back to the employees or are reinvested. It has proven to be a very successful model where ownership is combined with active participation and in that way the view and experience of the capital becomes different.

Since 2019, the Haier Group has called itself an ecosystem platform like Amazon's in which there are many companies that work together in one platform. Haier calls the small companies "entrepreneurs," when in fact they are gig workers. Since 2012, business has been done by competing through tenders, which happened when the organization introduced a structure with micro-enterprises (MEs). An ME can range in size from a few people to several hundred employees. These MEs also form an internal market within Haier, which means that they sell services and products to each other.

Haier is owned by the Chinese state and through an acquisition they came to the Hong Kong stock exchange in 2004. It is an example showing that it is important to analyze what is behind platforms that are presented as revolutionary, inclusive, and democratic. There are some blogs and social media articles that praise Haier as the largest self-organized organization in the world with around 80,000 people. This is without considering ownership, capital, and the business model. Haier has also been presented as being a network of cooperatives since most people own their ME. Claiming this is akin to saying that Airbnb would be a cooperative just because the people renting out their homes own them.

An example that deserves to be celebrated is Chobani, whose owner Hamdi Ulukaya, in April 2016, made all 2,000 full-time employees co-owners by sharing 10% of the company with them. The size of the shares was based on how long they had worked in the company. Hamdi is one of those business leaders who have nothing against listing the company on the stock market, but he points out that together with the shareholders' capital, there are often demands that might go against the people-centric principles that are the pillars of the company and of his leadership. For him, people always come first, and a company should serve people and society. Furthermore, he thinks that through ownership, the employees become part of the company and the financial security gives them a richer life.

Centigo has a similar view of ownership and the participation and strength this brings, but with the big difference that co-owners must buy shares for a large sum of money. They strive for ownership to be with the people who work in the organization, because their view is that people feel a greater commitment if they are a co-owner and at the same time an employee. This approach also creates a long-term perspective and that also sticks to the organization's principles. At the time of writing, a total of 36 people were co-owners, who together shape the organization's strategy. They have also created a structure for how to make decisions. This is done by forming six committees that deal with different types of issues, after which a group is formed by single representatives from each committee to make the final decision together. In this way, the decision-making process is made more efficient without all co-owners needing to have an opinion on every question. They compare their partnership system to a political system where, as in the Parliament, there are different types of committees. However, Centigo has not broadened partnership to all employees; people must be "qualified" to be offered partnership, which means that you must have been a senior consultant for some time and be able to finance your co-ownership.

In systemic organizations, capital and ownership must be aligned with the organization's values, principles, and purpose.

AN ECONOMIC ECOSYSTEM

In the future, we will see more and more economic ecosystems, and by that we mean organizations, companies, groups, and customers as well as individual professionals and businesses that work together and form an ecosystem.

A completely different type of economic ecosystem than Haier's is the NER group. The group acts based on principles that imply a common ethical approach towards society, the environment, and the employees. All companies that are part of the group commit to a series of actions and activities that involve being organized through self-organized teams, reducing the gap between the people who earn the most and the ones who earn the least, sharing a part of the profit with the employees, reinvesting, and the company having to give back to society or the world through social projects. Employees should also be encouraged to work as volunteers. In addition, employees cannot be dismissed due to financial problems and the companies in the group must help each other by "borrowing" each other's staff during crises and recessions. The group runs common social projects, has common agreements with other parties such as travel agencies, and companies both buy and exchange services and knowledge with each other.

At the time of writing this book, the group consisted of around 20 organizations that included more than 2,000 people and had a turnover of around 400 million euros.

The NER group's slogan is: *We take care of each other; we both learn and develop with commitment to people and to society.*

The NER group's view of ecosystems is that each company should run efficiently and provides the best for its customers. Each company also contributes with people who run social projects that in turn give back to the company and its customers in the form of a better society.

We believe that the financial ecosystem, similarly to what the NER group has, is what will be decisive in order to create a better future – a future with people who are committed, who feel good, and who enjoy what they do. It is also time for a paradigm shift in the way we relate to other organizations. It is not enough to change one's own organization and work with self-organizing, balanced salary systems, and other progressive elements, as there is a need for a wider perspective where relationships with other organizations and also society are included.

Holma, through its sociocratic organizational model, purpose, and principles, is another example that lives in balance with employees, students, clients, interest organizations, society, and the planet as such.

FINANCIAL STRUCTURE

Running a business includes having a financial structure, that is, how the company earns money from its revenues. There are many models that suit the organization differently depending on its nature, purpose, and market.

For consultant firms and providers of temporary workers, the salary model is often part of the financial model. For example, Centigo, which can be classified as a management consulting firm, has a model where after about three years, consultants receive a relatively low basic salary and 50–55 % is based on the income from the consulting assignments. Centigo takes the view that every consultant should be like a self-employed person but in a large organization. This means that the consultant has a form of income statement where their telephone, computer, and similar things are included. The founders' approach is that the consultants must understand that things cost money. Those who are customer coordinator receive a certain percentage of all sales, which means that part of the customer coordinator's sales ends up in their personal profit and loss account. The shareholders receive an extra portion in the form of a dividend.

Another, similar type of financial structure for consulting companies, which has spread in Sweden in recent years, is what is known as the 70/30 model. The basic principle in the model is based on the fact that employees should be considered more or less as entrepreneurs but are only employed when there is an assignment.

We illustrate the model with a real-world example of a company that we rename "X." Company X consists of several teams with different specialist skills and a central team of administrative staff and salespeople. The owners are part of the central team and have different roles based on their skills and interest. Each team has a leader who spends part of his or her time selling and part of the time working as a consultant.

The employees give 30% of their income to the central team and from the remaining 70% all direct costs linked to the consultant are taken. This includes healthcare, seminars, travel, computer, telephone, insurance, provision for occupational pension, and a pot for holidays and for possible sickness. The remaining amount of the 70% will be the monthly salary, which includes general payroll taxes for employees. The consultants are only recruited when there is an assignment, which means that they must generate revenue from day one.

The difference between X and Centigo's view that every consultant should be like a self-employed person is that Centigo wants the employees to feel freedom as if they were self-employed, but that they should feel secure in working at Centigo. X, on the other hand, wants to make money from the consultants by taking 30% of the revenue without investing or taking risks.

Think for a moment and answer the following questions:

> » **Is this a one-size-fits-all model?**
> » **Is it inclusive?**
> » **Are there any risks with such a model?**
> » **What is the strength of the model?**
> » **Is the model systemic and people-centric?**

The 70/30 model is classified as somewhere between having a real job and running your own business. The advantage is that people feel that they are in a context and receive help with administration and sales, which can be experienced as difficult when running your own company. On the other hand, the freedom, both financial and freedom of action, is significantly less than when you are self-employed. The model is based on an individualistic fundamental view instead of systemic values and can therefore only be considered modern, and perhaps even progressive, but not Teal or systemic.

Another type of financial structure is the one found at Buurtzorg, which is based on each team being financially self-sufficient, otherwise the team is dissolved. However, there is an acceptance of reduced income for a certain period of time. Their financial form is based on the fact that they are a foundation and not a profit-making company.

When a new team is to be established, they have about three months to get started. The nurses working in this team are paid from the first day they have a contract with Buurtzorg. This establishment period is considered an investment. The goal and expectation for the team is to be financially self-sufficient after the three months. But it is not that strict because there can be various reasons why a team does not have enough clients to take care of. In the case of financial difficulties, a coach from the central coaching team discusses different options with the team on how to solve the issues. This can be a process that goes on for several months, and if no solutions are found, the team is eventually discontinued.

The financial model works in such a way that the parent foundation invoices the insurance company (the customer) and in that way the income from all teams ends up in the same pot, and from that pot all salaries are paid, including coaches and administration. Thus, there is a form of solidarity if some teams have financial difficulties, e.g. when a new team has to find new patients or a team has reduced the number of patients for various reasons. However, there is a limit to how long a team can continue with a deficit before it has to be dissolved.

Part of the profit at Buurtzorg is reinvested in the foundation, and if it is over a certain limit, a bonus is awarded to all employees where the amount is based on the number of years of employment and the number of hours worked during the year.

Beetroot has a different financial structure, which is partly because the developers are located in Ukraine, even though it is a Swedish company. In Ukraine there is a form of business activity called Private Entrepreneur (PE), which is a kind of sole proprietorship and is more advantageous than being an employee. A PE only pays 5% tax plus a fixed amount of $45 (at the time of writing this book) for retirement savings instead of the 25% that is usual in the country. A very large proportion of the people who are active in the IT industry have a PE and are contracted with a fixed amount per month with another company who in turn has a contract with the customers. All people working at Beetroot in Ukraine (developers, administrative staff, and managers) run their PEs and are contracted by Beetroot. The company has only a few employees in Sweden, and it is these who are responsible for customer relations. The company runs an offshore operation and the developers are hired for a specific customer team.

The weakness of the model is that when a customer terminates their contract, or the contract comes to its end date, it is not possible to automatically move the developers to another customer team. Since Beetroot treats and considers these PEs as employees, they will do their best to recontract these people in another customer team. However, it is not always possible to do this. By changing the business model with their customers, Beetroot is trying to find a solution to move away from having customer teams and instead deliver entire projects or assignments. This would make it possible to move personnel between different assignments.

ProAgile AB from Gothenburg, Sweden is another company that has found a form of organization where they combine the freedom of having their own company and being able to be independent while being part of a larger context at the same time.

The organization consisted in 2019 of 14 agile coaches who were specialists and experts in agile methods and leadership connected to these methods.

The organization is built on an umbrella company, ProAgile AB, which has a business relationship with the customers including invoicing. All income thus goes into a common pot at ProAgile AB. In parallel, each consultant has their own limited company that the consultant manages on their own premises, e.g. salary level, type of computer, etc.

Each consultant works as much as they wish and then reports how many hours they have worked and gets compensated based on this. Nonbillable time such as client meetings, writing blogs, or representing the company is also considered working time. Compensation and profit sharing are decided together once a year. This process has been continuously improved and developed.

Unlike the 70/30 model, there is a basic principle for financial compensation that states that, as a minimum, they should be at the same level as what other companies offer, but preferably strive to be better. For example, they offer the same compensation in connection with sick leave and parental leave. Another difference is that health insurance, liability insurance, and costs for telephony, computers, and further education are taken from the common pot during possible parental leave or illness.

They see their collaboration as a relationship between people in a way similar to that of the NER group. Recruitment is mainly done through contacts and everyone in the group must agree that the person under scrutiny should become one of them. Otherwise, the company has no rules and descriptions, but they determine their future direction together and are then free to act within certain frames in an environment where there is complete trust.

The financial structure must be in balance between company and employees so that employees do not take too many risks and are not exploited. There must also be a balance between independence and vulnerability.

FINANCIAL CODE OF CONDUCT

In the same way as with the origin of the capital, a company must know and decide with whom it is doing business, who are the subcontractors, and with whom else the company cooperates.

We have mentioned this several times throughout the book, but we think it is important to point out that in a systemic approach, all parts must be in balance. One way to ensure that the financial aspects follow the values is to have a code of conduct that consists of principles around how these aspects are handled.

Questions that must be answered include whether the company should do business with dictatorships or cooperate with companies characterized by exploitation of labor and destruction of nature. It is not possible to call a company Teal, systemic, or sociocratic if these aspects are not in place and followed. Managing morality and ethics throughout the entire supply chain therefore becomes a must.

Media have drawn attention to the fact that there are unfortunately far too many examples of good companies that are not sufficiently knowledgeable about the ethics of their subcontractors. A company that has been shown to be lacking in this regard is H&M, where in 2018 it came to light that they had utilized subcontractors that exploited forced labor in the province of Xinjiang in China. The year before, the company had already seen a large loss of customers when they presented their new product set intended for millennials called "Nyden." For these products, H&M collaborated with a famous Swedish individual, Alexander Bard, who had made a series of condescending remarks about women and the MeToo movement. Consumers today have become increasingly aware of ethically produced goods and services. In addition, new information is constantly emerging on social media, where unfortunately there is also a lot of misinformation.

An organization must choose whom to do business with based on its values and principles.

COPING WITH DIFFICULT TIMES

A part of the financial model concerns how to handle difficult times. This book is being written during the Covid-19 pandemic where this aspect has become even clearer. What happens when the company experiences lower revenues or financial problems? In most societies there are laws that both regulate and guide when these problems occur, but we believe there is a need for principles and position taking from the company and its employees.

Talleres Arreche S.A. in Tolosa, Spain, which is part of the NER group, is an illustrative example. José Ignacio Amondarain, who is the owner, said the following when the Covid-19 pandemic paralyzed Spain and the production in the company:

During the strongest moment that came with the lockdown (when we were all at home) and when I heard in the media that there was a risk that society would almost collapse because of the health and economic uncertainty that we would suffer due to the pandemic, I wrote a letter that I delivered personally to all the people of Arreche. The intention was to reassure them as much as possible and to make them aware that together we can get out of this crisis. In the letter, I ratified my commitment as an owner: Leave no one behind. That is, no one will be fired, and all the economic and financial means available in Arreche shall be used to get out of the crisis. Also remind everyone of our shared commitment to make decisions together based on openness and transparency. Decisions that will be made based on personal freedom and the responsibility with the intention to seek efficiency, to take care of our customers more than ever, and to promote commitment to society at this time when there is the greatest need.

A series of measures with the aim of being able to have good liquidity were taken, among other things by securing bank loans to be able to pay both employees and suppliers. Another decision was that everyone would get their vacation in August as planned but with 85% of the salary, and to have temporary layoffs of 65% in May, and 70% in the remaining months. Another measure was to support each customer and set priorities that could contribute to helping the customers keep their heads above water.

The result was a strengthened solidarity and an even better feeling for the company, followed by tremendous achievements, both by the company and its customers, but also by the community. During the month of July 2020, the company started to receive more orders, and in November, the company received more orders than ever. Everyone could keep their jobs and are now working full-time again, and, in addition, three more people have been recruited. There were also plans for further growth even though at that time they were still in the middle of the pandemic.

For us, this is an example where it was easier to act because the principles were clear before the crisis came. One of these principles was not to dismiss anyone because of financial problems but rather to start finding a solution where everyone could find a way out of the crisis together, and that in all these kinds of situations, the owner would find a solution together with the employees. In addition to this, another principle was to see the customers as part of the ecosystem and that their needs should be considered when prioritizing. The result speaks for itself: It pays off to put employees and customers first!

In difficult times, sacrifices are required from both owners and employees in order for everyone to get by. This can also bring people closer together into a larger community, which in turn can generate new profits.

THE CUSTOMER AND SUPPLIER PERSPECTIVE

The financial model also includes the financial interaction with customers and suppliers. As the DP model is based on a systemic, people-centered, and progressive approach, this should be reflected in the relationships with customers and suppliers. Thomas Dagsberg, founder of Jayway, used to say: "If things go well for our customers, things go well for us." That may be true as long as the customer treats its suppliers in a healthy way.

In the section on sustainability and social responsibility, we reasoned that the organization has a responsibility for the whole as being part of a value chain or circular economy. This means that the best interests of customers and suppliers must also be taken into account, not just the interests of the organization. The traditional relationship between customer and supplier is based on a transaction model where compensation is given per activity or transaction. In many cases, a power-based contract is created that is based on conflicting interests as both actors want to maximize their profit. The business model can also be performance-based, where compensation is given based on performance or achieved quality requirements.

In many countries, the public procurement process suffers from the transactional model where the public sector tries to define its requirements and calls for tenders, after which the supplier with the lowest bid is awarded the deal. The problem is that it is not always easy to define the requirements clearly or to know exactly what is needed. The suppliers often misinterpret the requirements, consciously or unconsciously. It is rare that either party is satisfied once the agreement has been reached. In many cases with, for example, IT solutions, the final product will be much more expensive than initially agreed. The lowest bid is not always the cheapest.

The traditional contracts focus on the wrong things such as limitation of liability, compensation for damages, or price and fee changes. The financial risk usually lies with the supplier. If you look at the supply chain, in many cases the ownership of inventory is with the supplier until the customer needs the product. The inventory is usually at the customer's premises but is still owned by the supplier, the so-called *Vendor Managed Inventory*. It could in some cases be a shared risk for this type of warehouse but in most cases the financial risk lies with the supplier. The incentives for the customer and the supplier often lead to conflicts of interest. In cases where services or product development are sold based on time and materials, the financial risk is usually shifted to the customer, which means that there is usually no incentive for the supplier to keep costs down.

The agile movement has a greater focus on relationships and partnerships, for example working closely with its stakeholders who may be customers or suppliers. The relationship becomes the basis of the work, which leads to greater trust and partnership. A focus on trust and partnership leads automatically to a different business model based on results, i.e. compensation when a commercial result is achieved. This is where the agile contracts, which are based on partnerships, come in.

An agreement is needed even if the work is done according to the principles of the DP model. In many cases it is difficult to describe what you want in detail, especially if something needs to be developed. An agile agreement is based on objectives and scope, a holistic view, and shared responsibility between each party. The company does not always try to find the right product or service, but rather to find the right supplier. In the ecosystem, the relationship between parties in a partnership must work according to, and be based on, a common approach. Values and principles cannot be contradictory. The financial risk, but also the opportunities, are balanced and the value that is created is put in the center. You can also take in Sociocracy For All's slogan, "Good enough for now, safe enough to try," and stop developing the product or service earlier and share the "profit" (for example, the remaining budget).

Jayway is a company that has always tried to develop good relationships based on trust and openness with its customers. In most cases it has worked very well, however there are some examples when it has not worked that well because the customer has had a strong transactional approach based on power. This shows that both parties need to use the same relationship model for it to work, especially if the parties want to have a long-term business relationship.

Suppliers should be treated in the same way as customers. The customer cannot use power against the supplier in a long-term relationship between two parties. In addition, it is in the customer's interest that the supplier makes a profit, as a supplier with financial problems becomes a major commercial risk. During the pandemic, several cases of stressful conditions have come to light. Many companies have had difficulty with liquidity and customers have in many cases supported them in terms of earlier payments, or, on the other hand, the supplier has increased the payment period.

A relationship-based business model between customer and supplier leads to better and long-term increased profitability for both parties.

HYBRID BUSINESS MODEL

Hybrid business models are a mix between models that strive solely for profitability and models that strive to address some of humanity's urgent issues. This means that both nonprofit and for-profit perspectives are combined into one model. Such models also take away the categorization of private and public organizations where the private ones traditionally focus on profit and the public ones on serving the people of a society. Furthermore, hybrid models are based on the claim that neither traditional for-profit nor nonprofit models can solve existing social and environmental problems.

In an article in 2012, Nardia Haigh and Andrew J. Hoffman published their research on organizations operating under a hybrid business model, where they identified three key areas. These three areas deal with attitudes towards the environment and towards both people and organizations: (1) driving positive social/environmental changes as an organization's goal; (2) creating mutually beneficial relationships with stakeholders; and (3) interacting progressively with the market, competitors, and industry.

What characterizes the business model in hybrid organizations is that it is designed to address explicit social and environmental issues, whereby business cases are secondary. This is in line with what Laloux indicates, namely that the profit "comes by itself."

Companies like Patagonia use a hybrid business model and have been like this since the start.

Several steps need to be taken if an organization wants to move its business model from traditional to hybrid.

The first step is to re-evaluate the organization's mission and include some social and environmental issues. These must of course be supported by the board and management team, if one exists. Once the issues are identified, anchored, and included in the mission, the next step is to ensure that they are integrated into the real work. The third step is to review how the work is carried out so that it does not contradict or become inconsistent with the new mission. The last and perhaps most demanding thing is to review all relationships with suppliers, customers, and other actors.

We illustrate these steps with an example:

The company Y re-evaluates its mission, which is to produce cardboard boxes, and includes two new environmental and social goals, namely:

- CO_2 emissions must be less than x%
- The workforce must be characterized by diversity and inclusion

When these issues are identified and anchored, it is time to introduce them into the daily work, which will bring about some changes in working methods and working environments. To be able to include employees with disabilities, there must also be doors that are adapted for wheelchairs, elevators, telephones for the hearing impaired, etc. For everyone to feel included regardless of gender, the toilets must be made for everyone and not with the traditional division into men and women. People who belong to a religion where you do not show yourself naked in front of other people must have changing rooms that allow for privacy.

The next step is to look at how work is carried out and this may lead to changes having to be made to reduce material waste and thus reduce CO_2 emissions, which is also achieved through less or different ways of traveling. It could also be to change working schedules so that single parents want to take up employment where they can handle picking up and dropping off the children at preschool.

The relationship with the suppliers may need to be reviewed, and if they do not meet the requirements for CO_2 emissions or diversity and inclusion, the company may have to decide to change supplier. The suppliers shall, in the first instance, be influenced to make the same changes.

In addition to these steps, there may also be other projects or initiatives out in the community that work with these two goals, and which the company can support. Contributing financial support or freeing up working hours so that some from the company can participate can encourage people to participate as volunteers, much like K2K and the NER group do.

Voice from the field: Fredrik Palmgren – Co-founder of Centigo, Stockholm, Sverige

Fredrik Palmgren is co-founder of Centigo and Business Wellness Group. Fredrik believes that the traditional way of organizing and managing companies is a holdover from the Industrial Revolution and is the solution to the problems from that time. Today, we have completely different conditions and challenges. Fredrik has spent the last 20 years exploring how a modern company should work. Centigo is the result – an employee-owned, managerless, and ambition-driven company where engagement is the engine.

Here I share my thoughts on various areas relating to the financial aspects of business.

First, how I view financial structure such as ownership, capital, and investments.

Sweden is moving at high speed from a production economy to a service economy. Digitization means a turbo effect in this movement. However, many norms and rules in society remain in traditional industrialism. The classic conflict between work and capital is becoming increasingly diffuse, especially as the "capital" of the service economy is mostly knowledge and ability.

I believe that many service companies emerging today would be better off being employee-owned. In the long run, it is important for the development of society that companies act as positive social actors – the responsible company. I think it is best done if the owners, employees, and citizens tend to be the same people. For example, I think it would be good if companies in the healthcare sector could be employee-owned. We would then probably get a better balance between ethics, accessibility, and economy as decisions can be made with greater precision and in every situation.

If the legislature continues to reason that there are two distinct sources of income, labor and capital, and that these cannot be combined, then we will have continued increased economic inequality as capital yields so much more and belongs to so many fewer.

In service companies, investments are largely made in the abilities of employees. With the Internet, knowledge has become significantly more accessible. Therefore, the focus should be directed towards training interaction and developing the personal qualities of the employees. The value lies in getting employees to become more independent so they can handle more complex situations faster.

You can reason about this much like a football team. You play matches together with customers and you have a "training facility" at home.

A challenge when it comes to investing in the abilities of individuals is that the result depends on the motivation. In order to do this effectively, "training" should be voluntary and financed to a certain extent by the individual, preferably, compared to university studies where the time is paid for by the individual. Taking personal responsibility is absolutely key for the training to produce results. Increasing employee engagement is likely one of the biggest potentials in traditional companies. Then the people must be trained to understand interaction and their own role, their own ambition, their own need for development, and, above all, be able to make their own decisions.

Switching to a financial code of conduct, you have to think about who you collaborate with and whether there are any types of customers, suppliers, or partners you do or do not do business with.

Relationships, trust, and reputation are central values for service companies. Being a good social actor and following the rules decided by our elected officials is crucial. However, it is not always easy as many rules are based on a traditional business view. The development around us is moving so fast that it is difficult for politicians to keep up, especially as the lobbying organizations built up during industrialism are strong and the new modern companies that are emerging lack the corresponding influence. The result is often that rules that are meant to support companies are relevant for traditional industrial companies but become directly counterproductive for modern knowledge and service companies.

Rules in all their glory, there is also a question of ethics and morality. This question is more difficult as compliance is dependent on one's own conscience and one's own perception of what is right and wrong. The challenge lies in the polarity between finance and reputation. In other words, short-term and long-term results. With the concentration of influence that prevails in strictly hierarchical companies, this polarity lands on a few people in a senior position. At the same time, these are exposed to heavy pressure from the owners and the board. Then it can be tempting to "cut some corners." The result is major risks in the company and personal tragedies for individual employees.

Many solve this with beautiful objectives on the website and have a kind of balance argumentation by donating funds to worthy organizations as a kind of compensation for a bad conscience. I do not believe in that!

For long-term success, authenticity is important. Ethics and morals must be in the company culture, and through transparency and personal responsibility, you make the entire company ambassadors for the good company. This is more difficult in traditional hierarchies and more natural in modern networked companies.

Finally, some of my thoughts around business models.

It is still ironic that entrepreneurs in most cases praise free competition and the market economy. Nevertheless, most companies are structured quite precisely like a planned economy of the Soviet model. It is first and foremost a dictatorship with a clear hierarchy and a clear difference between managers and staff. Extensive financial planning is done in the form of multi-year plans (strategies) and budgets, and the little information that reaches the staff is always prepared. Managers think and decide, and the staff execute their orders. Control of the business is extensive and confidence in individuals' ability to solve dilemmas on their own initiative is low.

This model works well in a world where the direction of development is clear and where there are high barriers to entry. However, this world is a thing of the past. Today, development is often unpredictable and barriers to entry are constantly being lowered in step with digitization.

Today, creativity, innovation, and interaction are central values, and these are based on culture and the abilities and commitment of individuals rather than on structure and command. It is then necessary to create a joyful context with game rules that set an external framework and that provide a game plan where there is freedom for the individual to show their abilities, their creativity, and their ambition – very similar to a market economy with an interaction between free actors who in competition create value.

THE WAY FORWARD

In this part of the book, we will summarize the essence of previous chapters and present some approaches that facilitate the journey towards a new way of organizing work where people are at the center. There are also pitfalls. It is easy to fall down, or fall back, when it feels tough, and sometimes it would be nice to have a boss who just decides.... The DP model is not the end of a journey, it is something to lean on, a traveling companion on an ongoing journey.

IMPROVEMENT OR A NEW DISRUPTIVE PARADIGM?

We have previously described the DP model as a path to a progressive and systemic approach to organizing work. Are we facing a crossroads where we are moving towards a new way of looking at organizing or is the way forward a straight development of previous approaches?

We introduced Frederic Laloux and his book *Reinventing Organizations* in the introduction section. But before Laloux and Teal, there were many variants of progressive organizational forms that attempted to move organizations away from hierarchical power structures created during industrialization and heavily influenced by Taylor's theories of the organization as a machine. The way of working today has moved from a horizontal process to a network of interactions and relationships among people. The traditional matrix organization where you put a vertical function-oriented organization in a horizontal cross-functional process is difficult to apply when our world is becoming increasingly knowledge-intensive with many interactions and with an increasingly changing environment. In addition to, or perhaps together with, this, the digital and technical development has gone faster and faster, and today, technology and digital information are a natural part of most work. All this means that new ways of organizing work and looking at people are needed, which has been part of the background to the DP model.

Another area that we are convinced needs to be reformed is recruitment, which has become a long and administrative process, regardless of whether the organization is traditional or progressive.

First of all: All people have talents and potential. People will be happier, more engaged, and achieve better results if they get the opportunity to use their talent and potential.

In traditional forms of organizing, people are assigned tasks that in many cases are not linked to the individual's ability but rather to the position that the person is to fill. On several occasions, the recruiter tries to find people who match the position 100%, even though their previous experience does not automatically mean that they will do the work in the same way in a new workplace. As previously mentioned, most people do not want to do exactly the same thing they did before looking for a new job. We also see that new generations require a changed approach in order to be attracted.

The traditional way of centralizing power and decisions high up in a hierarchy means that the system becomes slow and sluggish and that a systemic approach becomes difficult. A systemic approach means that own organization itself, but also everything around it in an ecosystem, needs to be considered. Our belief is that this is done by distributing power and decisions out to the nodes and thus minimizing power. The word "power" is not needed if decisions are made by those who can and are close to those affected. If the group, the organization, the team, and the people know their area of responsibility, then it becomes natural for them to make decisions in this area, no power in terms of authority is needed.

Nevertheless, we call our model "Distributed Power." This is because we want to tear down the hierarchical power pyramids and let the people in the organization become responsible for their work and, not least, for how the work is organized. We are not saying there should not be hierarchies, which work very well for structuring work. However, we are moving from being process-centered to being people-centered. Processes for work will be needed but with people in the center. We see the DP model as part of the wave that is a new disruptive paradigm regarding how working is organized and also the view of work. Today, work is part of a person's whole, which also includes family, society, the outside world, etc. But the DP model can also be used by any organization that wants to make a change in one or some of the 12 areas that we have gone through in this book.

Many of the organizations we have studied have worked actively with one of these areas, even if they have not adopted a systemic approach.

In addition to having studied and, above all, talked to many organizations and people who want to act differently in terms of organizing, we have also talked to those who want to keep traditional forms of organizing and weave them into the whole. As Laloux writes about the evolution of organizational principles, we assume that there is a history that we bring with us when we are looking ahead.

In this part of the book, we will present some tools that facilitate the journey towards a new way of organizing where people are at the center.

MAKING THE JOURNEY SMOOTH

Using the DP model does not mean that you have to work with all the parts equally and at the same time. All organizations have strengths and weaknesses, and different prerequisites. What is typical is that the journey often starts in the culture. We see also that when purpose and principles are not in place, it is difficult to work with the other parts. One can choose to work with only certain areas of the model, for example decision-making models or sustainability and social responsibility, but other areas must be considered to maintain the systemic approach.

If a change is to be made in the organization, it will be easier if the majority of those affected accept the change. Several of those we have spoken to, and who have managed this type of change, claim that 70–80 % should be on board in order to start the journey. There are several ways to get people involved, for example visiting other organizations, holding seminars, training sessions, and meetings where people can ask questions, etc. Getting as many people as possible involved is a good prerequisite for success.

Actually, this is a "top-down" way of looking at change. However, our experience is that many initiatives can start from below, in a "bottom-up" procedure. We see that many cultural changes take place in groups, teams, and constellations. These are then followed by others in the organization. Many of those who say that management, boards, and others should be involved in order for a change to take place are schooled in a philosophy of change characterized by Kotter's theories where one of the first steps is to create a *"sense of urgency."* This is a traditional way of driving major changes and transformations and it is based on an old view that all structures are fixed and must be eliminated. Today, when the pace of change is already very high, most people are used to, and are more open to, change. The important thing is to clarify the principles for the organization and thus also accepted and nonaccepted behaviors. This can take place in organizational units in a larger organization, for example in a team or a department. In addition to this, never underestimate the force from "below."

It is essential that management is on board to consciously start a transfer that includes the entire organization. The board must also be involved if it is going to be a sustainable transfer. However, we have seen that in some organizations the journey has started in certain islands of the organization and then been spread.

Jurgen Appelo (known from the agile movement) described in his book *How to Change the World: Change Management 3.0* the following aspects of a change journey:

1. Make changes in small steps and adapt the journey based on steps taken (plan – do – check – act)
2. Consider the people in the organization. Everyone is different and it is the people who make the change
3. Stimulate the network, it is in the network that the change spreads
4. Change the environment by enabling and stimulating communication, transparency, and good behavior

The approach of being able to start small or anywhere in the organization is advocated by S3 and is what differentiates them from Holacracy and SoFA.

PITFALLS

Because cultural journeys are journeys that never end, they are difficult to describe, but above all, they cannot be copied. There is no complete description of the journey, instead each organization must have its own compass and find its way forward. There are some pitfalls, and since every organization starts from a different starting point and is different, these pitfalls can have a different level of impact. Below we list the most important of these, based on what we have seen in the various case studies and from the implementations we have participated in. Our hope is that you will be careful not to fall too far into these pitfalls. Note that the numbering does not refer to a ranking.

Pitfall #1 Not knowing why you are making the trip

A journey always starts somewhere. People do not always know when it starts and why, but there are different levels of engagement, understanding, and responsibility when it is initiated.

If it has been initiated from below, from a few teams, there is enormous power among those who are initiators but there is also a risk of creating a "them and us" if everyone does not understand what is going on and why the journey should be made. It gets even worse if different people or groups create different truths regarding why the change is happening. Furthermore, management can stop or oppose major changes if they see no point in making them. If a change is initiated from the top of the hierarchy but there is not a real majority on board with why and what is wanted to be achieved, it can lead to not getting anywhere or taking far too long. What is wanted to be achieved, why, and an overall explanation of what it will mean for everyone are essential elements to create engagement, identify resistance early, and be able to make something of the change.

Pitfall #2 Principles and prerequisites are not in place

Principles govern what the organization should be like and are the guidance that governs everything that is done in it.

Culture is based on principles, and it is not possible to make a cultural journey in a smooth way without having these principles clear from the beginning.

The more freedom people are allowed to have, the more clarity around the framework is needed. If operational and tactical decisions are to be made by those who have contact with the customers, the production organization, and/or the supplier, they must know what applies when making decisions. When these day-to-day decisions are not made by a manager, different people on the team must make their own, which also follows the principles. For example, if the principle is to always protect the brand and to have satisfied customers, a person in customer support can receive a defective product and decide to exchange it for something else even if the customer does not have a receipt.

Pitfall #3 Believing it is just a "behavioral journey"

Changing an organization and putting people at the center, giving everyone a voice, and thinking systemically represents a behavioral journey. But thinking it is just a behavioral journey is a big mistake. It is about being able to handle structure, working methods, decision-making, business acumen, and also having a high level of competence in both organizational theory and business models.

In those organizations that only focus on changing behaviors and attitudes, chaos is created, and the journey can be like a roller coaster. It takes longer and causes both stress and desperation despite good intentions. It is excellent to get help from psychologists and behaviorists to support the soft side of the transformation and to promote the needed skills. But do not forget to accept help from mentors who know organizational theories, have worked in organizations, have business skills, and who are not only coaches with behavioral science as a basis.

Pitfall #4 Past conflicts that have never been resolved remain

In most organizations there are conflicts and in the traditional hierarchies the managers sometimes act like mediators, which means that the conflicts do not blow up or spread further but are not resolved either. If there is not a culture of transparency, people do not normally talk about conflicts or undesirable behaviors. Starting a journey without having resolved these kinds of issues or tensions can exacerbate the situation, which can lead to bullying and sick leave, and resistance to the change journey can arise.

Pitfall #5 The belief that "we will find the way"

There are some proponents and leading figures in self-organizing who claim that there is no need for guidance, principles, or other means of control. They base their claim on the view that people are wise by nature and that adults should be able to find their way and see what is best for the organization and for themselves. Although this is a good way of looking at people, it is a naive approach. In some cases, it can be compared to leaving a group of inexperienced people in a sailboat on the Pacific Ocean and hoping that they will make it ashore under their own power.

Working with self-organizing and democratization of the workplace, and thus creating a systemic approach, is not the same as creating anarchy or as opening a water dam and then standing by and watching where all the water goes. It requires leadership and competence in the area, even in cases where the managerial role does not exist (see the section on leadership where we discuss the difference between the managerial role and leadership as an area of expertise).

Pitfall #6 The board is not on board

Many of those who write about this type of change journey say the same thing as all classic Change Management methods: "Management must be involved." We reasoned earlier that you can start the change only in a part of the organization, which is completely feasible. But if the change is to include the entire organization, then of course the board must be part of the journey. We have seen cases where the board thinks the change is interesting when it is going well, but if you don't show positive financial results, they can suddenly stop or demand a different approach. The board is part of the package if you want to go all the way. The members of the board must understand and accept that the organization will be governed by systemic principles and stand behind these.

Pitfall #7 The copy-paste syndrome

We have mentioned this before, but it is important to point out again: It is not possible to directly copy someone else's journey and think it will work. What works at Buurtzorg, where everyone has the same profession, does not work in exactly the same way in an organization with different professional groups and a different context. Our advice is that you should be inspired by other organizations, collect metaphors and examples, but not try to copy them. It is about finding a way that fits in a specific context and sometimes you have to experiment to find the right way.

Pitfall #8 Mix operational, tactical, and strategic decisions

As we have previously mentioned, there is a need to distinguish between different types of decisions. Not everyone can be involved in deciding everything. We have seen in some organizations that are moving from a hierarchy of authority to a more progressive form that the belief is that everyone must be involved in deciding everything. The result is chaos and discussions take a long time, which leads to frustration. Operational decisions must be made by those involved, which can also be a single person. Each unit must have a given area of responsibility within which decisions of an operational and tactical nature are made. Cross-functional groups usually work with tactical decisions regarding the development of the business. Sometimes, this can be rather difficult and the focus often shifts to operational issues. Strategic decisions should involve people who have complementary knowledge and who can come up with a proposal that forms the basis for the decision. Many forums and groups focus on the wrong things if these different types of levels are not clear.

Pitfall #9 Starting at the wrong end or trying to do everything at the same time

It is tempting to want to do as much as possible, to change and move as quickly as possible, but it is not recommended. Different stages or areas require different levels of maturity. Starting with the salary model and making everyone's salaries public, without having worked with culture, people, and communication, can end up in chaos. It will expose some injustices that have been going on for a long time. If the people do not have the tools to deal with the feelings that arise, it can provoke anger, frustration, and a desire to leave the organization.

Regular business must continue and starting many things at the same time can also cause chaos, stress, and a feeling that everything is floating around. Starting with one or a few areas but in early stages mapping the impact on the others is a good and agile approach.

Pitfall #10 Not training people enough or long enough
This pitfall is what many organizations starting the journey suffer from, even those that are aware that training is needed. It takes time to be self-organized, to let everyone have a voice, to understand that operational decisions must be made by those on the front line, to show one's vulnerability, to communicate openly, to let the strong egos go, etc. It is not enough to train a few, or to train once and think it is fixed. People will continue to work in other contexts where there are hierarchies of authority, the society around the organization is still working according to old norms and values, new employees are recruited, and similar things. For that reason, constant reminders and planned exercises will be needed for a long time.

APPROACH TO SUCCESS

The journey towards self-organizing and democratization of the workplace can be done in different ways and each organization must find its own. But regardless of which path is chosen, there are some steps that have to be taken. The DP model can be used as a guide where each part can be analyzed.

Figure 20 presents the 12 areas of the DP model having five levels each. This representation of the DP-model can be used to measure how far the organization have reached in each area and also to see possible gaps from a systemic point of view as well as visualizing the way forward.

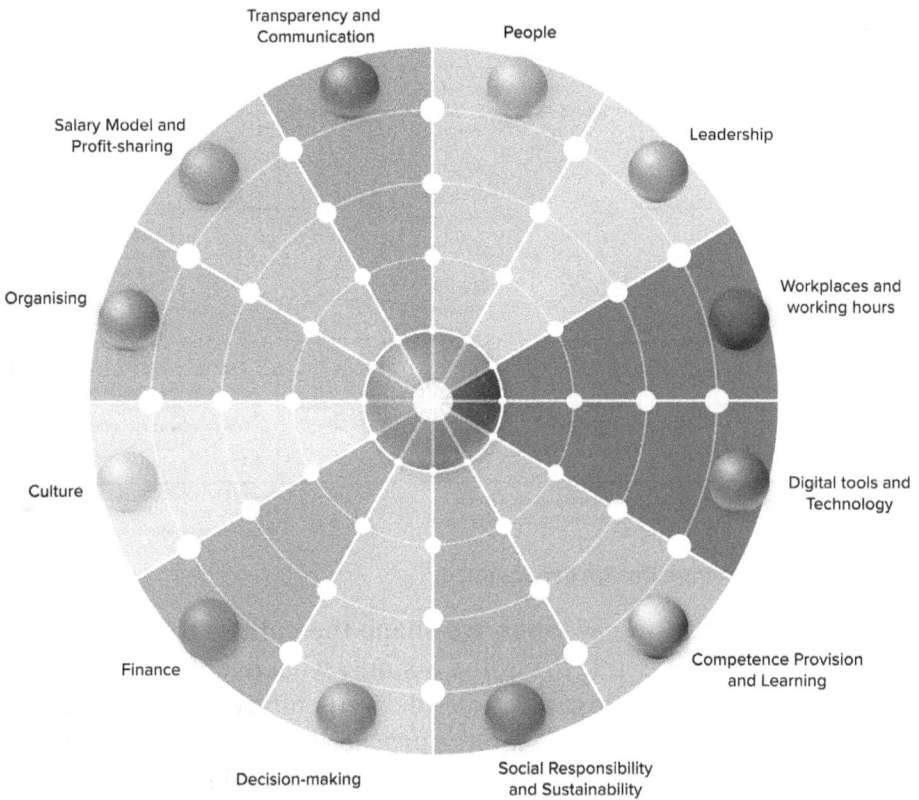

Figure 20. The DP model as a tool for measurement

There are also other tools and approaches that can be helpful, and in this section we present some of them that we highly recommend.

Culture Design Canvas

The journey starts in the culture and one tool that can be used is the Culture Design Canvas (see Figure 21), which was developed by Gustavo Razzetti (see further in the section on culture).

CULTURAL DESIGN CANVAS
Design a workplace culture that propels you into the future

Team name: [   ]   Date: [   ]

DECISION-MAKING	PRIORITIES	RITUALS
How is authority distributed? What methods do we use to make decisions?	Select the top three cultural priorities using even over statements	How do we celebrate our people, culture, and work?

PURPOSE
Why do we exist?

MEETINGS		FEEDBACK
How do we convene and collaborate?		How do we help each other learn and grow?

VALUES
What do we believe in?

NORMS & RULES	BEHAVIORS	PSYCHOLOGICAL SAFETY
How do we clarify expected behaviors without hindering autonomy?	What behaviors do we punish? What behaviors do we reward?	How do we encourage everyone to speak up? How do we promote participation and candor?

Designed by Gustavo Razzetti
FearlessCulture
www.fearlessculture.design

Figure 21. Culture Design Canvas (CDC)

This is a tool we use when we shape the culture to start the journey. It is possible to outline not only what it looks like right now, but also the organization's desired culture. The heart of the culture is the organization's purpose and what values it has. These form the basis of the principles, i.e. the rules and norms that must exist, which in turn govern what is accepted and not accepted in terms of behavior. The CDC describes which behaviors are rewarded and which are punished. The words "reward" and "punish" may feel harsh, but they mean which behaviors we give positive feedback to and which we do not accept. A rewarded behavior in an organization can be, for example, daring to make mistakes, while an undesirable behavior can be having a hidden agenda.

Other things that are addressed in the CDC are which methods are used to make decisions at different times, how meetings should work, rituals that exist, and how to feed back to each other to grow together. As part of the definition of the culture, we also go through the philosophy of prioritization, especially when you have to choose between two good things. Finally, we need a definition of how psychological safety (see the section on people) should work in our organization. What must be in place for people to be participatory and sincere and not driven to silence?

The CDC is a very efficient tool for defining the starting point and having a target of what you want the culture to look like. We see the tool as a more developed and modern way to develop a solution than the traditional As-Is – To-Be description (analysis of current situation and expected goal) that is generally used in organizational development.

The tool is suitable for use in workshop form, and we have seen that it also works very well in online workshops in combination with tools such as Mural, which we presented in the digitization and technology section.

You start by developing the current situation through the following steps:

1. Purpose and values as they are experienced today, perhaps not what is written in the document, on coffee mugs, or walls, but what is experienced as genuine.
2. Find out which behaviors are present in the organization today and which we encourage (reward) or signal as undesirable (punish). Which things do people think are good things to do and which are not allowed to be done?
3. When the behaviors are clear, norms and rules are drawn up in the organization. These are the behaviors that are expected.
4. The next step is to define how meetings are conducted. Is there a culture of many meetings? If so, do they have agendas? What do they result in? Who participates?
5. After analyzing the meetings, it is natural to think about how to make decisions in the organization. What methods are used and who are involved? Here you can consider the different levels of decisions that we discussed in the section on decision-making.
6. Prioritization is the next area. In this step it is important to think about how principles govern the priorities and form

sentences in *Even Over Statements*. These kinds of statements come from Holacracy and mean that you need to be able to prioritize between several things that are positive.

7. The next area is rituals. What things do you celebrate and how? Which symbols are important? What traditions are there?

8. How do we feed back to each other? Do we use direct feedback? Do we help each other? Is there a lot of collaboration? These are some questions that you can ask yourself. One should also think about the openness within the organization.

9. The last step is psychological safety. What does the organization do to make people feel safe in speaking their mind? Through all the steps it is easy to think about what you would like it to be like and that applies especially to this step. Here one should try to be honest and describe what level of psychological safety exists today.

By analyzing the results of the current situation, we continue to the desired situation by going through all the steps again. In this phase the focus will be on what we want each part to be like. It is surprising to see how quickly you can come to a picture of what the culture looks like today and how you want it to look in the future. The method can be advantageously combined with REPI as we describe below, and you can take reflection rounds to obtain a good result.

Tension Mapping

In an organization there are always tensions, things that cause small conflicts between people. In order to create openness and transparency, most of these tensions need to be resolved. One of the methods we successfully use in this area comes from Target Teal in Brazil and is called "Tension Mapping," a mapping that aims to bring out tensions that are not openly spoken about. In tension mapping, the following steps are taken:

1. Interviews with people individually or in groups. With individual interviews, there is a risk that people turn to complaining rather than giving a nuanced view. Group interviews are usually more effective and where various things bubbling under the surface can come to light. Here, it is important not to have the manager in the same group to avoid stopping people from expressing their thoughts.
2. Analyze the data from the interviews and create different types of codes and summarized concepts aiming to bring out patterns.
3. Group different areas and create some kind of diagram, for example an affinity diagram or mind map. This is to have different areas that can be given to different groups to work with. Here you can advantageously use the different areas of the DP model.
4. Create an action list with the prioritized actions. This is done both top-down and bottom-up.
5. Involve everyone in working on actions. Here it becomes important that people choose which area they want to work with. This is part of the journey where the people themselves must choose their tasks and not be assigned work.

The most important tensions will emerge by going through these steps and you can start working with them and thus create a better climate, but this is above all a start of the journey. In many cases, there are tensions between different teams or groups, which are based on a lack of communication, openness, and transparency. Actively working on this is a part of the journey.

REPI®

Within the DP model, we see that relationships and interactions between people are essential. Therefore, tools are needed that support these interactions. REPI stands for *Reflection, Elaboration, Practicing/Participation,* and *Investigation,* which are four different modes where learning and exchange take place in different ways. We have developed and worked with REPI in various ways since the early 2000s and the method supports a progressive form of organizing such as Sociocracy, Teal, Holacracy, etc.

REPI is a tool that has many areas of use: meetings, sharing knowledge, learning, brainstorming, co-creation, coaching, training, and more. Below we delve deeply into the basis of the method and then give examples of different areas of use.

Reflection means bringing together and constructing one's own thoughts and opinions within a given subject or situation. In this mode, associations with previous knowledge and experiences are created, and the person develops an opinion on the subject. People can reflect on mistakes, successes, new insights, what others have said, their own presentation, or anything else. In the reflection mode, previous activities are considered and seen from different perspectives, with the aim of learning from these.

Elaboration is the way or the activities in which the mind, with given information and facts, makes assumptions, interprets, and associates with other subjects. It can also be defined as being able to take an idea and improve it. The focus will be on adding new details and things to create a logical and comprehensible order within the information that exists. This mental process is highly selective and is linked to people's own preferences, current needs, and/or prior knowledge. In addition, it is about filling the information gaps through one's own thoughts without searching for new information.

Depending on the purpose and context in which REPI is used, P stands for either Participation or Practicing, or both. Participation is the mode where people share knowledge or interact with others, which means they actively participate in a discussion. It is also about sharing knowledge with others and expressing and discussing opinions. Practicing, on the other hand, is about testing ideas, and putting into practice newly acquired skills or insights. You can either practice alone or together with others and then share knowledge, solve problems, or try new and unknown things.

Investigation is about searching for information, facts, and experiences in addition to what is already available. It is about trying to use different sources such as the Internet, literature, benchmarking, analyzing how others do, good examples, case studies, and standards. If possible, discuss with others who have experience in the relevant subject area or make visits to study the subject.

In REPI there is no predetermined order, but you can choose the position that you think fits best at that particular moment. One can, for example, reflect after testing new ideas.

REPI MEETING

A REPI meeting is a meeting where the REPI method and a series of techniques are used, for example, to increase the group's competence in a specific subject, develop solutions and proposals, create consensus, co-create, and make decisions based on the group's joint proposals. The meetings usually have a goal and are managed by a REPI facilitator. These meetings are efficient, last 45–90 minutes, and ensure that all participants have a voice.

The following real-life cases illustrate how a REPI meeting can be used.

A team in a large company is working on the task of finding a new digital solution for recruitment that will replace the existing one. People from different departments, with knowledge and experience from different subject areas, are members of the team. They gather for the very first meeting.

The facilitator begins the meeting with the reflection mode by asking the team: "What do we want to achieve by choosing a new solution, and what are the strengths and weaknesses of the current solution?" In addition, the facilitator presents some facts such as the number of recruitments currently being made, the time it takes to complete a recruitment, and the average cost of recruitment. Based on this information, the team is given a few minutes to reflect on the questions and these facts. In the next step, the REPI facilitator asks the team to share their reflections as a first round. In the second round, participants are given the opportunity to comment on the reflections that have been presented. This is the Participation mode from the REPI model. An important thing at this stage is to facilitate everyone's participation and create a constructive, open, and genuine interest in the subject.

The next step is Elaboration, which is carried out by having the participants work for a short while in small groups or individually, using a technique called "parallel thinking." This technique means that the groups work in parallel on the same task after having delved deeply into the available information. In this case, the team worked on three main questions:

1. Where do we want to be when the work is done?
2. What are the needs that the new solution will fulfill?
3. What are the most important aspects to consider?

After this, the groups worked on different areas. One of the groups delved deeply into the financial aspects and the time for completing a recruitment. Another group chose to look at the usability of the solution with a focus on satisfied users and the reduced need for support. Finally, the third group focused on efficient communication, transparency, and collaboration when implementing a new solution. The groups carried out their work by developing proposals through discussion in rounds and with consent as a decision model.

After Elaboration in the groups, a new Participation activity was started in which all groups presented the conclusions they had reached, and several new insights were presented. The groups had worked without specified instructions, which allowed them to be innovative and tackle the task from different points of view. The meeting ended by agreeing that the team members, for the next meeting, would look for solutions, read HR articles focusing on recruitment, contact some consulting companies and ask them to share their experiences, and conduct benchmarking of what other companies have done in the field. This meant entering Investigation mode. The next REPI meeting started with a round where the team members shared what they had found. This was followed by a round of reflection regarding how the investigation had been carried out and what had been concluded so far.

The work progressed according to this process to gradually arrive at a proposal where no one had any objections.

This is an example of how you can use REPI to gradually produce proposals for decisions within, for example, Sociocracy. Of course, REPI can be used regardless of organizational form, but a culture based on openness and equality gives a much better result. The method involves everyone, supports innovation and participation, and creates safety in that everyone can express their thoughts and ideas.

COACHING AND MENTORING

A session can be considered a REPI meeting as above but with only two participants – the coach/mentor and the person. The session can start by reflecting on a certain topic and by discussing reflections and questions. This session can be followed by Elaboration, where you develop a possible solution that the person could put into practice. The next session may begin by reviewing the experiences of what has been practiced, followed by reflection on what can be improved or incorporated as part of normal work. Depending on the purpose of the coaching or mentorship, the individual may be asked to read a book that will be discussed later, or to visit another company to gain new knowledge (Investigation).

There are many ways to approach coaching and mentoring based on REPI, but the basics are for people to reflect, develop ideas, practice, and search for new information and knowledge.

COMPETENCE DEVELOPMENT

Using REPI for competence development for individuals or groups follows the same flow as for meetings and coaching according to REPI. The purpose of the competence development activity is to develop a person's competence in a specific subject, area, or situation. Competence development takes place in everyday life and active learning is what creates continuous and lasting learning. In the real example of the REPI meeting previously presented, the aim was to gain deeper knowledge regarding not only a new specific solution for recruitment but also this kind of solution in general. Here people reflected together, developed new ideas, sought information, and tried out. This can also be done individually by reflecting on the area you want to develop, finding new angles and information, practicing, and gradually reaching new insights.

This way of developing people's competence can be used as support for development talks and similar.

TEAM BUILDING

A team can use REPI to create a stronger connection by addressing various topics that affect the team, reflecting, developing new ways of working, seeking new information, testing new things, and in this way strengthening the cohesion of the team. The Tension Mapping work described above can be carried out with the help of REPI and thus strengthen the cohesion in the organization.

TEACHING

REPI has its basis in teaching and learning where the course participants work with specific tasks and where they are given tasks that are high level without detailed instructions. The students work in groups with the task, reflect on what they have reached, seek information from different sources, develop new proposals, and so on. This approach also creates active learning as opposed to passive learning when you have a lecture or similar.

The power of REPI lies in the fact that it provides people with a technique to learn, refine, and build new skills, understand, and gain insights about each other and about different subjects. A team that uses REPI meetings continuously uses each meeting as an arena for learning, for sharing, for innovative thinking, and for collaboration. In a self-organized team, the REPI facilitator role can shift between different members of the team.

R&F – Retrospective & Feedforward

We presented the best-known methods of feedback in the section on communication and transparency. Feedforward was one of these and the strength of this particular method is that it is forward-looking and solution oriented. What is missing in the method is an objective analysis and reflection over the past, and therefore the learnings are lost.

We have also seen that, above all, in organizations dominated by the "green paradigm" (Laloux's definition), where people are able to experiment, there is an environment that allows mistakes but where the focus is almost solely on the future. This often leads to very quickly drawing a line across what has been and rushing on to do things in a different way. This is absolutely not optimal. The advantage of experimenting and being able to make mistakes lies in the learning process that the mistakes lead to, but without reflection, learning is reduced and mistakes can be repeated.

On the other hand, only looking back and thinking about what has happened, and why, rarely leads forward. Within agile methods, you analyze what has happened and how tasks have been performed. This is called Retrospective, which we combine with Feedforward, which, according to Marshall Goldsmith, is a human-to-human coaching process. With these combined, we have developed a method that we call "R&F" (Retrospective & Feedforward).

The method is efficient because it does not take much time and can be used for one-on-one meetings and in teams. It is based on two simple steps:

1. The conversation begins with a retrospective part, without any element of feedback, where it is important to listen to each other without evaluating. The further the group has come in its openness and trust, the easier it becomes to both talk and listen. It is neither about criticizing nor encouraging, but only about presenting in an objective and constructive way what did not work and thus explaining what needs to be solved. No in-depth details are needed, but rather a simple description of the impact of what needs to be resolved.

2. When what did not work has been presented, the conversation moves to Feedforward, that is, to looking ahead. The focus here is to find solutions and think of various concrete steps that can be taken to improve what is not working satisfactorily. The central idea here is that each person suggests and takes on what they should do themselves. There is no one assigning tasks or actions to anyone else, which automatically creates ownership of the activities needed to be done.

R&F is based on the REPI model, and if R&F is to be used by teams, rounds are included.

Sociocratic agile – governance model for Scrum

In this section, we present a method that can help organizations working with agile methods to take the next step in their journey towards self-organizing. As we mentioned in the section on progressive organizational models, the governance model is the weakness of most agile methods and frameworks. We also mentioned that agile is more of a culture, while there are different types of methods and frameworks for development, for example Scrum (see Figure 22).

Today, there are several software and product development companies that use different methods to connect different agile teams while trying to create some kind of overall governance. Reviewing these methods is beyond the scope of this book. However, we have seen that these methods do not work satisfactorily in other types of companies or in large companies where the different backlogs must be connected, even if they are not part of the same product.

Sociocratic agile is a combination of Sociocracy and agile where we combine these two into a method for working agile but supplement it with the governance model according to Sociocracy.

Scrum is based on one or more teams working systematically with iterative deliverables, so-called "sprints." There is a product owner who, together with the team, prioritizes in a backlog (to-do list) and the team independently chooses which tasks to do during the next sprint, which can be one to four weeks. There is a Scrum Master, who is the coaching leader of the team. The difficulty arises when there are many dependencies between different teams who have different priorities in their backlogs and different product owners who own the backlogs. The process is visualized in Figure 22 below.

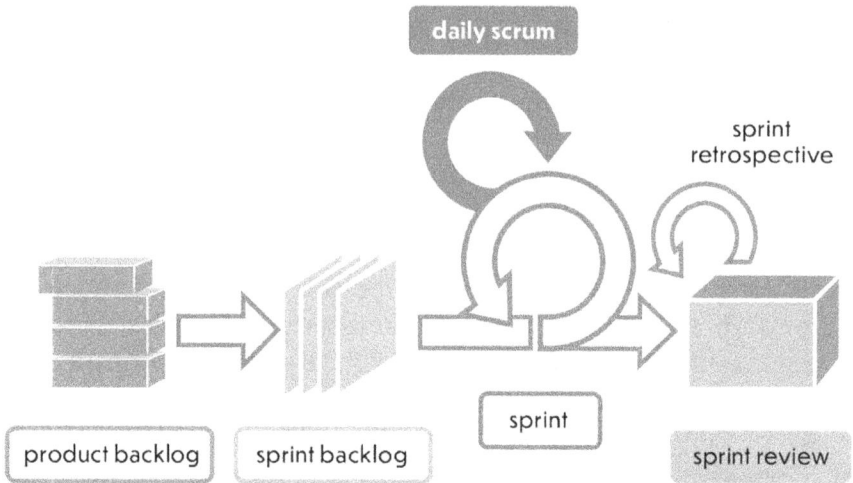

Figure 22. The Scrum process

Since Sociocracy is built up by different teams called "circles" where the team is self-organized, and where one of the roles in the circle is the facilitator, a circle is very similar to a Scrum team and the facilitator is similar to the Scrum Master.

In Sociocracy, the parent circle (1 in Figure 23) appoints a leader for the subcircle (2 in Figure 23). The leader's focus is that the circle performs its tasks in line with its purpose and goals, and with future issues. The leader creates the circle and is responsible for communication from the parent circle to the circle. This role is similar to the Product Owner role in Scrum. Since Sociocracy is based on double-linking (3 in Figure 23), the circle appoints a delegate as a representative in the parent circle. The scrum team can appoint a person with deep knowledge of the product or solution they are working on, thus ensuring that there is domain knowledge of the product/solution in the parent circle. The delegate can also be the Scrum Master, which is up to the team to decide.

As the parent circle can have many subcircles (4 in figure 23) with leaders and delegates from each subcircle represented, you get the whole. Dependencies that are not resolved within the Scrum team can be taken up for decision in the parent circle

(1 in Figure 23) and solution proposals are developed through the consent method. If dependencies must be investigated, a support circle (5 in Figure 23) with relevant members can be established. The support circle can be connected directly to the parent circle or to the subcircles involved in the investigation. In this way, the overall prioritization between different Scrum teams is managed and, in addition, the governance model for decisions, prioritization, etc. is ensured.

Depending on the complexity of the organization, several parent circles can be connected to an additional level to ensure the whole (6 in Figure 23).

A parameter to take into account is that a person can be a member of several circles; that is, there is no restriction that one person must belong to a specific circle or team.

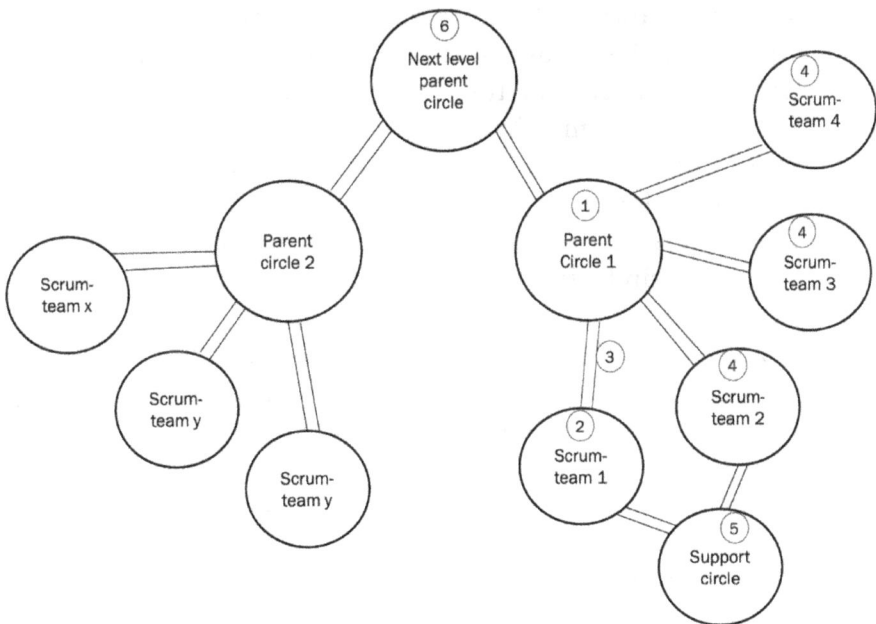

Figure 23. Comparison of Sociocracy and Scrum

Comparison of roles and concepts between Sociocracy and Scrum

Sociocracy	Scrum
Leader	Product Owner (Scrum Master can in some cases take all or part of this role)
Facilitator (manages meetings and the decision-making process)	Scrum Master
Secretary	Scrum Master
Delegate	Does not exist as a role in normal Scrum. Selected by the team
Circle	Team

Approach in a traditional organization using Scrum

1. The parent circle appoints a leader of a subcircle, who is the product owner. The team must consent to this role.
2. The Scrum Master takes the roles of facilitator and secretary, which means that the Scrum Master facilitates and documents joint meetings, for example *daily stand-up*, *sprint planning*, *review* meeting, and *retrospective* according to Scrum principles.
3. The team selects a delegate who becomes a full member of the parent circle. In a digital development team, this could be, for example, a system architect or product specialist. It can also be the Scrum Master. Selecting a specialist means that you bring in-depth knowledge in the domain area to the parent circle, which can facilitate decision-making there. However, the team should consider what type of competence it wants to bring to the parent circle. The parent circle must give its consent to the elected delegate in order for him or her to become a full member of the parent circle.

Approach in a progressive or self-organized organization

The difference to a traditional organization using Scrum is that the team proposes a leader to whom the parent circle must give its consent. Since a leader in Sociocratic agile is what Scrum calls a "product owner," the proposed leader must have this competence in order to be part of the decision-making process according to the consent model.

The same applies to the roles of facilitator and secretary, which correspond to the Scrum Master's competence profile. The team chooses these roles, and they can be rotated over time. Here perhaps the responsibilities of the roles should be considered as these can be rotated among the team members without there being a need for a specific Scrum Master role, as any team member can perform the tasks of a Scrum Master. This is because in a self-organized team the focus is on the task and not the role.

FINAL WORDS

We have come to the end of the book, which will hopefully be the beginning of your journey towards self-organizing and the democratization of working life where organizations are healthy and people are at the center.

The book is based on a research project but is not a research report and therefore it is written in a language that hopefully suits many people. It contains stories, metaphors, and facts presented in a way that differs from the rigidity required by academia. In addition, it is characterized by our belief in research and our desire to make it useful and accessible to many people.

LEARNINGS FROM OUR JOURNEY

At the beginning of our research project, we thought it was about finding progressive organizations, meaning those that use new and radical approaches, or organizations that have progressive areas. We were a bit discouraged and disillusioned after visiting and interviewing people from these organizations. In many progressive organizations we found that people were not feeling well.

What we also found in many of these organizations was that the progressive methods rested on a very raw capitalist approach, where people can be replaced if they are not always at the top of their game or if there is someone who can do better. Netflix is often used as a positive example of a progressive company. However, we found that behind the positive words and notions such as "entrepreneurial spirit," other things were hidden such as uncertain employment terms and strong individualism.

Other examples include the Chinese company Haier and several Swedish consulting companies.

We visited a company that defined itself as a Teal organization where the CEO told us that they only hired "red people" (one of the personality types according to Disc personality test), which meant that they only wanted strong, outgoing people. Other personality types were considered by the CEO to be weak and incapable of moving the successful company forward. The more we looked, the more we experienced that what looked good on the surface was hiding something else, and that much of what was written in articles or blogs and told in podcasts was not true. We also saw that several of the most famous cases, those that had put self-organizing in the spotlight, had reverted to power hierarchies and traditional forms of organizing.

These new insights made us rethink. It was not only about organizing according to progressive forms, but it was also about the whole, about the systemic approach. In particular, it was about values, about people, and the planet having to come before economic profits and growth.

We also learned that it is important to differentiate between the organizations that are on a change journey because they want to market themselves as modern and want to keep up with the trends, and the organizations that start the transformation because they want to work in a people-centric way. For some, it is fun and trendy to call yourself "Teal," "bossless," "self-organized," and so on. Many also want to be there to increase their profit margins or to attract new employees. After all, many of them remain in the old paradigm, maybe because of a lack of deeper understanding. In some cases, they really believed they were working according to the new principles when in reality the opposite was the case!

There were many people and companies who opened their doors and gave us all the keys so that we could open everything, interview whomever we wanted, and see financial figures and strategic plans.

We also found some closed doors, for example Swedish companies that won the "Best Place to Work" award but did not want to talk to us, not even by phone.

During the trip we also found many stories and there is a clear trend where storytelling becomes part of the marketing. There are many who have found what they call the "new way" or "new life" while being somewhere in Spain. Yes, Spain in particular is actually overrepresented in these stories. The stories are about people who, while sitting in a chiringuito, a bar, or on a mountaintop, got insights that we only have one life, that there is only one planet, and that they wanted to do something else in this life. Many have also shared that they have been burned out, have collapsed, and had everything but were not happy. Therefore, they now do something else (or maybe the same thing with a different name).

In conclusion, we can say that we found some hypocrisy and some wannabes, but above all we found great people who were genuine, who have been on a journey where it may not always have been perfect, but it was authentic. The DP model has risen from these great stories and good examples, and we have integrated these realities with theories and research findings. We thank all the people who have opened their doors and given us so much information, for their trust, and we are feeling honored to have experienced the openness they have shown.

We have experienced what Frederic Laloux, Tomas Björkman, and Robert Kegan call "the movement." There we have found people and companies in all parts of the world who, independently of each other, work to democratize the workplace and see organizing from a systemic perspective. It has been fantastic to visit so many workplaces and talk to so many people from all over the world. During the journey, we have both learned and, in some cases, relearned.

Our final words are about our own journey and what we have learned out in the field.

The biggest issue that emerged during our journey and which we want to highlight is the paradox that arises when people are to be selected to be a part of the organization. In all the case studies, especially in the organizations that had progressed further in self-organization and democratization of the workplace, we learned that recruitment and the way people are selected were extremely important. It appeared that the organizations spent a lot of time on this selection and many interviews were conducted in the search for "the right people." Most companies have said that not everyone is suited to work according to self-organizing principles. There is a huge fear of bringing in the "wrong" people who can destroy the beauty that has been created. How is it possible that these good organizations, who believe in the potential of people, do not believe in the potential of ALL people? If only some fit in, what will happen to the rest? Here we all have to rethink again, even the organizations and business leaders who have come quite far on the journey and stand as our good examples.

This book was written during the Covid-19 pandemic, which has led to changed ways of communicating within organizations and not least leadership. People and organizations have realized that it is possible to do things differently. We hope and believe that the leaders who assume that people do not work if the leaders do not see them will disappear forever.

We also hope to be part of your journey and share your experiences. Therefore, we would like to ask you to write to us and tell us about your experiences via *mystory@foosweden.se.*

Alicia and Rolf

AUTHORS' THANKS

Now is the time for us, the authors, to thank the people who have made our journey in the creation of the DP model and the writing of this book possible.

We would like to begin by thanking those who exceptionally and without reservation opened the doors of their organization and gave us access to interviews, allowed us to attend meetings and get access to documentation, and who have invited us in every way: Anna Elgh, Fredrik Palmgren, Javier Salcedo, Karin Tenelius, and Gustav Henman.

We also want to thank all the experts who gave us their time and shared their knowledge. We would especially like to mention Jos de Blok, Ted Rau, Maximilian Tropé, Gustavo Razzetti, Tanya Stergiou, Andreas Jonsson, James Priest, Dunia Reverter, Madelon van Tilburg, Mette Aagaard, Cristina Sánchez, and Charlotte Petersson Troije.

So many of you have shared your stories and allowed yourselves to be interviewed, and also it is unbelievable that so many business leaders have shared material and information with us. There are several hundred of you, but we would like to mention in particular Tõive Kivikas, Ulf Svensson, José Ignacio Amondarain, Pascal Dulex, Mats Lindblom, Philip Kron, and Brita Forsström.

Thanks to Bertil Löfkvist, who meticulously read the first draft of the Swedish script and gave us invaluable feedback that contributed to improvements.

We also want to thank Hoi Publishing and our publisher Carola Rääf who made the original version (in Swedish) of this book possible.

There are also other people who have indirectly made this possible.

I, Alicia, also want to especially thank Manne Lidén, who extended a hand and helped me in 1991 when, due to my non-Swedish surname, I could not find a workplace where I could do my thesis. Thanks also to Gunnar Meller, who gave me my first permanent job as a systems engineer in 1992. Finally, thanks also to Dr. Sven Haidl, who since 2003 has helped me stay healthy.

This book is about organizing based on faith in people and letting them test and try. That's why I, Rolf, want to thank Olof Thorsell, who hired me as a newly graduated engineer at SSAB Oxelösund and gave me space to grow and learn new things. A memory forever is how Lena Larsson and Agneta Agnemyr, during a job interview at Ericsson, made me talk about what I had failed at in my previous jobs, and because of that hired me in my first manager role. This laid the foundation for my belief in openness and trust, and I think my journey towards the view of this book started there.

Then there are all those people who have crossed our paths through life and who in many different ways have inspired and given new insights. You all deserve our eternal gratitude'. Teal, trust, and transparency make the world a better place.

SOURCES AND LITERATURE

During the three years that the project has been going on, we have read lots of books, scientific articles, blogs, newspapers, and websites. We have also listened to podcasts, speakers, and watched videos. The source list is a selection of books and scientific articles that are cited in the book or that we believe have been of great importance during the research project.

Andersen, L. & Björkman, T. 2020. *The Nordic Secret. A European Story of Beauty and Freedom*. Falun: Fri Tanke förlag.

Andrén, T. 2018. *Om chefen är sjuk – vem tar då hand om personalen? Ohälsa bland personer med ledande befattning*. Stockholm: Saco.

Appelo, J. 2012. *How to Change the World: Change Management 3.0*. Rotterdam: Ojo Ventures BV.

Arbetsmiljöverket och Statistiska centralbyrån (SCB), 2018. Serie: Arbetsmiljöstatistik *https://www.av.se/globalassets/filer/statistik/arbetsorsakade-besvar-2018/arbetsorsakade_besvar_2018_rapport.pdf* (Hämtad 20200614).

Bockelbrink, B., Priest, J. & David, L. 2020. *A Practical Guide for Evolving Agile and Resilient Organizations with Sociocracy 3.0*. Ebook. 2021.0314.2147.

Bringselius, L. 2018. *Tillit – en ledningsfilosofi för framtidens offentliga sektor*. Helsingborg: Komlitt AB.

Bruzelius, L. H. & Skärvad, PH. 2004. *Integrerad organisationslära*. 9:7 uppl. Lund: Studentlitteratur.

Bruzelius, L. H. & Skärvad, PH. 2018. *Management: Att leda verksamheter och människor*. 2. uppl. Lund: Studentlitteratur.

Burns, J. M. 2003. *Transforming Leadership: A New Pursuit of Happiness*. New York: Atlantic Monthly Press.

Burton, R., Håkonsson, D., Nickerson, J., Puranam, P., Workiewicz, M. & Zenger, T. 2017. "GitHub: Exploring the Space Between BossLess and Hierarchical Forms of Organizing". *Journal of Organization Design*, 6(1), s. 1–19.

Carlzon, J. & Lagerström, T. 2018. *Riv pyramiderna! : En bok om den nya människan, chefen och ledaren*. Stockholm: Volante.

Clark, Timothy R. 2020. *The 4 Stages of Psychological Safety: Defining the Path to Inclusion and Innovation*. Oakland CA: Berrett-Koehler Publishers.

Dirks, K. T. & Ferrin, D. L. 2002. "Trust in Leadership: Meta-Analytic Findings and Implications for Research and Practice". *Journal of Applied Psychology*, 87(4), s. 611–628.

Edmondson, A. 2019. *The Fearless Organization: Creating Psychological Safety in the Workplace for Learning, Innovation, and Growth*. New Jersey: John Wiley & Sons Inc.

Edmondson, A. & Lei, Z. 2014. "Psychological Safety: The History, Renaissance, and Future of an Interpersonal Construct". *Annual Review of Organizational Psychology and Organizational Behavior*, 1(1), s. 23–43.

Graeber, D. 2018. *Bullshit Jobs: A Theory*, New York: Simon & Schuster Inc.

Greenleaf, R. 1970. *The Servant as Leader*. Oakland CA: Berrett-Koehler Publishers.

Gullers Grupp Informationsrådgivare AB. Är svenskt management konkurrenskraftigt? VINNOVA – Verket för Innovationssystem Rapport VR, 2007:13.

Haigh, N. & Hoffman, A. J. 2012. "Hybrid Organizations: The Next Chapter of Sustainable Business". *Organizational Dynamics 41, s. 126–134.*

Herbst, P. 1976. "NonHierarchical Forms of Organization". *Acta Sociologica, 19(1), s. 65–75.*

Hersey, P., & Blanchard, K.H. (1969). Life cycle theory of leadership. *Training & Development Journal, 23(5), 26–34.*

Kegan, R. & Lahey, L. 2016. *An Everyone Culture: Becoming a Deliberately Developmental Organization.* Boston: Harvard Business School Publishing.

Kegan, R., Lahey, L., Fleming, A. & Miller, M. 2014. "Making Business Personal". *Harvard Business Review.*

Kelloway, K & Barling, J. 2010. "Leadership Development as an Intervention in Occupational Health Psychology". *Work & Stress, 24(3), s. 260–279.*

Kivikas, T. 2009. *Det du vill men inte vågar. Läsebok för anställd och chef.* Stockholm: Debutantförlaget.

Laloux, F. 2014. Reinventing Organizations: A Guide to Creating Organizations Inspired by the Next Stage of Human Consciousness. Bryssel: Nelson Parker.

Lawrence, P. & Lorsch, J. 1967. "Differentiation and Integration in Complex Organizations". *Administrative Science Quarterly, 12(1), s. 1–47.*

Lee, M. Y. & Edmondson, A. C. 2017. "SelfManaging Organizations: Exploring the Limits of LessHierarchical Organizing". *Research in Organizational Behavior, 37, s. 35–58.*

Lopez, E. & Medina, A. 2016. *Ethics and Governance in Project Management: Small Sins Allowed and the Line of Impunity,* Boca Raton: CRC Press – Taylor & Francis Group.

Madestam, J. 2009. *En kompispappa och en ytlig djuping: Partieliters ambivalenta partiledarideal.* Stockholms universitet. Statsvetenskapliga institutionen.

Manpower. 2019. *Work Life 2019 Drömarbetsplatsen.* [faktablad] insikt.manpowergroup.se/dromarbetsplatsen2019.

McGregor, D. 1960. *The Human Side of Enterprise.* New York: McGrawHill Book Company, Inc.

Medina, R. 2018. *Managing Project Competence – The Lemon and the Loop.* Boca Raton: CRC Press – Taylor & Francis Group.

Medina, R. & Medina, A. 2018. *"The Linkage between Learning Capabilities and Innovative Capacity – A Case Study".* Journal of Leadership, Accountability and Ethics, 15(1), s. 125–142.

Medina, R. & Medina, A. 2018. *The Linkage between Learning Capabilities and Innovative Capacity – A Case Study.* Glasgow: Euram.

Northouse, P. G. 2007. *Leadership Theory and Practice* (4:e uppl.). London: Sage Publications.

Priest, J. & Bockelbrink, B. 2015, *Sociocracy 3.0.* sociocracy30.org/thedetails/whysociocracy30/ (Hämtad 20180114).

Rau, T. & Koch Gonzalez, J. 2018. *Many Voices, One Song. Shared Power with Sociocracy.* Amherst: Sociocracy For All.

Riksrevisionen. *Karriärstegsreformen och lärarlönelyftet – högre lön men sämre sammanhållning*, RiR 2017:18, s. 75.

Rosenberg, M. 2003. *Nonviolent Communication: A Language of Life: Create Your Life, Your Relationships, and Your World in Harmony with Your Values.* London: PuddleDancer Press.

Scharmer, O. 2018. *The Essentials of Theory U: Core Principles and Applications.* San Francisco: BerrettKoehler Publishers.

Scharmer, O. 2007. *Theory U, Leading from the Future as it Emerges: The Social Technology of Presencing.* Cambridge: SoL Press.

Schein, E. H. & Bennis, W. G. 1965. *Personal and Organizational Change Through Group Methods: The Laboratory Approach.* New York: Wiley.

Schutz, W. 1994. *The Human Element.* San Francisco: JosseyBass.

Scott, K. 2017. *Radical Candor: Be a Kick-Ass Boss Without Losing Your Humanity.* London: Macmillan.

Stanford, N. 2015. *Guide to Organisation Design: Creating High-Performing and Adaptable Enterprises.* London: Profile Books Ltd.

LINKS

Below is a compilation of the links we refer to in this book.

www.sociocracyforall.org

www.holacracy.org

www.linkedin.com/company/teal-for-teal-sweden

www.tealpodden.se

www.linkedin.com/company/tealpodden

www.hep-online.se

www.sociocracy30.org

INDEX OF ORGANIZATIONS

INDEX OF PEOPLE AND CONCEPTS

U

Ulukaya, Hamdi **46, 295, 306**

V

van Tilburg, Madelon **240, 359**
Villines, Sharon **54**

W

Weber, Max **154**
Wilber, Ken **59**

ABOUT THE AUTHORS

Alicia Medina was born in Montevideo, Uruguay. She moved to Sweden in 1982, got her Master of Science in mathematics and computer science from Gothenburg University in 1991, spent the next 20 years in corporations like Ericsson, AstraZeneca, Sony Mobile, Ikea and some consultancy firms in technical and management positions. Her interest in people and the human side of organizations led her to study part-time in parallel with her work and complete a degree in organizational psychology from Lund University. Seeking knowledge and a deeper understanding of organizations, she re-entered academic life in 2009 without leaving the business world.

In 2012, she completed her PhD in strategy and management at SKEMA in Lille. Until 2021, she worked part-time at Umeå University in Sweden and was a visiting lecturer at SKEMA in France as well as Universidad de Montevideo (UM) in Uruguay. Considering herself a boundary spanner between academia and the business world, she spent over a decade working as an organizational developer and advisor in combination with being a lecturer and researcher within leadership, organization design, entrepreneurship, multicultural diversity, project management, and change management. She has co-authored a book on ethics in organizations and written many scientific articles on organization, leadership, competence, and learning.

In 2019, she co-founded Future of Organizing Inc. with the aim of helping organizations to move to a new paradigm beyond Command and Control. Currently, she spends her time providing services about self-organizing and Teal as well as writing and speaking about new ways of organizing, leading and collaborating.

Rolf Medina is a Swedish Doctor of Philosophy in management and a frequent speaker and debater on topics related to organizational design, culture, leadership, and innovation.

With a background in computer engineering after graduating in 1989 from Halmstad University in Sweden, he worked professionally in different technological areas, after which he moved on to various management positions where he also had the honor of establishing new business areas. Since 2002, when he left Ericsson, he has run his consulting company Quini and worked with a number of different clients, such as Sony Ericsson, GN ReSound, Skånetrafiken, Sony Mobile, Vattenfall, and IKEA.

Parallel to his business activities, he has during the last ten years worked in academia as a lecturer, module leader, and researcher at the School of Economics at Umeå University in Sweden, SKEMA in France, and UCL in London, UK. He has been fascinated by the mechanisms behind the management of complexity and the fact that everybody has a talent.

He has written several scientific papers and is the author of the book The Lemon and the Loop, which presents new ways of managing and defining competence and how to improve organizational learning.

He is co-founder of Future of Organizing Inc. and Highly Engaged People Inc. Nowadays, he devotes all his time to his consulting activities, in which he focuses on digital journeys, competence-centered organizations, and supporting companies to move to the new organizing paradigm.

www.ingramcontent.com/pod-product-compliance
Lightning Source LLC
Chambersburg PA
CBHW050237270326
41914CB00034BA/1958/J